PUBLIC ENTREPRENEURSHIP, CITIZENSHIP, AND SELF-GOVERNANCE

In this book Paul Dragos Aligica revisits the theory of political self-governance in the context of recent developments in behavioural economics and political philosophy that have challenged the foundations of this theory. Building on the work of the "Bloomington School" created by Nobel Laureate Elinor Ostrom and Public Choice political economy co-founder Vincent Ostrom, Aligica presents a fresh conceptualization of the key processes at the core of democratic-liberal governance systems involving civic competence and public entrepreneurship. The result is not only a reassessment and re-articulation of the theories constructed by the Bloomington School of Public Choice, but also a new approach to several cutting-edge discussions relevant to governance studies and applied institutional theory, such as the debates generated by the recent waves of populism, paternalism, and authoritarianism.

Paul Dragos Aligica is a Senior Research Fellow in the F. A. Hayek Program for Advanced Study in Philosophy, Politics and Economics at Mercatus Centre at George Mason University where he teaches in the Economics Department. He received his PhD in Political Science at Indiana University-Bloomington, where he was a student of Vincent and Elinor Ostrom at the Workshop in Political Theory and Policy Analysis. He has published extensively on institutional and governance theory, being the author of six books and numerous academic articles, exploring both the foundational and the applied side of alternative governance systems.

CAMBRIDGE STUDIES IN ECONOMICS, CHOICE, AND SOCIETY

Founding Editors

Timur Kuran, *Duke University*
Peter J. Boettke, *George Mason University*

This interdisciplinary series promotes original theoretical and empirical research as well as integrative syntheses involving links between individual choice, institutions, and social outcomes. Contributions are welcome from across the social sciences, particularly in the areas where economic analysis is joined with other disciplines such as comparative political economy, new institutional economics, and behavioral economics.

Books in the Series:

Public Entrepreneurship, Citizenship, and Self-Governance

PAUL DRAGOS ALIGICA

George Mason University

CAMBRIDGE
UNIVERSITY PRESS

CAMBRIDGE
UNIVERSITY PRESS

University Printing House, Cambridge CB2 8BS, United Kingdom

One Liberty Plaza, 20th Floor, New York, NY 10006, USA

477 Williamstown Road, Port Melbourne, VIC 3207, Australia

314–321, 3rd Floor, Plot 3, Splendor Forum, Jasola District Centre,
New Delhi – 110025, India

79 Anson Road, #06–04/06, Singapore 079906

Cambridge University Press is part of the University of Cambridge.

It furthers the University's mission by disseminating knowledge in the pursuit of education,
learning, and research at the highest international levels of excellence.

www.cambridge.org
Information on this title: www.cambridge.org/9781107186095
DOI: 10.1017/9781316888728

© Paul Dragos Aligica 2019

First published 2019

Printed and bound in Great Britain by Clays Ltd, Elcograf S.p.A.

A catalogue record for this publication is available from the British Library.

ISBN 978-1-107-18609-5 Hardback
ISBN 978-1-316-63701-2 Paperback

Cambridge University Press has no responsibility for the persistence or accuracy of
URLs for external or third-party internet websites referred to in this publication
and does not guarantee that any content on such websites is, or will remain,
accurate or appropriate.

Contents

Acknowledgments

This book owes immensely to the support and encouragement that I have received over the years from my colleagues at Mercatus Center at George Mason University. I would like to express my deep gratitude to all of my Mercatus colleagues for creating such an extraordinary intellectual environment, and my special thanks to Peter Boettke, Tyler Cowen, Virgil Storr, and Daniel Rothschild for their leadership in this respect.

I owe much gratitude for his help on elaborating the concept of public entrepreneurship to Ion Sterpan, student and friend, tragically and prematurely departed before this book was completed. Individual chapters of the book were read and most helpfully commented on by Peter Levine, Brent Never, Brenda Bushouse, Robert K. Christensen, Paul Lewis, Hartmut Kliemt, Filippo Sabetti, Richard E. Wagner and Vlad Tarko. Their criticism is gratefully acknowledged.

The book includes previously published or publicly presented material: "Citizenship, Political Competence and Civic Studies: the Ostromian Perspective" in *Civic Studies*, edited by Peter Levine and Karol Soltan, Association of American Colleges and Universities, 2014. I thank the Association of American Colleges and Universities for permission to reprint from this material. "The 'Neither Market nor State' Domain: Charting the Nonprofit Territory through Ostromian Theoretical Lenses" in *Nonprofit and Voluntary Sector Quarterly*, volume 45, number 4, 2016. "Addressing Limits to Mainstream Economic Analysis of Voluntary and Non-Profit Organizations: The 'Austrian' Alternative" in *Nonprofit and Voluntary Sector Quarterly*, volume 44, number 5, 2015. I thank Sage Publishing for permission to reprint from these materials. "The Two Social Philosophies of Ostroms' Institutionalism" (with P. Boettke) in *Policy Studies Journal (PSJ)*, volume 39, number 1, 2011. I thank John Wiley & Sons for permission to reprint from this material.

Chapter 2 is a revised version of "Public Entrepreneurship: The Notion and Its Implications," presented with Ion Sterpan at The Association of Private Enterprise Education (APEE) Annual Conference, 2016. A previous version of Chapter 6 was discussed at the "Fact/Values/Strategies" conference organized by the Tisch College of Civic Studies, Tufts University in 2016 and later published in *The Good Society*. I am grateful for the comments received then from Lauren Swayne Barthold, Paul Croce, Mary E. Hess, James Johnson, Susan Orr, Larry M. Jorgensen, David Eric Meens, Timothy J. Shaffer, Karol Edward Soltan, Peter Levine, and Trygve Throntveit. Chapter 3 contains a fragment of "Revisiting Theories of Nonprofit Entrepreneurship: Ideological Entrepreneurship. Implications for Public Policy" presented with Cameron Harwick at the "Philanthropy and the Economic Way of Thinking" conference at Troy University in 2014. The comments received then from Lenore Ealy, Robert F. Garnett, David Ellerman, Adam Martin, Mark Frazier, Amanda Achtman, Laura Grube, Daniel Sutter, and Stefanie Haeffele-Balch are acknowledged with pleasure and gratitude. Chapter 5 and sections of Chapter 8 are based on "Institutional Design, Social Norms, and the Feasibility Issue," presented at the "Learning and Changing Social Norms" conference organized by *Social Philosophy and Policy* at the University of Arizona in 2016 and later published in *Social Philosophy and Policy*, Cambridge University Press, volume 35, 2018. The comments received on that occasion from Christina Bicchieri, Fiery Cushman, Jerry Gaus, Daniel Kelly, Gerry Mackie, Ryan Muldoon, Shaun Nichols, Carol Rose, David Shoemaker, John Thrasher, Chad Van Schoelandt, and Peter Vanderschraaf are hereby acknowledged with much appreciation. I am very grateful for the invaluable help received in preparing the manuscript from my research assistant, Thomas Savidge, and my colleague McKenzie Robey. At Cambridge University Press, Kristina A. Deusch and Neil Ryan helped me and the manuscript to smoothly navigate the publishing process. I most sincerely appreciate their efforts. The contributions of Virginia Bowen and Karthik Orukaimani were vital in preparing the final version of the text for publication, and their efforts are most gratefully acknowledged. I have been profoundly impressed by Virginia Bowen's amazing copyediting work, and I would like to extend my special thanks to her. A unique sort of debt is owed to one person at Cambridge University Press: Karen Maloney. Her encouragement was decisive in my determination to put together the proposal leading to this project, while her kind and supportive attitude during the last stages of my work on the manuscript, mobilized me to complete it. This book is in large part an outcome of her professionalism, kindness, and optimism. It has been a real privilege working with her.

Jerry Gaus deserves my special gratitude for providing a source of inspiration, an intellectual benchmark, and a challenge for so many of the ideas presented in this volume. In a sense, this book could be seen both as a contribution to the research program advanced at Indiana University, Bloomington, by Vincent and Elinor Ostrom, and as an essay in applied theory, resonating to the direction of the intellectual agenda advanced at the University of Arizona, Tucson, by Jerry Gaus.

Needless to say, I remain responsible for any errors.

Introduction

The political economy and institutional theory associated with the Bloomington School, created by Nobel Prize in Economics recipient Elinor Ostrom and Public Choice Political Economy cofounder Vincent Ostrom, has been widely recognized for its contributions to a whole range of domains, from the fields of institutional design and public administration to the study of collective action, social cooperation, and common pool resources management. There is, however, one aspect of their work that, despite its centrality, has seldom attracted the attention it truly deserves: the pivotal and intriguing place the issues of public entrepreneurship and citizenship have in their writings. The Ostroms' interest in public entrepreneurship and citizenship as well as their institutional corollary – the idea of a polycentric domain of voluntary associations and enterprises as an intrinsic component of a viable self-governance system – is rather unique among the new institutionalism scholars who, in the second half of the twentieth century, reinvented and rebuilt institutional theory using political economy and public choice economics.

Public entrepreneurship not only had a special place in the Ostroms' work but the Ostroms were also genuine pioneers of its social scientific investigation. Elinor Ostrom's 1964 UCLA doctoral dissertation "Public Entrepreneurship: A Case Study in Ground Water Basin Management" is probably the first major study undertaken in this respect, while Vincent Ostrom's 1950s and 1960s writings on competitive and democratic governance systems (some of them together with Charles M. Tiebout and Robert Warren) have prepared the grounds for one of the most fruitful theoretical frameworks incorporating and conceptualizing the public entrepreneurship function. In a sense, in the Ostroms' view, public entrepreneurship is a governance ideal and an important political virtue, a feature of citizenship. It is sufficient to

1

recall, in this respect, Vincent Ostrom's lecture occasioned by the receipt of the 2005 John Gaus Award conferred by the Public Administration Society "to honor the recipient's lifetime of exemplary scholarship in the joint tradition of political science and public administration." The lecture summing up his lifetime contribution was tellingly entitled "Citizen-Sovereigns: The Source of Contestability, the Rule of Law, and the Conduct of Public Entrepreneurship." In it, Vincent Ostrom made unmistakably clear the crucial position of public entrepreneurship in his view of governance: our intellectual challenge, he explained, is to convert as much as possible of what is known as "public administration" into "public entrepreneurship." Even more tellingly, one can find instances in Elinor Ostrom's writings of truly passionate pleas for public entrepreneurship, with a strong normative connotation:

> To unlock human potential, we must unlock the way we think about non-market institutional arrangements. We need to open the public sector to entrepreneurship and innovation at local, regional, national, and international levels ... Given that the benefits of public goods and common-pool resources are dispersed within a community, many scholars ignore the possibility of local public entrepreneurs devising effective ways of providing, producing, and encouraging the co-production of these essential goods and services ... The presumption made by many policy analysts is that without major external resources and top-down planning, public goods and sustainable common-pool resources cannot be provided. This absolute presumption is wrong. While it is always a struggle to find effective ways of providing these services, public entrepreneurs working closely with citizens frequently do find new ways of putting services together, using a mixture of local talent and resources. (E. Ostrom 2005b)

In a similar way, the Ostromian vision of governance and normative political economy is strongly anchored in a notion of civic competence and a well-defined view of citizenship and civic behavior (Levine 2011; Soltan 2011; Sabetti 2011; Sabetti, Allen, and Sproule-Jones 2009; Aligica and Boettke 2009). Once the themes of political competence, citizenship, and civic knowledge get introduced into the picture, the Ostroms' work instantly gains an entirely new dimension. It is, hence, a great loss that their contribution in this regard has seldom been recognized, although in the end, it occupies just such an essential position in their theoretical system. After all, the Ostroms defined the very mission of their work in terms of a direct contribution to an "art and science of association" to be used by citizens in the exercise of democracy:

One of our greatest priorities at the Workshop has been to ensure that our research contributes to the education of future citizens, entrepreneurs in the public and private spheres, and officials at all levels of government. We have a distinct obligation to participate in this educational process as well as to engage in the research enterprise so that we build a cumulative knowledge base that may be used to sustain democratic life. Self-governing, democratic systems are always fragile enterprises. Future citizens need to understand that they participate in the constitution and reconstitution of rule-governed polities. And they need to learn the "art and science of association". If we fail in this, all our investigations and theoretical efforts are useless. (E. Ostrom in Aligica and Boettke 2009, 159)

The most remarkable and important aspect of the Ostroms' work in this respect is that their interest went beyond identifying and isolating public entrepreneurship and citizenship as two phenomena of concern in the effort to understand institutional order and change. In their view, the two are part and parcel of a broader theory of governance. The Ostroms have advanced a specific approach to governance that builds on political economy and public choice elements but also goes beyond them. It is an approach that constantly puts citizens at the center of the governance system, while simultaneously trying to extend the analysis of entrepreneurship in nonmarket and collective action settings. The result is a unique way of reinterpreting and reconstructing the theory of governance as one of self-governance. It is a theory of both positive (explanatory) and normative (applied) relevance. Self-governance (the problem, its analyses, and the institutional dimensions) is the major underlying theme of the Ostroms' work and is often recognized as such by commentators and followers of the Ostroms, but its assumptions, nature, and implications are seldom systematically explored.

The theory of self-governance is, by its very nature, unavoidably centered on social actors. Although heavily inspired by political economy and public choice, the problems of actors' heterogeneity, imagination, capabilities, skills, values, cultures, contextual decision-making, etc. are essential. Self-governance is about actors operating in diverse and complex dynamic circumstances, using the resources available to them in trying to solve collective action and coordination problems. That requires an approach making use of basic rational choice models (homo economicus and related models of man and action), but it also has to move beyond those models. The Ostromian system tries to balance the tension between, on the one hand, the structural factor as conceptualized by the political economy/institutionalist dimension and, on the other hand, the agency factor as conceptualized by the social actor and the human capability dimension. The problem of citizenship and public entrepreneurship emerges naturally at the interface between structure and agency.

The ultimate question motivating the intellectual endeavor to construe a self-governance system, explains Vincent Ostrom, is straightforward and could be expressed in almost individualized, personalized terms: "If you and I are to be self-governing, how are we to understand and take part in human affairs?" (V. Ostrom 1997, 117). In response, the Ostroms advanced an approach

in which a science and art of association rather than a science of command and control was viewed as constitutive of democratic societies. This fundamental difference of perspective has radical paradigmatic implications in addressing the question "Who govern?" in the plural rather than "Who governs" in the singular. A minor distinction in language may have radical implications for theoretical discourse in the same way that a shift in perspective from a revolving sun to a spinning and orbiting earth had profound implications for many different sciences, professions, and technologies. (V. Ostrom 1997, 282)

In brief, the Ostroms place at the core of their research program an issue that combines positive analysis with a straightforward normative stance: self-governance. Governments should not "exercise tutelage over Societies and steer and direct those Societies." And if "people are to rule," then "members of society should know how to govern themselves" (V. Ostrom 1997, 3, 271). The Ostroms' work is avowedly meant to contribute to the creation of a collective cumulative knowledge base for citizens to apply in governance processes. In fact, they saw their efforts as part of "the central tradition of human and social studies," contributing from today's perspective (i.e., using the intellectual tools of the age and the historical insights gained so far) to a long tradition of creating relevant knowledge about self-governance (Aligica and Boettke 2009).

This book is an attempt to revisit the theme of self-governance and advance the approach to it from an Ostromian perspective. The objective is to contribute to the theory of self-governance along the lines defined and inspired by the Ostroms' work. At the core of the effort will be the focus on what is considered in the book to be two essential elements of the theory of self-governance around which the entire Ostromian system pivots: public entrepreneurship and citizenship. The book pinpoints, clarifies, and further develops these key concepts and the cluster of issues and phenomena they designate and illuminate. In doing so, it will be revealed that the two imply an entire theoretical apparatus and conceptual system. They entail and are entailed in a theoretical dimension defined by notions such as polycentricity, collective action, and competitive governance. Following the logic of exploration of and elaboration on this concatenation of issues, notions, and models, the very theory of self-governance advances naturally on both its analytical-conceptual and its normative sides. The book presents the insights thus emerging, and in so doing, elaborates and refines the ways we think about self-governance. The result is not only a reassessment and rearticulation of the theoretical apparatus constructed by the Bloomington School of Public Choice, but also a fresh approach to several cutting-edge research domains and contemporary debates relevant to governance studies and applied institutional theory.[1]

When it comes to the contemporary debate, the argument of this book could be read first and foremost as a contribution to the defense of a certain form of liberal democracy, the ideal of a system of governance centered on a normative individualist recognition of the primacy of citizens' values, interests, and preferences and pivoting on the institutional and epistemic processes generated by the citizens' participation in governance endeavors. To fully understand the magnitude and relevance of the challenges to which the arguments advanced in the book aim to respond, one needs to be more explicit about what is at stake.

A self-governance doctrine assumes that the tension between the notion of government by experts – or "guardians" as Robert Dahl (1989) calls this model – on the one hand, and government by adult citizens who take responsibility for the collective decisions in their communities and societies, on the other, has already been settled in favor of the second. Hence, the emphasis is on citizens and civic action, seen as both the normative sources and as the main causal drivers of political order and change. This citizen-centered governance theory pivots on the interrelationship between the institutions of governance and civic and political competencies (i.e., the skills, values, strategies, knowledge, and beliefs needed by citizens to operate the institutional and procedural apparatus and to generate and maintain the social relationships necessary for good governance).

---

[1] The term *public choice* is used in this book in two ways. The first designates an activity, a social phenomenon in real-life public affairs. The second meaning designates the discipline, the area of study and inquiry, a domain of academic and public discourse. We refer to, on one hand, "public choice," and on the other hand, "the field of public choice" or "Public Choice." The first denotes the activities and institutions by which a society makes collective choices – how people make choices in groups as opposed to individually. The second denotes the academic field at the interface between economics and political science that studies how collective choices can be made efficiently.

To locate the citizen-centered approach on the conceptual map of governance doctrines and systems, one should imagine their range on a continuum. At one end, "tutelage" and "guardian" systems, "seeing like a state" structures, pivot on the ruler–ruled relationship. At the other end, systems in which power, authority, and hierarchy are more fluid and modular, broken into polycentric countervailing structures and forms of association and in which "seeing like a citizen" is the dominant governance vision. Obviously, these are ideal types. But they capture well what is at stake. The image could be translated rather coherently into the terms of a conceptual framework: the closer one moves on the continuum to the citizen-centered perspective, the more citizens' competence and an institutional and social environment of voluntary action and association take the forefront, while the hierarchies of power, authority, and control shift to the background. The reverse move leads to reversed saliences.

Turning from the analytical to the normative side, the citizen-centered approach gives expression to the perspective of "seeing like a citizen" as opposed to the "seeing like a state" perspective. The result is an ideal theory, a model of a governance system and a direction for practical aspiration. The normative exercise is meant to drive political reality as much as possible in that direction. The analytical exercise is meant to illuminate the factors that may be supporting or hindering that drive. Thus, both analytically and normatively, it indeed represents a distinctive and significant approach to current political philosophy and governance theories.

The assumption is that rule by the citizens is both desirable and feasible. But crucial for the very idea of a self-governance system is the fact that it is considered that social actors have the political or civic competence on a scale and scope that makes self-governance possible. It is further considered that an affirmative answer has already been given to a particular set of foundational questions: Do social actors, when assuming the roles of citizens, have the capacity to play that role effectively? Do citizens have the knowledge and skills to put facts, values, and strategies together in effective ways, given their self-governance objectives? Do they have what it takes to self-govern? In brief, these are questions regarding the very *competence* of citizens at mastering facts, values, and strategies while aiming in rational and moral ways toward certain social and political objectives. The entire architecture of this approach hinges on this feasibility assumption; it places the entire discussion in the realm of the possible as opposed to the realm of the utopian.

The problem is that recent developments in behavioral economics and political philosophy have profoundly challenged the very foundation of the self-governance argument. The ideal of rational, active, and informed democratic mankind was subjected to a variety of empirical and conceptual criticisms. The realism and feasibility of self-governance were questioned on the grounds of the very limits of citizens' competence. The emerging view suggests that any governance theory based on citizens' capacities and on expectations of public entrepreneurship is doomed to be unrealistic and unfeasible – the epistemic and competence resources of citizens are rather limited, and public entrepreneurship is far from able to effectively overcome collective action problems. In fact, it is rarely triggered, given the incentive structure of the public action arenas and the ways social actors perceive and react to those incentives. And, thus, a revival of revamped antidemocratic doctrines shifts attention toward various forms of epistemic-asymmetry-based alternatives to liberal democracy.

The growth of a new form of paternalism is not just a figment of the speculative and theoretical imagination. The literature already features concrete applied formulas that materialize it: at the most basic level is the so-called nudge technology of public policy, as an example of the elemental policy intervention unit (basic building block) of the approach. Then there is "libertarian paternalism," as the theory justifying the technique and the intervention. And finally is the so-called epistocracy, as a larger doctrine of governance, within which technical social engineering interventions on the architecture of choice, such as nudging, or normative justifications, such as paternalism, combine to generate a model or ideal of a defensible system of governance (Thaler and Sunstein 2003; Brennan 2016a, 2016b, 2016c). There is no doubt that the idea of self-governance is seriously put on the defensive in light of the theories and doctrines noted above, as well as of the resurgence of more traditional, authoritarian, and collectivistic views, reasserting in the global arena.

Confronted with this massive challenge, the defenders of the self-governance tradition are left with basically two reactions: The first is containment and accommodation, admitting the veracity of the challenge and acknowledging that all one can do is try to minimize the scale and scope of the epistocratic paternalist designs on the private sphere of citizens' lives. More concretely, the response can be to try to encourage, out of the many paternalist designs, just those that are comparatively less intrusive in an attempt to preserve as much as possible some space for individual choice and responsibility. The second reaction is bolder: to try to push back, to renew the citizen-centered vision, to update the conceptual and normative stance behind it in light of the newest developments in social science and philosophy, and to redouble efforts to bolster the institutions and civic capacities needed for self-governance. One might say that it is very difficult to draw a line between the first approach and the second approach. And indeed, there is a vast overlapping space between them. Yet, in the end, even if it is a matter of degree and emphasis, one still has a clear choice between the strategy of accommodation and the strategy of pushing back.

In this respect, probably the most constructive approach is one where before succumbing to the middle ground of pragmatism (which means accommodating and tinkering within a broad climate of opinion and institutional designs dominated by epistocracy, paternalism, and even authoritarianism), the supporters of self-governance have the duty to push back first. Their strategic task is to articulate new arguments for the viability of the self-governance, citizen-centered approach. They need to update and upgrade the theoretical and normative framework supporting the desirability and feasibility of governance systems that are democratic in the traditional (Tocquevillian) sense, not epistocratic or technocratic. Even if, in the end, one is just strategically positioning for making concessions from a better position when adjusting to the policies and reforms inspired by epistocratic paternalism or authoritarianism, one still needs a renewed vision to orient the effort. "Seeing like a citizen" (not like a state, an enlightened despot, or an expert advising the latter) needs to be operationalized in the process of negotiated accommodation and pushback. If one gets into this process sharing with the other side the "seeing like a state" vision, then the results are easy to anticipate.

If that is the case, then the question is what should the main directions of this response be? What ideas, conceptual instruments, and normative notions should be used as vehicles of first order? This book will address this challenge from a perspective shaped by the Ostroms' work. Their approach can offer resources and lessons in this regard in a way that few authors working at the interface between foundational and applied theory could. It is well known that the Ostroms have contributed to the empirical side (metropolitan governance, common pool resources, public services provision, etc.) of the themes that are at the core of that discussion. Yet, in addition to these empirical and analytical aspects, they have also dedicated ongoing attention to a dimension that is foundational and normative. In fact, it is precisely this normative engagement that is ultimately motivating the analytical and empirically focused efforts. Responding to the challenges of paternalism means that, sooner or later, one has to search for resources in this area in which theoretical framing, normative ideals, and institutional design principles intertwine. It is a complex and messy domain in which it is very hard, if not impossible, to draw a line between the theoretical and the applied.

The special relevance of the Ostroms' work comes from the fact that their empirical and analytical contributions are deeply permeated by a normative dimension solidly bolstered by a social philosophy of civics in which citizenship, public entrepreneurship, and self-governance are intertwined. They approach things from the perspective of the applied level, defined by an unmitigated interest in institutional design and policy intervention. Such a position bridges the theoretical world and the world of practice. Its distinctive feature is that it mobilizes and uses the relevant insights from foundational work – theoretical, normative, and empirical – and does so with a view not to solve theoretical puzzles or empirically test some hypothesis generated in the workings of one research program or another, but to orient feasibility and desirability judgments and to bolster the analytics and heuristics of applied-level approaches. This type of position is usually associated with the notion of applied theory or, when the normative and conceptual framing dimension has a decisive role, of applied philosophy. Seen from a political philosophy angle, this type of perspective could be associated with the increasingly influential debate and literature on "nonideal theory." It is a messy area in which philosophical and theoretical matters overlap and combine with empirical and operational aspects, intertwining in complex ways in multiple dimensions (Gaus 2016, 1–2). Yet it is a crucial area to chart and explore because it is the very area where the relevance of our philosophical and scientific endeavors is decided. This is the space where the debates about the desirability and feasibility of self-governance and its alternatives have to be settled.

This book will show that many of the questions and doubts that are salient – and perhaps impossible to respond to – if public entrepreneurship and citizenship are approached separately and in isolation as distinct phenomena, have to be reconsidered as soon as one grasps the bigger picture of the theory of self-governance that is connecting them to the other elements of the theoretical framework: polycentricity, coproduction, competitive governance, voluntary association, etc. The Ostromian approach both encourages the analysis of these particular phenomena and, at the same time, shifts the emphasis to this broader systemic view and the process aspect related to it. That, as Vincent Ostrom has explained, "has paradigmatic implications."

The core insight is that a self-governance system is not mainly about the framing and channeling of preexisting social actors' skills, knowledge, and political competencies and entrepreneurship. It is also about generating them. The participation of social actors as citizens in the governance process is essential. Self-governance is about the interrelationships between the institutional structure and processes and the psychological, attitudinal, and epistemic features of social actors interacting with those institutional arrangements. At this point, one could recognize the contours of the Tocquevillian participatory democracy paradigm within which the Ostromian self-governance theorizing has deep roots. In this intellectual tradition, citizens' competencies are endogenous to the governance process, not exogenous conditions reflected in abstract assumptions that are easy to question anytime by simply evoking the real-life, concrete, empirical evidence. As Carole Pateman put it:

One might characterize the participatory model as one where maximum input (participation) is required and where output includes not just policies (decisions) but also the development of the social and political capacities of each individual, so that there is feedback from output to input. (Pateman 1970, 4–5)

The participatory democracy paradigm responds to the problem of the limits of citizens' capacities – information, rationality, resources – and by implication, the concerns for the stability, resilience, and feasibility of a self-governance system by pointing to the process itself.

Thus there is no special problem about the stability of a participatory system; it is self-sustaining through the educative impact of the participatory process. Participation develops and fosters the very qualities necessary for it; the more individuals participate, the better able they become to do so. Subsidiary hypotheses about participation are that it has an integrative effect and that it aids the acceptance of collective decisions. (Pateman 1970, 42–43)

In this paradigm, public entrepreneurship and citizenship become pivotal elements of the system. At the same time, they are effective ways of conceptualizing and translating in applied terms the very idea (or ideal) of "participation." The Ostromian approach could thus help the response to the paternalist and epistocratic challenge through its contribution to the reconstruction of the Tocqueville–Mill–Popper tradition that links institutional structures, political acts, and habits of mind and heart, while placing them at the core of a dynamic model of democracy (as an open society) and of democratization (as an open process).

This book does not harbor the ambition of offering a complete or general theory of self-governance, much less "The Theory" of self-governance. It is a contribution from one specific angle out of many possible angles, traditions, and schools of thought, advancing a defense of liberal democracies and citizen-centered governance systems. It is an attempt to present a possible take on the complex universe of self-governance, always mindful of the public choice and institutionalist context and origins of the Bloomington School. The goal is to get a more fine-grained understanding of essential aspects of self-governance arrangements by improving the theoretical lenses used to approach them. At the same time, there is the hope to reassert the stance, identity, and desirability of self-governance as one of the alternative doctrines of governance and political theory.

With this end in view, the volume is organized into three parts. Each is focused on one of the three key themes that are at the core of the volume: public entrepreneurship, citizenship, and self-governance.

The first part is dedicated to public entrepreneurship. It revisits and reconstructs the contributions of Vincent and Elinor Ostrom to the study of entrepreneurship in nonmarket settings. To advance the case for self-governance, one needs to understand in more nuanced ways the structures and processes at work in such governance systems that are driven by citizens' participation and initiative. Public entrepreneurship, or more precisely, the phenomena and processes designated under the notion of public entrepreneurship, opens up insights that otherwise may not be captured in the absence of the conceptual apparatus associated with the theory of entrepreneurial actions and functions. Part 1 of the book looks at how one could conceptualize public entrepreneurship and how that conceptualization generates a series of insights regarding the institutions and processes of self-governance.

Chapter 1 starts by presenting the basic vision of public entrepreneurship emerging from the Bloomington scholars' work and then moves on to elaborate by connecting it to significant developments in the relevant literature. It thus goes a step further from where the argument was left by the Ostroms and their collaborators. It explicitly spells out the underlying theoretical assumptions and parameters of that vision, with a special emphasis on its implications for the ways one understands the relationship between entrepreneurship and governance systems. The result is (i) a fresh understanding of public entrepreneurship as a compounded social phenomenon, described via a theoretical apparatus built around notions such as competitive governance, polycentricism, public goods, collective action, Wicksellian efficiency, disequilibrium, and process theory and (ii) a nuanced understanding of its role in the complex competitive ecology of government, for-profit, and voluntary and nonprofit institutions.

The second chapter takes it a step further by outlining the building blocks of a theory of public entrepreneurship seen as a phenomenon intrinsically related to the problems of collective action. While the first chapter looks at the structural conditions, Chapter 2 looks at the substantive, endogenous collective action related processes. Within the parameters of collective action theory, the chapter imports critical mass theory. In carving a path from the theory of collective action to a theory of public entrepreneurship, it shows how, given a collective action situation and the potential for a necessary critical mass to solve the problems posed by it, a contribution interdependence, the production function, and the heterogeneity of preferences, resources, and information create the conditions for both the emergence of public entrepreneurship as well as for its identification, definition, and analysis. The resulting insights cast the problem of entrepreneurship in public action arenas in a new theoretical light and open up a fresh theoretical view on the relationship between entrepreneurship and political processes in general.

Both the problem of polycentrism and of collective action illuminate the degree to which public entrepreneurship is intrinsically linked to the issues of voluntary association and institutional diversity, the institutional settings and action arenas within which public entrepreneurship may emerge and operate. The next chapter (Chapter 3) charts that territory consisting of domains of voluntary action that are defined by significant degrees of freedom of exchange, choice, and association. Using political economy and public choice as the main conceptual vehicles, the Ostroms' work offers the conceptual instruments to map at multiple levels (micro, mezzo, and macro) and, from different angles, the diversity of settings defined by polycentric overlapping of the cooperating and competing arenas of collective action. The chapter reviews all of that, illuminating the structural aspects of self-governance systems and recommending a conceptual toolkit for their description and analysis.

As one advances in explaining and elaborating upon public entrepreneurship, a second dimension emerges in addition to the structural one. The logic of self-governance requires that public entrepreneurship be channeled by social actors who are operating under specific profiles and social roles. Underlying themes of public entrepreneurship are gradually morphing into a profile of a social actor who has to play a role in a specific institutional environment, with a specific set of manifest and latent functions, and assuming a certain set of political skills and capabilities. The analysis is sliding into the territory and themes of citizenship. At a closer look, public entrepreneurship, seen as a key to self-governance, is intrinsically linked to the idea of "citizen." Entrepreneurial drives have to be channeled in constructive and productive directions, avoiding the unproductive entrepreneurship trap. Citizenship, and the roles, expectations, and norms associated with it, does precisely that. Public entrepreneurship and citizenship are two facets of the same set of phenomena. The first points to an institutionally contingent function or process, and the other to a social actor role defined by certain norms, expectations, and capabilities. To understand one, we need to understand the other.

The second part is dedicated to the problem and the concept of citizenship, mainly as framed through Ostromian lenses. Chapter 4 overviews the ways the twin themes of citizenship and civic/political capabilities are reflected in the Ostroms' work. Starting with their more visible and relatively better-known views regarding citizenship and civic and political competence, the chapter will move to the less-known and less-understood dimension in which a philosophy of social order and change pivoting on citizenship and the "art and science of association" takes center stage. Next, the chapter connects the issue of citizenship to public entrepreneurship, identifying as a potential link and vehicle the notion of "ideological entrepreneurship." A closer look at how one conceptualizes ideological entrepreneurship shows how the analytical focus could be moved from the functional-structural analysis of the entrepreneurial process to the social role and the social actors' motivations, capabilities, and beliefs. In doing so, it illuminates the general pattern of the theoretical move that links the domain of public entrepreneurship theorizing to citizenship theory. While noticing the huge potential of cross-fertilization at the interface with the political theory and philosophy of citizenship and civics, the chapter also notes that the Ostromian perspective is grounded mostly in the political economy, public choice, and institutionalist domain rather than in political philosophy and theory of citizenship. Last but not least, the chapter could also be read as an argument – using textual evidence – for why the Ostroms' interest in citizenship and public entrepreneurship should not be seen as a mere footnote or marginal extension of their main work but as part and parcel of their institutional theory and their core message regarding self-governance.

The next two chapters illuminate some of the main features of the citizen-centered approach by placing them in the larger context of the recent developments in research programs and the literature that are germane to the citizen-centered approach. The key is the theme of the "social agent," bearer of social and political capabilities for collective choice and collective action. Starting from an angle based primarily in political economy and public choice institutionalism, first are engaged the evolutions that offer intellectual ammunition to the citizen-centered approach: social sciences developments that came to focus on social actors and their profiles, features, capabilities, and contextual collective action situations. Next are engaged social science and political philosophy developments that challenge and undercut the citizen-centered approach to governance.

Chapter 5 looks at the research programs focused on institutions and collective action that have revolutionized social sciences over forty years and which have inadvertently pushed to the forefront the problem of social roles – a problem that lies at the foundation of citizen theory. The chapter traces the evolution of a stream of insights and findings that make necessary the conceptualization – within theoretical political economy parameters – of social actors as bearers of culture, social norms, and ideology, acting as agents who operate with rules, values, and strategies in specific contexts and circumstances. The chapter shows how the need for agency (bearers of certain profiles and sets of capabilities) emerges from a research program that initially was supposed to look more at structure and collective action arenas and less at the individuals' profiles, social roles, and capabilities. A fascinating logic is revealed: the more the analytical attention moved on the heterogeneous set of informal institutions, social norms, values, beliefs, rules, cultural factors, and contextual factors, the more the need for a social agency model able to meaningfully operate in such a complex environment became apparent.

The next chapter, Chapter 6, looks at the opposite developments coming from the research programs, which generate findings, insights, and arguments that challenge the citizen-centered approach and the ideals of self-governance. The chapter deals with the already mentioned developments taking place in behavioral sciences and political philosophy that have profoundly challenged some of the key assumptions regarding civic and political competence of normal citizens operating in the normal circumstances of a democratic-liberal system. Alternative governance theories, some of them profoundly challenging the very notion of self-governance – such as libertarian paternalism and epistocracy – are considered. The chapter charts the nature of those challenges and tries to show how a response to them may look once one adopts the position inspired by the theoretical and normative stance advanced by the Ostroms. Part 2 will, thus, offer three ways of approaching the multifaceted problem of citizenship from an Ostromian perspective, giving a better sense of its relevance in a manner that is fully anchored in the current developments and debates of the relevant literature.

Part 3 of the book takes a broader look at the very idea of a doctrine or theory of self-governance in light of the insights brought to the table in the previous chapters. The question is, what kind of system is more precisely the governance system whose contours and elements have been touched upon again and again in the previous chapters while exploring the issues of public entrepreneurship and citizenship? Where should one place self-governance systems in relation to other governance systems? How could one classify them in the context of, perhaps, more familiar political doctrines and ideologies? These are very important questions. In the end, both the public and the scholars frame and understand a topic like the one discussed in this book using the shortcuts and heuristics of ideology. Governance ideas are, sooner or later, interpreted through the lenses of a standard taxonomy based on the more familiar and traditional ideological and doctrinal positions. This part of the book is an attempt to answer that particular challenge, and it engages the task on two dimensions.

The first dimension (Chapter 7) takes as a reference the classical, traditional anarchy versus Leviathan, state versus libertarianism, "seeing like a state" versus "seeing like an individual citizen" set of dichotomies. It is the system view of governance in which the contrast between the nature and role of the state (seen as the governance system, by definition) and its negation shape the ways one thinks about various alternative approaches to governance. In our case, the profile of the self-governance position is drawn by contrasting it to the statist, anarchist, and libertarian stances. The chapter will show why the self-governance position is neither statist nor anarchist/libertarian and why classical liberalism is the closest construct in the range of familiar political doctrines. Textual evidence will be used in an attempt to establish the grounding of the conceptual reconstruction and interpretation developed by this argument and by this volume in general.

The second direction takes as a reference point a policy view. Chapter 8 will shift its focus from a political system perspective, based on the place and role of the centralizing authority in governance systems, to the different stances one may take toward social change implemented by and via the state through social intervention. The developments in social sciences – institutionalism, public choice, behavioral economics – and in social and political philosophy have converged in raising important questions in this respect. The chapter tries to respond to one of them – given these developments and the insights they bring, how are we to interpret and translate the basic dichotomy between the interventionist and the conservative status quo orientations? Where should we place the self-governance approach, given this dichotomy? Is self-governance a progressive or a conservative project? Responding to these challenges, a nuanced stance will be articulated, navigating through the conservative resistance to change and the progressive interventionist enthusiasm toward a special position that revives and reconstructs an older tradition anchors participatory democracy elements into a classical liberal framework.

To sum up, the three parts of the book illuminate, from different but converging angles, the complex and vast array of problems, social mechanisms, and processes associated with self-governance as an ideal and as an applied institutional arrangement. The emerging set of conceptual tools and insights helps us to get a better understanding of the nature of the phenomenon and the various ways one could conceptualize it. Thus, it puts us in a stronger position to respond to the challenges raised by the refurbished ideas and doctrines that question key foundational assumptions of self-governance or the very idea of the feasibility of self-governance systems. The Ostroms' work offers an impressive set of insights regarding self-governance and its associated phenomena of public entrepreneurship, citizenship, polycentricism, and voluntary governance.

Thus, the book demonstrates an ability to inspire the response to the challenges fueled by the current developments in behavioral sciences and political theory – such as epistocratic paternalism and authoritarianism. In overviewing and discussing these insights, we need to keep in mind one important thing: the Ostroms warned us against panacea. They were keen to emphasize, again and again, the perils of thinking in terms of universal solutions. Each of their many contributions came with a reminder that what they offered is not "The Solution." Their work shows that we may be able to consistently and constructively respond to paternalist and epistocratic challenges from a civics perspective, incorporating lessons and insights from historical experience, social sciences, and philosophy. But in the end, we should never forget that we are confronted with "a world of possibility rather than of necessity," that in thinking and practicing governance, "we are neither trapped in inexorable tragedies nor free of moral responsibility" (E. Ostrom 1998, 15–16). Institutional order is not predetermined; we live in an open universe in which time and circumstances matter, but even more decisive are human deliberation, responsibility, and ideas. Humans are moral agents able to imagine alternative scenarios and create alternative strategies combining facts and values to achieve those scenarios through acts of public entrepreneurship shaped by the norms and aspirations of citizenship. Ultimately, we bear the responsibility for the alternative courses of action we design and set into motion.

PART I

PUBLIC ENTREPRENEURSHIP

The structure and functioning of any self-governance system are intrinsically dependent on the initiative and problem-solving capacities of the participating citizens. Irrespective of how one designates the factors that link the initiative of social actors with the dynamics and problem-solving capacity of the system, they represent a key to understanding self-governance. Using, as an inspiration, the scholarly literature that has explored similar factors in the context of the market process, the notion of entrepreneurship renders itself an excellent vehicle in this respect. However, extending the study of entrepreneurship from market to nonmarket settings brings to the fore a set of theoretical and methodological challenges deriving from the fact that the emphasis has to be not so much on commonalities but on the specific differences between public forms of entrepreneurship and the more familiar forms taking place in market settings. Part I advances the Ostromian approach to a new stage of identification and conceptualization of entrepreneurship in nonmarket settings. It puts together the building blocks of a conceptual apparatus that leads to an analytical and functionalist–structural perspective that is more theoretically coherent and consistent with already existent, more advanced, theorizing of entrepreneurial action in market settings.

Following the work of Elinor and Vincent Ostrom, the approach builds on three insights:

(a) Public entrepreneurship is institutionally contingent. It is a phenomenon whose emergence, structure, and dynamics are not purely individual, behavioral, and psychological but are a function of a specific institutional ecology and the decision arenas created by that. To be able to identify the public entrepreneurship function, one

19

needs to identify and use the logic of the institutional setting and the social ecology in which the action takes place.

(b) Public entrepreneurship is a phenomenon intrinsically related to collective action, and the problem of collective action is part and parcel of its identification, definition, and analysis. The problem of collective action is the ultimately defining reference point for the public entrepreneurship function. More precisely, the Ostromian approach opens the way to an innovative approach to public entrepreneurship seen as a second-order collective action problem: a collective action induced process that aims at solving collective action situations.

(c) The concept of public entrepreneurship implies a theory of voluntary association. The diverse institutional settings and action arenas within which public entrepreneurship may emerge and operate are all domains of voluntary action, defined by significant degrees of freedom of exchange, choice, and association. The Ostroms' work offers the conceptual instruments to chart, at multiple levels (micro, mezzo, and macro) and from different angles, the diversity of settings that are defined by polycentric overlapping, cooperating, and competing arenas of collective action. The articulation of these multiple dimensions, levels, and angles allows us to isolate and illustrate the public entrepreneurship function in ways that are more nuanced, theoretically precise, and empirically relevant.

The crucial insight is that following the Ostroms' approach, the concept of public entrepreneurship brings to the limelight a set of theoretical and conceptual elements associated with and implied by it. The concept has a clear descriptive and analytical meaning only when seen in the context of those assumed and implied elements. In this part of the book, they are grouped under three clusters: (i) polycentricity and competitive governance related (Chapter 1); (ii) collective action related (Chapter 2); and (iii) voluntary action and association related (Chapter 3). In conjunction, they offer a unique, coherent, and nuanced understanding of how some of the basic intuitions and insights surrounding the notion are, in fact, elements of a conceptual system that (a) anchors the theme in an area extremely relevant for the current governance theory debates, (b) puts in a new theoretical light the problem of entrepreneurship in public action arenas, and (c) may even open up a fresh theoretical view on the relationship between entrepreneurship and political processes in general. The notion of public entrepreneurship reveals itself as a most constructive and fruitful entry point into the complex conceptual universe of self-governance theory.

1

Public Entrepreneurship, Competitive Governance, and Polycentricity

The Ostroms' interest in public entrepreneurship as a key element of governance processes is one aspect of their work that, despite its centrality, has never attracted the attention it truly deserves. It is quite surprising that, so far, the relatively recent wave of interest in social and public entrepreneurship that spans disciplines hasn't delved into the important contributions made by the Bloomington scholars in this respect. This chapter revisits the Ostroms' contribution to the study of the function or category of public entrepreneurship in order to draw attention to its noteworthy place in the context and evolution of contemporary political economy theorizing. At the same time, it aims to further elaborate the conceptual and theoretical dimension of this neglected aspect of their contribution by putting together its existent but disparate and, in many cases, just left implicit, pieces. With this goal in mind, the chapter will start by presenting the basic vision of public entrepreneurship emerging from the Ostroms' work. This is a much-needed act of restoring their thoughts on the matter to their proper place in the political economy literature, an act taking place at the boundary between an exercise in history of thought and one in conceptual reconstruction. Next, based on that, it will go a step further by engaging in an effort to specify and articulate the underlying theoretical parameters of that vision as well as some of its implications.

The focus will be on the polycentricity and competitive governance preconditions of public entrepreneurship as an institutionally contingent phenomenon. What will become clear is not only (a) the measure in which polycentricity and competitive governance are operating as conditions for public entrepreneurship but also (b) the measure in which self-governance itself is a function of the polycentric and competitive nature of the institutional environment, able to engender incentives and opportunities for entrepreneurial initiatives in the public arenas.

PUBLIC ENTREPRENEURSHIP IN THE OSTROMS' VIEW: THE BASIC PERSPECTIVE

In her 1964 dissertation, "Public Entrepreneurship: A Case Study in Ground Water Basin Management," Elinor Ostrom starts by noting that the political science and economics literature "has given little consideration to the strategy used by individuals in organizing public enterprises to provide public goods and services." Economists largely confined themselves to entrepreneurship in private markets, while political scientists largely took the existence of a governmental organization as a given. Hence, the phenomena related to the undertaking of new public enterprises providing public goods and services failed to be systematically investigated. Yet, the existence of entrepreneurship in the private sector, notes Ostrom, "raises the question of whether there is a comparable function performed by those who undertake to provide public goods and services in the public sector, which might appropriately be characterized as public entrepreneurship." At least *prima facie,* in the United States, the conditions are in place for that function to manifest itself: "Concepts of home-rule, local self-government, and local autonomy in the conduct of local governmental affairs, reflect some of the same elements of freedom and openness which provide the essential conditions for the exercise of an entrepreneurship in the public sector" (E. Ostrom 1965, 5).

One may already notice that, from the very beginning, the Ostromian conceptualization of public entrepreneurship had two distinguishing components. The first is that public undertakings meet and express a demand for goods with special properties: they require collective action in order to be secured. Some goods can only be supplied if many people align their contributions. Public goods and commons have features leading to collective action, and social dilemmas factor into their demand, supply, and consumption. Public entrepreneurship is intrinsically related to solving such problems (Chapter 2 will focus on this dimension). The second is that successful public entrepreneurship depends on how open the institutional environment is to initiative. Its institutional context is presumed to be of such a nature that individuals can act relatively freely in organizing new undertakings.

Both components reflect a political economy and institutional theory in the nature of an "ecological rationality" (Smith 2008). Each type of entrepreneurship is a function of its social, institutional, and natural environment. That is to say, in their view, entrepreneurship is a truly social phenomenon; it cannot be defined or specified independently of its social context and environment. When defining or describing entrepreneurship, one always assumes an environment with certain properties. It is true that public entrepreneurship, as explained by Elinor Ostrom (1965), can be seen at one level as simply reflecting the aspects made well known by the standard economics models: Knightian, where the entrepreneur is taking the task of dealing with uncertainty (Knight 1921), Schumpeterian, in which innovation and the innovative function are central (Schumpeter 1976), and the classical notion of the entrepreneur (as the organizer and administrator of a going concern). Hence, at one level, public entrepreneurship is defined by a combination of all these three well-known functions as "a particular form of leadership focused primarily on problem-solving and putting heterogeneous processes together in complementary and effective ways" (Ostrom 2005b, 5). However, at another level, public entrepreneurship manifestations differ from the more well-known and better understood private entrepreneurship: the specificity of an entrepreneurial form is a result of the types of physical environments, objectives, and action arenas in which it manifests. From an "ecological" perspective, entrepreneurship is part and parcel of a combination of natural and social processes.

As genuine institutionalists, the Ostroms emphasize in this respect the working rules governing the behavior of entrepreneurs. To be more precise, certain institutional settings create the opportunities, incentives, and deterrents for social actors "to engage in public entrepreneurship by organizing new enterprise to secure appropriate forms of community action in providing common goods and services" (Ostrom 1965, 5). The capacity to engage in public entrepreneurship is obviously enhanced when "there are ground rules which stress the right of local communities to self-determination," thus laying a framework for public enterprise activities of individuals and groups (Ostrom 1965, 5).

This is not to say that only legislative enactments and public rules and regulations "provide the working rules which public entrepreneurs must follow in proceeding to undertake a new enterprise." In a sense, that is true for any enterprise. But more interestingly, public entrepreneurs have specific capabilities; they can exercise "fundamentally different powers to develop, control and allocate resources than private entrepreneurs." Public entrepreneurs "have access to the use of such powers as eminent domain and taxation which extend the range of activities in which they can engage." For instance, one of the thirty-two parties involved in the Californian Raymond Basin stipulated agreement (a key case study used by Ostrom in her analysis) never signed to the stipulation. Yet, the

Californian authority enforced a bottom-up initiated written agreement that followed a strenuous collective negotiation and litigation process (Ostrom 1990, 113). The proportionate cutback in water pumping was arguably the efficient solution to the problem of water depletion.

Aside from special access to coercive legal instruments, another feature peculiar to public entrepreneurship is a wider spread of entrepreneurial effort among beneficiaries. The absence of a unique residual claimant of the ensuing gains makes it so that entrepreneurial effort is more dispersed among actors in the case of public than in the case of private entrepreneurship. Even though some actors play a stronger role than others, most cases feature a shifting configuration of entrepreneurs. In the case of the Raymond Basin, sixteen of the parties had a single lawyer to represent them in litigations; yet, the lawyer was not the only entrepreneur. Because only some parties know how to best approach certain other parties, considerable amounts of dispersed tacit knowledge are needed to reach collective agreements (Ostrom 1990). With public entrepreneurship, bringing people together with an aim of providing public goods, various actors can hold different keys.

These are only two of the features that distinguish public from private entrepreneurship. In general, the different working rules of the market and the public arena affect the motivations, behaviors, and strategies of public and private entrepreneurs in different ways. Beyond the differences, the Ostroms' work drew our attention to the fact that an institutionalist or "ecological rationality" perspective on entrepreneurship – be it private or public – speaks in favor of shifting attention from the purely individual features associated with entrepreneurship toward the operating environment, the action arenas in which those behaviors or attitudes manifest. We are dealing with an institutional and broadly defined "political" phenomenon; hence, one cannot reduce entrepreneurship to a mere set of psychological or behavioral features or to occurrences of "discovery" or "innovation." Entrepreneurship can be understood as such only as a composite phenomenon emerging in the interplay between the individual and social–institutional aspects. The specific differences between various types of entrepreneurship have their source primarily in this interplay. Entrepreneurship is not only about individual motivation but also about institutional channeling, and not only about social conventions but also about the natural features that define the various degrees of publicness of a service. All these must be analyzed together. The very definition of entrepreneurship has to be adjusted to the composite and process features of these phenomena we associate under that label. In brief, to get analytical traction and to be a meaningful social science concept, public entrepreneurship needs to be embedded in a well-articulated conceptual and theoretical framework capturing this compounded process.

POLYCENTRICITY AS A CONDITION FOR PUBLIC ENTREPRENEURSHIP

Vincent Ostrom, a pioneer of the theory of competitive governance and polycentricism, has provided precisely that broader framework able to capture the configuration of the operating environment and able to specify the functional nature of public entrepreneurship. To take a step further in understanding this approach to entrepreneurship, one needs to place it on the background given by Vincent Ostrom's work on competitive governance and polycentricity, its proper intellectual context.

Vincent Ostrom's theoretical and normative perspective was built around units of observation and empirical case studies provided by the US metropolitan governance. This environment was described as a quasi-open institutional system in which a citizen can opt for jurisdictions that offer the more highly preferred bundle of local public goods and services. It was observed that polycentricity – the existence of multiple and overlapping centers of decision-making and governance – allows citizens to pressure local governments that act as suppliers. Threatened by their subjects' increased effective choice, governance units had to stay competitive to secure their citizens' loyalty. These observations could be generalized. The more open to entry and exit jurisdictions are, the more competition is induced in the system. The increased rivalry musters entrepreneurial forces toward a better calibration of public services to the demand. A better calibration or adjustment of supply to demand means increased welfare and greater efficiency in providing public goods. Public entrepreneurship emerges naturally in such polycentric environments, and with it emerges an entire range of organizational and associated forms, many of them nonprofit and voluntary, most of them associated with the "neither markets nor states" "third sector" (Aligica 2016). Public entrepreneurship is a force that fuels change and institutional adaptation to change in a wider system with an increased range of supply. As the Ostroms repeatedly noted, competition in the public goods economy – vying for citizens to resolve problems and procure services in an urban neighborhood – may be a method for reducing opportunistic behavior and taking advantage of localized knowledge. Allowing citizens to form neighborhood-level collective consumption units encourages face-to-face discussion and the achievement of common understanding as well as better monitoring, coordination, and self-governance. Public entrepreneurship is both a condition and a consequence of this institutional environment, imperfectly but clearly illustrated by US metropolitan governance.

In a word, public entrepreneurship (under this particular definition extracted both deductively from political economy theory and inductively from the metropolitan governance research) seems to be associated with a particular form of social order that is pluralist, complex, and dynamic. Given the diversity of environments, preferences, values, and interests in a heterogeneous and dynamic society, one may anticipate that the result of this type of order is a process leading not to "a single, most efficient pattern of organization but to a continual search for more efficient ways to perform" (Oakerson and Parks [1988] in McGinnis 1999, 320; V. Ostrom 1987). This process is fueling a diversity and complexity of competing and overlapping organizational forms. To conceptualize the nature of such a system, Vincent Ostrom has introduced and elaborated on – as we have already noted – the notion of polycentricity:

[The notion suggests that] a system of ordered relationships underlies the fragmentation of authority and overlapping jurisdictions that had frequently been identified as "chaotic" and as the principal source of institutional failure in the government of metropolitan areas. We identified a polycentric political system as having many centers of decision making that were formally independent of each other. A "system" was viewed as a set of ordered relationships that persists through time. (V. Ostrom [1972] in McGinnis 1999, 53)

In a similar vein, Elinor Ostrom notes that the structure of rich polycentric systems induces self-organization, initiative, and institutional adaptation, phenomena associated with public entrepreneurship:

While all institutions are subject to takeover by opportunistic individuals and to the potential for perverse dynamics, a political system that has multiple centers of power at differing scales provides more opportunity for citizens and their officials to innovate and to intervene so as to correct maldistributions of authority and outcomes. Thus, polycentric systems are more likely than monocentric systems to provide incentives leading to self-organized, self-corrective institutional change. (E. Ostrom 1998)

Two observations based on all of the above are in order. First, the logic of metropolitan governance cases and patterns on which the Ostroms based their insights could indeed be generalized to other social domains. It makes intuitive sense to conjecture that public entrepreneurship is more likely to emerge in recognizable forms in systems that are open and polycentric.

Polycentric systems engender multiple forms of organization: for-profit, nonprofit, and mixed. Second, one can see how the Ostroms' view of the concept of public entrepreneurship fits as a crucial piece in the architecture and analysis of the nature and dynamics of polycentric systems. Public entrepreneurship emerges as a function in a complex arrangement with several moving pieces. The dynamics of polycentric systems can only be explained by a conjunction of voice, exit, competition, and public entrepreneurship. In the absence of public entrepreneurship, citizens' voices and exits alone are unable to operate effectively as a mechanism for "translating jurisdictional fragmentation and overlap into relatively efficient outcomes" (Kuhnert 2001). At its turn, the polycentric system gives function and meaning to competition, voice, and exit. In the absence of polycentricity, competitive forces take different forms that channel and shape entrepreneurship in other directions.

We have now a better sense of the place of the notion of public entrepreneurship in the broader theoretical and conceptual architecture of the Ostroms' thought. Far from being a mere construct of shallow theoretical substance, floating on quasi-commonsensical research questions meant to be answered empirically in contextual research settings, the notion of public entrepreneurship was, in the Ostroms' view, part and parcel of a broader effort to articulate a vision of social order and social change in specific social circumstances and institutional conditions. The notion cannot be understood and elaborated on independently of the theory articulating this vision. That theory functions as its conceptual background and its semantic context and engenders a specific model of the relationship between different forms of organizing the production, financing, and provision of goods and services. Identifying and using the theoretical lenses articulated by the Ostroms gives us a better sense of the relationship between the market, the state, the third sector, and their components as part of the public economy within which public entrepreneurship comes to play its function. The link to the underlying theme of self-governance is evident.

THE UNDERLYING THEORETICAL ASSUMPTION: COMPETITIVE GOVERNANCE

The previous sections have outlined the basic elements of the Ostroms' vision of public entrepreneurship, and in doing so, it pointed toward a particular model of the social process associated with it. Using the Ostromian approach as a vehicle, one can take a step further and specify the features of the underlying model as well as identify more systematically the processes at work. We'll make explicit what has been implicit while relying at the same time on textual evidence from their work.

We have seen that the theoretical framework within which the notion of public entrepreneurship acquires meaning and substance is predicated on the idea of a relatively open polycentric system in which competition within the rules of the game creates favorable conditions for choice and for the phenomena we describe under the label of "public entrepreneurship." The next step in analyzing this cluster of phenomena is to make explicit the assumptions implicit in the theoretical framework employed to capture it.

The most effective way to approach this task is to start with the Tiebout model, the core of Vincent Ostrom's apparatus (Ostrom, Tiebout, and Warren 1961). This construct captures some usually taken for granted elements, in the absence of which significant facets or manifestations of public entrepreneurship would simply not be imaginable. As already suggested, the model is predicated on the presumption that citizens could (and in many real-life situations either do or threaten to) vote with their feet. Citizens are in the position to exercise their exit options from a jurisdiction. When dissatisfied with the bundle of goods or services in place, they simply leave – or threaten to leave – prompted by a cost–benefit calculus. This simple assumption focuses our attention on an entire set of phenomena surrounding and intrinsically associated with public entrepreneurship, either as its conditions or as its consequences.

At the same time, it forces us to think in unorthodox ways. The argument could be advanced a step further by specifying the components of the social mechanisms at work. For instance, the possibility of exit is, indeed, a key condition. But there are limits to the measure to which citizens' exits alone can be effective. Geographical exit (physical relocation) could be very disruptive and costly. Second, the loss of tax revenue and the decline of the real estate market are longer-term phenomena, with no immediate effect on local officials. Hence, one needs to see the Tiebout effect in a broader context in which exit is not simply geographical and where it operates in conjunction with alternatives like voice or voting.

"Voice" signals and articulates dissatisfaction with the existing situation and complements the sorting process, forcing local officials to adapt to citizens' preferences and align the qualities and quantity of services with costs (taxes), and the other way around as well. Voice and exit operate in a mutually reinforcing way. Both help shape the demand for and supply of (public) goods and services. Both create the conditions for public entrepreneurship to manifest. In conjunction with electoral signaling and voting, they foster the exercise of *initiative* by the citizens in expressing demand, as well as the response of the officials in meeting that demand. The tendency toward alignment of supply and demand in a complex and diverse system is, as we shall see in the section entitled "Public Entrepreneurship, Efficiency, Equilibrium, and Process Theory," an emergent result of these working processes. In such a system, demand is revealed not only through the ballot box and via representatives and elected centers of power, but also through informal channels and via nonelected and purely administrative centers of decision-making involved in the production of goods and services.

This is the environment within which public entrepreneurs emerge on the supply side, responding to the demand revealed and manifested in a wide variety of forms. As Oakerson and Parks, two important collaborators of the Ostroms, succinctly put it, "Organizational innovations, especially those that involve multiple jurisdictions, emerge from discussions and negotiation – processes that enable individuals to discern common interests among diverse communities." Yet, innovation requires time and effort. There are significant costs involved: "Some individuals must be willing to incur those costs if a complex metropolitan area is to function effectively. This is the work of individuals we call 'public entrepreneurs' namely, persons who propose ideas and carry the burden of ensuring discussion, compromise, and creative settlement" (Oakerson and Parks [1988] in McGinnis 1999, 320).

As one may immediately realize, the model is part of the family of competition models. It is an instantiation of the theory of competition extended to nonmarket settings. At this juncture, one could use this theoretical framework, following Breton's (1996) trailblazing work as a vehicle, to move the discussion via the Ostromian notion of polycentricity to another level.

As in most competition models, an individual has preferences for a service or goods, has some meaningful freedom of choice, and will tend to choose based on quality and cost. In the polycentric world, there are multiple suppliers of diverse goods and services: for-profit market-based, state, and nonprofit organizations (or if there are not many, there are no significant barriers to their emergence). That is to say, we are now moving beyond the limited "markets versus states" dichotomy perspective. The model assumes product differentiation in response to a larger diversity of demand, and hence, in it, diverse nonprofit organizations emerge because, in some circumstances, they have a comparative advantage in providing certain collective goods that otherwise are less efficiently provided by either state or market organizations. They respond to niches of demand of quantities and qualities that are not covered by commercial or governmental organizations.

The fact that all services are, to some extent, similar or substitutes entails that all organizations compete with all others on some margin (Breton 1996). There are no goods that are, by their very nature, a market or government monopoly. For instance, something having features of a "public good" is not necessarily and exclusively deliverable through the state. This assumption is transparent in the ways the Ostroms treat the very idea of government and governance services and functions. One should not think of "government" or "governance," they write, as "something provided by states alone."

Families, voluntary associations, villages, and other forms of human association all involve some form of self-government. Rather than looking only to states, we need to give much more attention to building the kinds of basic institutional structures that enable people to find ways of relating constructively to one another and of resolving problems in their daily lives. (V. Ostrom in Aligica and Boettke 2009, 146)

One may start with a more realistic assumption that, in real life, there are complex mixed economies that contain public and private enterprises, for-profit and nonprofit organizations, and that emerge in a wide variety of provision, production, and financing formulas:

Public services need not be provided by a central government or the state. Many streets, roads, and other thoroughfares; fire protection; police services; and other such services may be arranged by local communities. These arrangements may rely on private entrepreneurs, but under terms and conditions that are communally specified. (V. Ostrom in Aligica and Boettke 2009, 146)

The goods may be provided at different costs, in different bundles, and in different qualities and quantities by different organizational forms, families, churches, humanitarian bodies, cooperatives. Yet, ultimately, they are essentially similar to those provided by states and markets or are close substitutes for them.

That, indeed, means that, assuming a relatively open system, all these organizations will become more and more engaged in some form of effective *competition*. We have thus come to identify even more clearly the major unifying feature of the architecture of the theoretical framework: the functional and structural link between *polycentricity, public entrepreneurship, and competition*. The system that the Ostroms assume in their theoretical articulations of public entrepreneurship is based on a model of competition extended to nonmarket settings. It is a system of competitive production of goods with different features (public, private, commons, toll, club goods) done by a variety of market, governmental, and nonmarket voluntary organizations. It is a system based on choice and engendering choices. This conclusion is fully consistent with both the spirit and letter of the Ostroms' work.

When people exercise their prerogatives as citizens under a properly constituted system of government, they are able to take into account how their decisions may affect the productive and consumptive possibilities that will be available to them under the institutions they fashion. This implies that individual choice is not limited to choice on the basis of price in a market, but involves a broader range of calculations extending to the choice of terms on which alternatives become available under diverse institutional arrangements, including both market and non-market institutions. (V. Ostrom in Aligica and Boettke 2009, 146)

In light of all of the above, one can also understand the implications of the fact that all organizations in a system that displays polycentric features are potentially in a rivalrous relationship at multiple levels and in many forms. The simple existence of multiple producers within the same geographic region changes the dynamics of the relationship between citizen and public official as well as the relationship the state has with other forms of governance or collective goods production and organization. However, competition in such cases may not take the same forms as market competition. To compete at all, organizations do not need to compete on the same margin. They use their comparative and competitive advantages to differentiate their products or operational domains. Nor do organizations need to compete on the same terms. Shifting the terms of competition is itself a form of competition. This dynamic process creates the conditions for the emergence, growth, evolution, and decline of an entire range of organizational forms, many having features that transcend the markets versus states dichotomy, thus continuing to fuel and restructure the core of the so-called third sector.

This chain of observations leads to the next key point. Public entrepreneurship as theorized by the Ostroms has to ultimately be seen in a competitive context that gives it an efficiency-enhancing propensity. "When there is an environment that enhances their capacities to organize, mobilize resources, and invest in public facilities," they write, "local public entrepreneurs can develop a wide variety of efficiency-enhancing solutions to local collective-action problems" (V. Ostrom in Aligica and Boettke 2009, 155). Pinpointing the efficiency-enhancing properties opens a further avenue for elaboration of the model. However, to conceptualize this tendency toward efficiency, the market model helps only up to a point.

Writing about the history of the notion of polycentricity, Vincent Ostrom notes that it was never intended "to develop a strict market model for the supply of public goods and services to individual buyers." Nor was it intended "to present an economic analogy based upon classical economic theory." The intention was to point out that "quasi-market mechanisms were operable in a public service economy" and that reality "would imply important new dimensions for a theory of public adminis-tration" (V. Ostrom [1972] in McGinnis 1999, 54). The section entitled "Public Entrepreneurship, Efficiency, Equilibrium, and Process Theory" will deal with this challenge.

Summing up the argument so far: the major contribution of the Ostroms' position, as emerging in the light of our discussion, has been to draw attention to the fact that to make sense of public entrepreneurship as a meaningful social science notion, one has to assume an institutional environment engendering a *nonmarket* form of competition, driven by individuals that are self-interested and relatively rational in calculating costs and benefits of producing and consuming certain goods and services. To speak about public entrepreneurship in the absence of reference to the underlying forces and forms of competition engendered by the demand, production, and supply of various goods and services in communities that have to make private and public decisions regarding competing uses of scarce resources is to project the notion outside the sphere of the social and economic phenomena from which it derives its ultimate meaning.

PUBLIC ENTREPRENEURSHIP, EFFICIENCY, EQUILIBRIUM, AND PROCESS THEORY

Putting the pieces together and articulating explicitly the links between them, one may take yet another step further in elaboration. Using the broad notions of "competition" and "competitive systems" as benchmarks, one may construe a spectrum of ideal-type social systems. At one end are monolithic systems, closed to competition. At the other end are composite, compounded systems with power and decision-making divided between multiple centers, thus engendering competition. We have shown how the Ostroms assume for their treatment of public entrepreneurship a situation closer to the competitive end of the spectrum. In such systems, public entrepreneurs "are given both incentive and opportunity to configure and reconfigure   productive   organizational   and   inter-organizational arrangements" (Oakerson and Parks [1988] in McGinnis 1999, 326). We have also seen that the Ostroms noted the efficiency-enhancing properties of systems that allow for experimentation with such diverse organizational and institutional reconfigurations. As noted by Oakerson and Parks ([1988] in McGinnis 1999, 326), public entrepreneurship as a response to citizens' preferences in competitive conditions can explain the "efficiency-inducing properties of polycentricism." Addressing the problem of this tendency toward equilibrium in matching resources to needs, and toward efficiency in provision, takes us to the last step in fully specifying what the Ostroms' view of public entrepreneurship entails.

Mainstream economics insights provide a benchmark and a starting point that could be transcended with a broader political economy perspective. In neoclassical economics, the logic of a competitive system operating on supply and demand of goods and services leads toward a well-specified equilibrium. That equilibrium is explicitly associated with various criteria of efficiency. Once we shift attention from market competition to competitive governance, one implicitly faces the following question: What is "efficiency" and what is "equilibrium" in a nonmarket competition mode of the type hinted at by the Ostroms? What is the nature of the equilibrium (if any) toward which competition in this broader action arena is pushing? What is the meaning and nature of efficiency in such a case?

By all accounts, although the Ostroms did not elaborate on this line of argument, it looks like one concept of efficiency expounded in the traditional literature is closer than any other to their intuition. This is the Wicksell–Lindahl efficiency or Wicksellian efficiency: In the Ostroms' perspective, the connection between the costs and the benefits of publicly supplied goods and services is crucial. In their view, citizens try constantly to assess the costs and benefits of various public goods and services, weighing them and acting accordingly. But this is precisely the feature of what is known as the Wicksellian approach to efficiency. This approach takes us to the link between (a) the tax price citizens pay through taxes for the goods and services provided by governments and (b) the valuation the same citizens place on those goods and services. The closer the match, the more efficient the system. By definition, the better aligned the price and the valuation are to each other, the closer the system is to efficient equilibrium.

In its purest form, the model postulates a collective decision about expenditures and a collective decision about revenues, made simultaneously and unanimously. The connection thus formed between costs and benefits is of such a nature that the resulting collective decisions are Pareto-efficient (Breton 1996, 23). This Wicksellian optimum is an ideal situation, an imaginary state helping us as a benchmark or a heuristic device. It is built using a set of assumptions typical of neoclassical economics, including the full information and rationality of the decision-makers. The problem is that, useful as it is, the benchmark itself says little about the process leading to the alignment of demand and supply of public goods and the efficiency-inducing features of this process. It is pointing in the right direction, but it is not a fully satisfying solution. For instance, Wicksellian efficiency assumes that the objects of choice are already available. The solution set, in the form of public services or in the form of organizational means to provide those services, is assumed to be already discovered and in place. Entrepreneurial actions are, thus, simply assumed away. Here is where the limits of neoclassical economics inspired models become palpable. The difficulties in conceptualizing entrepreneurship within the neoclassical framework are notorious. If competition in the public goods economy is a quasi-market process, then we must be able to specify a theory of a quasi-market process and an explanation of the tendency toward equilibrium that creates room for entrepreneurship and its theorization.

The last step in our argument will be dedicated to that task. In our efforts to delineate the firmer contours of the Ostroms' perspective, we need to introduce a notion and theory of competition that departs from the mainstream version while retaining some less stringent version of the conceptual benchmarks (such as equilibrium, rationality, and efficiency) that have been so useful thus far as a heuristic and definitional instrument. Fortunately, a theory that fits the description has already been advanced in social sciences by an important school of political economy initiated by Carl Menger during the second half of the nineteenth century. It was continued via Ludwig von Mises (1920; 1922) and Friedrich A. Hayek (1945) and relabeled in the second half of the twentieth century by Israel Kirzner as a "process" theory (Kirzner 1992, 1973; Boettke 2010; O'Driscoll and Rizzo 1985). Its conceptual apparatus provides the needed element in our elaboration of the Ostromian perspective on entrepreneurship theory.

Its distinctive feature lies in its interpretation of equilibrium and disequilibrium amid rivalry and competition as a background for a clearly stated theory of entrepreneurship. The approach changes the emphasis: while the neoclassical approach focuses on optimal resource allocation problems and the mechanics of equilibrium, the Austrian approach focuses on the process of adjustment itself and on the path toward equilibrium, including the variety of disequilibria on the way. The static properties of the system in equilibrium are replaced with alertness, change, discovery, invention, and creativity – and importantly, with an emphasis on the processes related to them. The neoclassical mechanist and algorithmic perspective is thus replaced by a process view. Competition itself becomes more realistic and not a mere abstract assumption for a formal allocation modeling exercise.

Seen in this light, the market and the competitive process are not a matter of efficient allocation configurations but a matter of *dynamic adjustment*. For instance, when it comes to market processes, prices serve as the basis of economic calculation "only in the context of a process of competition brought into being by what formalism assumes away: disequilibrium" (Boettke 2010, 280–281; O'Driscoll and Rizzo 1985). Various states of disequilibrium and their competitive features become crucial. On the one hand, there is the tendency to depart from equilibrium. Discovery, error, changes in the environment, or acts of Schumpeterian entrepreneurship fuel it. On the other hand is the tendency toward equilibrium via the price system fueled by "arbitrage," (Kirznerian) entrepreneurship that acts in the direction of matching resources to demand and thus pushing things toward increasing efficiency.

In brief, this so-called Austrian approach offers a theoretical framework that gives meaning to entrepreneurship both/either as a force operating on the tendency toward equilibrium or as a factor in disequilibrium. Kirzner (1997, 81) clarifies that this theory "makes no claim that the market outcomes at any given date are efficient and socially optimal (in any sense in which traditional neoclassical welfare theory would use these terms)." Instead, the market works as a system of incentives and information conducting actors to adjust their behavior and engage in error correcting. Thus, it is inducing a tendency toward equilibrium. "We appreciate that there are equilibrating forces but that doesn't mean that an equilibrating process is at all times in progress." Therefore, explains Kirzner, "the social significance of a market system does not reside in the beauty of the allocation pattern under equilibrium conditions." Instead, "it rests upon the capacity of markets to translate the errors made in the immediate past into opportunities for pure entrepreneurial profit of direct interest to potential entrepreneurs."

For our purposes, it is important to also note that Austrian theorists go to lengths explaining that this process and its capacities are a function of a particular institutional framework. It is not only the signaling and production and dissemination of relevant knowledge that we typically attribute to the market. The institutional environment also may help or hinder this adjustment-and-discovery process by improving or diminishing the chances for entrepreneurial discovery. Kirzner (1997) calls this ongoing institutionally induced process of adjustment, alertness, discovery, learning, and error correction taking place within a secure system of property rights the "entrepreneurial process."

Based on all of the above, it is understandable how the argument outlined above could be relatively easily extended outside the domain of the market. In fact, Austrian theory inspired scholars have developed a rather concrete series of applications to problems outside of the typical sphere of the market. Christopher Coyne's (2013) work on humanitarian interventions is paradigmatic for the application of Austrian ideas to concrete case studies of direct relevance to voluntary, nonprofit social actions and institutions. Applications related to the problem of interventionism and civil society have been made for the problem of disaster relief and recovery using research designs operationalized in field research and in-depth case studies (Chamlee-Wright 2010; Grube and Storr 2013; Storr, Haeffele-Balch, and Grube 2015).

It is rather plausible that the competitive governance situations theorized by the Ostroms and their settings conceptualized as polycentric engender a sufficiently powerful competitive dynamic to justify the use of the Austrian heuristics. Hence, this view, once extended and calibrated to public and nonmarket settings, seems to be the appropriate context for the concept of public entrepreneurship. The process may be less effective, less dynamic, and further from equilibrium than in the case of the market. Yet, polycentric systems, via competitive governance, may create the forces and mechanisms pushing toward equilibrium through a dynamic, equilibrating adjustment process. The Wicksellian equilibrium may never be realized, but the tendency should nonetheless be more or less present as long as the minimally supportive institutional environment is in place. While the end result of this process will never actually be a stable most efficient pattern of organizational configurations, polycentricity still predicts a continual search for more efficient ways to perform. We may easily conjecture that the more a system encourages initiative and decision, the more productive public entrepreneurship will emerge, as long as we stay within the rules of the game. This tendency itself is the stable outcome, and it is in this sense that we can speak of a structural trend toward efficiency.

We are now in the position to restate succinctly the essence of the argument in light of its latest elaboration: the Ostromian approach defines and analyzes public entrepreneurship as a phenomenon emerging in the specific environment of a competitive governance system of a polycentric nature in which the social mechanisms at work have at least a minimal tendency toward Wicksellian efficiency. In such systems whose operations are best captured through "process" competition theory, entrepreneurship manifests itself in multiple ways: public, private, and mixed forms that generate a diversity of initiatives and arrangements. The state and state-based arrangements are, thus, competing with other non-state (market, nonprofit, voluntary) organizations. As a result, the analogy with the standard market process is warranted. Given a minimal set of favorable conditions, a dynamic process of entrepreneurial adjustment and innovation is set into motion. The process itself is always imperfect and fallible. Yet, when certain minimal conditions are in place, its emergence engenders a sufficiently forceful drive toward a form of Wicksellian equilibrium. Last but not least, in this approach, entrepreneurial action is pivotal: it is both a driver and a consequence of this process. That allows us to describe the relevant competitive governance phenomena using the Schumpeterian and Kirznerian models and, thus, to fully and robustly connect the Ostromian perspective to the mainstream entrepreneurship literature.

IMPLICATIONS AND CONCLUSIONS

The Ostroms' work opens up a deeper and richer perspective on public entrepreneurship and, by extension, on the relationship between entrepreneurship and public governance systems in general. As a result, it identifies a crucial missing link between political economy and entrepreneurship studies. Its thrust resides in more than the observation which states that in order to describe the nature of entrepreneurial endeavors, one needs to describe the political–institutional environment itself, the functional relationships between institutional arenas and the social actions that give structure and meaning to those endeavors. The Ostroms' concept of polycentricity converts that observation into a viable theoretical instrument and takes the discussion to a new level. We are, thus, led to a more systematic understanding of the dual relationship between entrepreneurship (in its multiple facets) and the institutional structures that define a public administration or governance system, as well as the processes emerging from that interaction. Seen in this light, public entrepreneurship doesn't seem anymore to be a secondhand entrepreneurial manifestation, an imperfect and struggling entrepreneurialism in an uncongenial setting. It is part and parcel of modern pluralistic governance systems. Its role is pivotal: Given a set of minimal conditions, including the relative openness to entry and exit across domains and jurisdictions as well as some room for rivalry, contestation, and voice, public entrepreneurship emerges as a major driver of change and adaptation.

The second set of lessons and insights brought to light by our exploration of the Ostroms' views relates to the very problem of conceptualizing and theorizing entrepreneurial actions and situations. We are led to the observation that "entrepreneurship" may be a label for a type of institutionally contingent and composite phenomena. Entrepreneurship seems obviously more than a set of psychological or behavioral features of social actors and more than events and incidents (of discovery, creativity, invention) of a significance to be more or less arbitrarily determined ex post. To call something entrepreneurship (be it public, private, social, or political) requires more than an appeal, a showcase of acts of invention, creation, discovery, alertness, etc. The notion evokes a structural context, a specific institutional configuration that allows us to assign a phenomenon to the class of instances of entrepreneurship. No context or description of it serves the cause of entrepreneurship and its analysis. The "context" has mainly to do with multiple supply and demand centers; their various forms of competition; efficacy in purposeful, goal-driven, instrumental rational actions; a systemic tendency toward efficacy induced into the system; and a general tendency toward (a broadly defined) equilibrium. In the absence of all these, it makes sense to speak only of innovation, discovery, etc. To qualify the latter as entrepreneurial or entrepreneurship requires evoking at least some of the aforementioned elements. To detach the elements from the concept, to reduce it to attitudes and motivations or to psychological traits or actions related to them, is to void the concept of its very essence.

In brief, by following the Ostroms and extending their views, one may be able to articulate an approach in which public entrepreneurship is studied as a compounded phenomenon, a composite social fact in which a structural dimension (described in precise economic and social theory terms) is combined with a psychological or behavioral one. Given the fact that the dynamic, dialectic element is unavoidable, that leads to a process perspective. That doesn't mean that other perspectives that focus on psychological features, attitudes, behaviors, actions, and events are not legitimate. It means that the Ostroms' inspired approach draws attention to a different angle, a complementary and perhaps more comprehensive and systemic approach.

Last but not least, the current discussion in this chapter has repeatedly touched on the normative dimension, although it did not fully explore it in all its implications. We have seen that there is a robust conjecture that rivalry and competition in such dynamic, entrepreneurial governance systems defined by polycentricity may induce a tendency toward efficiency.

At the same time, it may lead to checking opportunistic and corrupt behavior and encouraging civic, voluntary, and philanthropic attitudes. It is important to note that the Ostroms themselves had a strong interest in precisely this normative aspect that is at the core of their views about self-governance systems, and one cannot conclude this discussion without mentioning this fact, which will require a repeated discussion in itself. In the Ostroms' view, public entrepreneurship is a governance ideal and something of a political virtue, seen in conjunction with citizenship. A self-governance system could hardly be understood in its functioning in the absence of an understanding of public entrepreneurship and its operations within polycentric, competitive institutional arrangements. Focusing on public entrepreneurship opens a series of insights into the deep structure of self-governance.

To sum up, the Ostroms' case for the study of the entrepreneurial function in political processes and governance systems is rather compelling, both in its positive theory and normative dimensions. This chapter elaborated on that case by going back to the Ostroms' work on polycentricity and public economies and showing how they opened a possible conceptual avenue toward the integration of the entrepreneurial function in political economy theorizing and, through that, toward the analysis of self-governance systems. As a result, it has only touched the surface of a rich territory waiting to be explored at the boundary between social science analysis and normative theory. Chapter 2 will take a step further by focusing on the collective next dimensions of public entrepreneurship.

2

Entrepreneurship and Collective Action

Chapter 1 revealed the measure in which public entrepreneurship is institutionally contingent, assuming and implying a polycentric institutional structure and competitive governance processes. The public entrepreneurship function emerges and flourishes in such institutional environments. In this chapter, we take a step further in focusing on the second functional dimension of public entrepreneurship as outlined in the Ostroms' approach: the one related to collective action. The conceptual space becomes thus clearer. On one axis is the monocentricity–polycentricity dimension; on the other axis is the private–collective action dimension. The more one moves to the polycentric collective action area of the conceptual space, the more likely the emergence of public entrepreneurship is, given the institutional configuration in place. We are now at the core of the problem of self-governance. The success of self-governance systems depends on the measure in which such systems are able to solve collective action problems. Most arguments against self-governance are pointing precisely to the problem of collective action as the reason why such systems are not viable. The analysis of public entrepreneurship in collective action situations is one of the most perceptive ways to fathom what is going on in those situations and to test and reject such criticisms.

While revisiting some key aspects of Mancur Olson's (1971) classical treatment of the problem of collective action, the approach advanced in this chapter combines three major relevant intellectual elements: First, the underlying methodological assumption is based on Ludwig von Mises's functional and formal understanding of entrepreneurship as a praxeological concept. We have already noted how Mises (1998, 61) applied his dual epistemology of social sciences conjoining history with theory and distinguishes between two meanings of entrepreneurship and two corresponding ways of doing entrepreneurship analysis. The first is associated with a historical and typological–psychological interest in a type of human individual, the entrepreneur as social actor, and in the features and activities of that ideal type as instantiated in personalities and historical circumstances. The second meaning is functionalist and formal: entrepreneurship is a category of human action. Entrepreneurship thus makes the object of a social science approach in which theory and conceptual development are the main drivers. In this formal social theory, as opposed to historical and typological research, we look at how actions – described only by their formal features – interrelate, as driven by the logic of purposeful human decisions. If we bring this interrelatedness of actions to the foreground, we understand entrepreneurship as a social phenomenon, a phenomenon with a certain function that gains contour in certain webs of interactions generated by acting human beings. If so, then entrepreneurship must take a private or a public form, depending on the nature of the social web in which it manifests. As Shockley (2009) and Klein et al. (2010) observe, it is the logic of the web that defines the functional features of entrepreneurship.

Second, it extends this implied Misesian perspective by looking at a particular web of interactions: the collective action situation. Public entrepreneurship, understood along the lines suggested in Chapter 1, is intrinsically related to collective action and has a compounded nature: (a) the attributes and behavior of the individual, (b) the structural–environmental circumstances, and (c) the intended and actual consequents. Entrepreneurship is an individual action-driven process that occurs in a certain kind of environment, aiming at generating a certain type of change in that environment. As a compounded phenomenon, entrepreneurship depends on all three components: its analysis is complete only when the entrepreneurial aspect of human behavior is seen in connection with the environment that makes it possible and with the result that it feeds back into that environment. Collective action is the feature that most distinctively defines both the structural circumstances and the intended results of entrepreneurial activities in public settings.

Third, to achieve the chapter's objective, a particular theory of collective action needs to be imported. This chapter introduces in its treatment of the problem of collective action the critical mass theory perspective. From the pioneering work of Pamela Oliver, Gerald Marwell, and their collaborators, it adopts the notion of a critical mass of contributors able to ignite the completion of collective action. A critical mass is the critical level of resource contributions to a collective good that must be reached for the collective good to come into existence (Oliver, Marwell, and Teixera 1985).

It is assumed that (a) group members are heterogeneous in their interests and (b) their actions are interdependent in the sense that individuals take account of how much others have contributed in making their own decisions about contributing to collective action. These are the basic factors that determine contributions and, through contributions, the level of effectiveness of group actions in pursuit of a collective good. These factors explain the probability of a collective good's provision, a collective good's level of achievement, or the extent of a collective good. Intermediate contributions produce intermediate probabilities of success.

This is, broadly speaking, the framework of the approach. Within this framework, we are able to identify the parameters of the public entrepreneurship function in nonmarket settings; specifically, in the circumstances of collective action. The chapter shows how combining the process–functional understanding of entrepreneurship with the critical mass approach to collective action (a) helps us conceptually identify and pinpoint with even more accuracy the function of public entrepreneurship, (b) opens the way for the development of a theoretically driven empirical approach to the study of public entrepreneurship, and (c) gives us a more precise understanding of what happens at the microlevel in the process of self-governance and how public entrepreneurship is essential in solving the collective action dilemmas that are at the core of any governance system.

THE COLLECTIVE ACTION SITUATION AND THE CRITICAL MASS APPROACH TO IT

As already mentioned, the approach looks at public entrepreneurship as intrinsically connected to collective action situations and their correlates, such as public goods and services production, distribution, and consumption. A collective action situation is one where members of a group have a common interest in a collective good, but there is a mismatch of individual interests. Hence, the members are unable to collectively reach the goal without additional coordination and cooperation. The problem may be described as a *collective efficacy* problem, where individuals lack sufficient cohesion and willingness to provide the common good. It can also be analyzed as a *free rider* problem, where each individual holds back their contribution, expecting that a sufficient number of others will take care of it with theirs. Needless to say, solutions to collective action problems are costly and involve trade-offs. The literature distinguishes between first-order collective action problems – associated with providing the basic, targeted public goods – and second-order collective action problems –

"problems of orchestrating the coordination and/or enforcement needed to render agreements for resolving first-order CAPs [collective action problems] credible" (Ferguson 2013, 5).

From the very beginning, the discussion of collective action started by Mancur Olson (1971) in 1965 has led to the identification of entrepreneurship as one of the possible keys to understanding collective good provision. As Richard Wagner (1966) observed in his review of Olson's trailblazing work, the tasks of solving first-order dilemmas can be handled impersonally or fall on political entrepreneurs who act from inside or outside the group. Since then, although the literature on collective action has evolved considerably, the entrepreneurial element intrinsic to it has not received the full elaboration that it deserves. In exploring the parameters of the public entrepreneurial function in the context of collective action, we shall keep in mind that the literature is now acknowledging that collective action situations have many different structural characteristics, each carrying a different logic (Ostrom 2000; Marwell and Oliver 1993; Aligica 2014, 14). There is no single problem of collective action and, obviously, no single solution. There are many kinds of collective action situations at each level. These observations are pointing to the fact that in the interim, the literature has moved far from the initial generalization of "the" logic of collective action to a more contextual and nuanced approach.

One manner of describing these structural differences within the diverse family of collective action situations and problems is, for instance, Heckathorn's (1996) game-theoretical taxonomy that uses as organizing principles the prisoner dilemma games, the chicken game, the assurance games, etc. Other manners identified by Marwell and Oliver (1993) are single-actor models that treat the group behavior as given; models of interdependent aggregation of individual choices into a collective action; models of the collective actions of individuals with different interests; and models of the dynamic interaction among collective actors and their opponents. As one may expect, identifying the niche and the parameters of the public entrepreneurial function depends on the nuances in our description of the problem situation. And, needless to say, each model captures a specific facet of the phenomenon of interest, while the utility of each varies with the specific research question.

Without denying the usefulness of other models and approaches, the current argument takes a specific direction: it employs a simple critical mass based approach to the collective action problem. The hope is that the strategy illustrates the strength of the broader, more general class of approaches that relate collective action to public entrepreneurship.

In addition to that, and as the literature has made clear, it is relatively easy to link the logic of this approach with the other ways of conceptualizing collective action situations and dynamics (Kuran 1997; Granovetter 1978). The key observation behind critical mass theory is intuitive and simple (Oliver and Marwell 2001, 296): a critical number of group members must act convergently in a certain direction to trigger further actions. The sequence of in-group contributions adds up to solve the collective action problem only after a critical number of contributions are first secured. According to this view, the solution to the collective action problem lies in the creation of a subgroup sufficient to create that mass.

The notion of a critical mass is intuitive in describing participation in a riot or revolution, and hence, such extreme cases are the typical illustrations of the notion. The first group member to riot is a maverick and someone who values change exceptionally highly; hence, he pays great costs and takes great risks. The more people are in the street, the more the chances of success increase and the less risky and costly it becomes for others to join the riot. Once a critical mass of rioters are out in the street, we move toward a new social equilibrium. Collective action has been achieved. Cleaning the sidewalk makes another simple example: A neighborhood collective good involving collective action. A critical number of residents clean the part of the sidewalk closest to their homes, and once a critical mass of residents contribute, subsequent efforts at keeping the sidewalk clean become increasingly likely. Manifestly, interest group members are not equally interested in the provision of a public good. For all the first resident who decided to clean her part of the sidewalk knows, other residents may not have any interest in changing the situation. But once a critical mass is reached, the collective action in providing the public good of a clean sidewalk becomes increasingly possible. A different example is when first movers produce a noticeable effect at low cost to themselves, while late contributors might make little marginal difference at great cost. A group of residents attempt to overturn an unfavorable local government regulation by exercising their capacity to exit. The most mobile residents act first, while the least mobile are the slowest to act. Business owners who can easily shift registration to the neighboring county will make the first move. Tenants might move next. Homeowners, who usually lose about 10 percent of their home's value, will move last. Perhaps at that point, the local government has already decided to think the matter over such that the marginal effect of the last contributor to the collective good will be practically null. Yet another example offers an additional angle on the phenomenon of interest: funding a mutual insurance fund. Without some kind of assurance contract (with a money-back guarantee), the first in a sequence of contributors find it difficult to overcome the risk that they will be the only ones contributing while others will benefit. Once the fund is off the ground and a sufficient mass of contributions are paid, others find it increasingly less risky to also contribute.

One can already see, from a mere list of illustrative cases, how the contours of the public entrepreneurial space start to intuitively emerge. In light of the view offered by these cases, the function of the public entrepreneur is that of identifying and pushing the group toward the relevant critical mass. If we compare the entrepreneurship here with market process entrepreneurship, we note an important difference. In the market setting, the entrepreneur reaches a sufficient ex post alignment of participants to a process that reaches or breaks an equilibrium. In a public setting, the entrepreneur reaches an ex ante alignment of participants sufficient to match in-group supply with in-group demand. The particular differences between the two types of entrepreneurial processes need to be, and could be, further specified. To take a step further in our effort to identify the contours of public entrepreneurship, we need to introduce three notions of crucial analytical relevance (interdependence, production function, and heterogeneity) that, while helping us chart the structures and patterns of collective action situations, will at the same time help reveal the conditions, features, and functions defining public entrepreneurship.

PARAMETERS AND CONDITIONS OF THE PUBLIC ENTREPRENEURSHIP FUNCTION

Before delving into the production function and the problem of heterogeneity, let us first emphasize the issue of interdependence, because despite its essential role, it is neglected most of the time in many discussions of collective action, being taken for granted or merely mentioned as an implicit assumption. However, the interdependence of contributions is the decisive difference between Olson's conjectures on collective inaction and the theoretical explanations of collective action. As we'll see, when it comes to understanding public entrepreneurship, a lot hinges on interdependence.

a. Contributions' interdependence

To see why interdependence is so important, let us recall Mancur Olson's analogy between real-world large interest groups and firms in a competitive market. Olson's first assumption is that in real-world large groups (just like in perfectly competitive industries) no individual firm's output decision is enough to determine a price change, and no individual withdrawal is enough to produce a significant increase in the burden for any other dues-payer. This is equivalent to saying that any individual withdrawal has a sufficiently small impact on public good production, that all members who care only about the individual withdrawal's effect on the public good will safely ignore the individual withdrawal.

Olson's second assumption is that (just like in perfectly competitive industries, where an industry-level marginal increase in quantity sold would not justify the ensuing marginal decreases in price as practiced), a group-level marginal decrease in contributions would, indeed, be large enough to prevent public good production. In a competitive industry, whenever some temporary disequilibrium makes it so that an individual firm's marginal cost has not yet reached the price, an individual firm will increase output until marginal cost does reach the price, relying on assumption 1. And since all firms increase output relying on assumption 1, their actions, taken together, amount to a marginal increase of output on an industry level. That, by assumption 2, lowers prices to a level that makes each firm worse off than if none of the firms or almost none of the firms had increased their output. Similarly, reasons Olson, in real-world large groups, one member's efforts or lack thereof "will not have a noticeable effect on the situation of his organization." If so, any member reasons "he can enjoy any improvements brought about by others whether or not he has worked in support of his organization" (Olson 1971, 15–16).

Critical mass theory nuances the approach and questions assumption 1. It relaxes the assumption of individual negligibility. There are multiple ways in which one could show how various degrees and forms of non-negligibility have a chain effect on collective efforts. In its strongest version, it claims that the loss of one dues-payer may have a significant impact on whether other dues-payers pay their due. The amount of one withdrawal can be critical for the entire collective effort. Critical mass theory questions negligibility because it believes contributing efforts are, in the real world, interdependent. Interdependence becomes a key critical issue.

Interdependence could be very clearly illustrated by imagining a simple model where contributions are made in sequence, and everyone pays their contribution as long as the person right before them (or a certain number of people, subjectively determined) has contributed. When Olson addressed assumption 1, he claimed that "a rational person would not believe that if he were to withdraw from an organization he would drive others to do so" (Olson 1971, 12). But in our model, this is clearly false. One person's failure to pay their dues will be noticed by their neighbor, the next contributor in sequence. The rational person will foresee that the neighbor will drive their own neighbor to not contribute, and so on, in a domino effect, where one individual failure determines collective failure. With dominoes, if pieces are arranged to concentrate the impact of one piece's fall on the piece next to it, so that the impact is entirely felt by that next piece, the impact is enough to bring down the next piece, and so on. But other forms and patterns of chain events may be imagined. The bottom line is that interdependence matters.

A comprehensive approach to collective action uses both Olson and interdependence critical mass types of formulas. Robust collective action analysis will reason either, like Olson, from negligibility of impact or, like Oliver and Marwell, from critical mass, depending on how social ties are regulated in the situation in question. If the initial distribution of social ties regulates impact to equally divide that impact onto other group members, then Olson is right, and the analogy with firms in a competitive market works well. If, on the other hand, the initial distribution of social ties regulates the impact as in a domino effect, then genuine collective action may be possible.

For the purposes of our argument, the main observation is that interdependence offers us an indication of the direction in which one may search for manifestations of the public entrepreneurship function. Searching for ways of fostering, creating, and using interdependence emerges as one of the major modes of identifying entrepreneurship in public collective action settings. Interdependence becomes a key element orienting our inquiry strategy. Empirical studies may thus be oriented and focused using the theoretical lens that isolates and frames the problem of interdependence as well as the causal chains it illuminates.

Seen in that light, the entrepreneurial task need not be excessively difficult. In situations of potential domino effects, the successful entrepreneur may aim to arrange interdependence to form a critical mass. In a sequential model, the entrepreneur may convince sufficient contributors that their own individual defection will be enough to jeopardize the final collective outcome due to link-by-link interdependence continuing down the chain. Sometimes, the ties are already such that everyone finds it natural to imitate the person who makes a move before they make their own move. When this mechanism is imperfect, successful entrepreneurship is to make it clear to everyone that the contributor next to them will valorize their potential defection's negative impact on the public good highly enough to respond by also not making the contribution. As opposed to Olson, this solution does not necessarily involve distributing selective incentives for non-collective goods over and above the collective good in question. It merely involves making contributors believe that the next one in line cares about the collective good enough to contribute if the person before them also does, but not enough to still contribute upon noticing that the person before them has defected. In short, the public entrepreneur will have to convince members that others care about the collective good. Related to these types of situations and their analyses, Timur Kuran's (1997) classic work on the process of collective beliefs formation and their social consequences is exemplary in this respect. Merely expressing a framing perception activates a chain of reactions in the social network. The increasing availability of that perception makes increasingly plausible the social evolutions as framed. Kuran and Sunstein (1999) even note that availability entrepreneurs engage in deliberate attempts to engineer availability cascades.

However, Olson might retort that this is a special case of selective incentive provision by the entrepreneur. Contributors' concern with their neighbors is a concern over and above the concern for the public good in question. If so, then the entrepreneur's shuffling contributors' positions around still counts as distributing selective incentives. After all, the entrepreneur is providing new social ties, new things to care about; in other words, new attractions and sanctions. It is not the objective of our discussion to delve into this debate. The point is merely to show that an awareness of the crucial role of interdependence could orient our efforts in the course of research to identify, isolate, conceptualize, and analyze public entrepreneurship phenomena.

b. The collective good's production function

Let us move now to how the analysis of the production function helps further reveal and specify the domain of public entrepreneurial action. The production function relates contributions toward a collective good to the achievement of that collective good. It gives a formal treatment to the relationship between contributions and the collective good's level of achievement. To operationalize the idea that actions are interdependent, one needs to consider decisions as sequential. The production function charts what outcomes may be expected for marginal contributions. Outcomes are measured in level of achievement or probability of success, while contributions in dollars, votes, intensity of effort, etc. are registered on a simple individual contributor basis. Oliver, Marwell, and Teixera (1985) gave the example of homeowners in a neighborhood of 1,000 homes who suddenly learn that their neighborhood school has been scheduled to close. The total group losses are much higher than the cost of a hired lawyer who would win the case for them with certainty, but no individual owner incurs private costs high enough to pay the lawyer's full fee of, say, $100,000. By hypothesis, reaching the $100,000 target brings the probability of winning the case to a full 100 percent, but this does not mean that each additional $1,000 contributed will linearly increase the probability of winning the case by 1 percent. Perhaps the first thousand dollars will increase the probability by a little less or more than 1 percent. At any point in the contribution sequence, a given dollar amount will raise the probability of winning by either proportionately more or proportionately less.

The idea is amenable to a very clear and telling graphic illustration. The slope at each point, how far the inflection point lies behind the target contribution, and other properties of the production function are contingent to each case, but the standard in the literature is the intuitively simple didactic S-shaped curve, first accelerating, then decelerating. One could use these shapes to organize important insights about the collective good production process. In the first region of the S-shaped curve, the function is increasing at an accelerating rate: it plots increasing marginal returns to contributions until the inflection point. In the second phase, it is increasing at a decelerating rate, which means it plots decreasing marginal returns on efforts. The area before the inflection point favors late contributors over initial contributors. For example, the marginal contribution made closer to the inflection point achieves more than the marginal contribution made earlier and further away from it. Each contributor increases the marginal return of the next. On the other hand, the area of the function beyond the inflection point favors early over late contributors. Each contribution decreases the marginal return of the next.

A closer look at the two components – treated separately for analytical reasons – will provide a series of insights advancing our understanding of the entrepreneurial function in the production of goods and services in collective action problem-prone settings.

Let us start with the dynamics induced by the decelerating function (or the decelerating region of the S-shaped curve). In the diminishing marginal returns region, contributions are negatively interrelated in the sense that each contribution reduces the marginal return of the next. Hence, in decelerating regions, early contributors are favored over late ones. In such a circumstance, some collective action may take place, but if too many contributions are needed to reach the critical mass, there is a danger that the collective good will not be provided.

But herein lies the function of the public entrepreneur, and the logic of action reveals it with clarity. Because, in the diminishing marginal returns region, the impact or return to the first contributors are higher, even unconcerned members can be co-interested in contributing in the initial stages. An entrepreneur might induce dispassionate members to start first and initiate the production, hoping that their marginal returns in terms of (perceived) impact on the level of achievement or probability will compensate for their low level of interest. As the favorable initial production stages of this region are being completed and the production function enters the increasingly decelerating region, the subgroup that cares most about the provision and that has withheld its contribution will move ahead, only to save the day at the later stages of the region. The relatively more concerned will make contributions even when marginal returns are less enticing.

Hence, when the production function is decelerating or has a decelerating region, the public entrepreneurship function is to induce an order in the sequence of contributors from the less willing members to the more willing. The willing subset is induced to postpone their contribution. They do this either as a result of a tacit contract or because they are themselves part of the entrepreneurial core. Either way, the total level of contributions is maximized if entrepreneurs find ways to bring participants to contribute in a certain order, starting from the least to the most interested. In brief, for the diminishing marginal returns region, the collective action problem may be solved if individuals with low levels of interests make the contributions first and those with high levels of interest make them later.

In regions where the production function is accelerating (or the accelerating region of the S-shaped curve), the logic is different. Contributions have positive effects on subsequent contributions. In accelerating regions, late contributors are favored over early ones. In the initial phase of a region where marginal returns to contributions are increasing, the first units of contribution have a very limited impact on the (perceived) level of achievement of the collective good. Since initiation is not favorable, the willing subset – the group that cares most for the provision – has to act first in the sequence if any chances of successful action are to be created. However, as we move along the function, the slope increases, and so do the prospects for the collective good. Because each subsequent contribution becomes more enticing, one could set into motion a snowball effect. In such situations, individuals highly interested in achieving the critical mass should find it profitable to contribute first. Initial contributions lower the interest necessary for subsequent contributions. The total level of contributions is maximized if entrepreneurs find ways to induce participants to make contributions in a certain order. The collective action problem is solved if individuals with low levels of interest are channeled to make contributions later and those with high levels of interest make them earlier.

Marwell and Oliver (1993, 88), the authors who drew attention to this effect, noted that "a pool of highly interested and resourceful individuals willing to contribute in the initial region of low returns may therefore become a 'critical mass' creating the conditions for more widespread contributions." More importantly, they basically identified the public entrepreneurship role without, however, naming it as such: "If even one such person exists, she may begin a process in which a continuously increasing number of group members find that the contributions of others have changed the situation to one in which they too wish to contribute" (Marwell and Oliver 1993, 88). They called that person "the initiator." But the entrepreneurial function is obvious: "The bandwagon may roll, started by a single person. For the process to start, however, this initiator must have an extraordinarily high interest in the collective good, perhaps several hundred times greater than that necessary to initiate collective action for a decelerative good" (Marwell and Oliver 1993, 8). The interest need not be solely related to the public good in question. A specific mix of motivation – both intrinsic and extrinsic to the collective action arena – may be at play. As we have already seen, the initiator's role is even more important in decelerating function situations. In both cases, the public entrepreneurship role is crucial, although its modus operandi differs.

All of the above amply illuminate the reason why microanalysis of collective action via the production function is useful for our purposes. The shape and size of collective good production functions obviously define, at least in part, the public entrepreneurial task. In their initial paper, Oliver, Marwell, and Teixeira (1985, 530) assumed information was complete and uniform and only considered how the production function creates room for strategic competition among potential contributors. There was no explicit discussion of entrepreneurship linking these insights with the classical literature on entrepreneurial action. But in the third paper of the series on critical mass theory (Marwell, Oliver, and Prahl 1988), the authors used the notion of "group organizer." There, they concluded that centralization of social ties in a group organizer positively affects collective mobilization. Their explanation was that the organizer selects those contributors known to be more interested and forms a critical mass while avoiding organization costs. One could take the argument from there and proceed in several directions, all of them not only compatible but also convergent with the sociological analysis of entrepreneurship phenomena, thus opening an entire line of empirical inquiry framed by the conceptual apparatus developed here. Social network theory and social capital theory become key elements in explaining the operating environment, resources, and strategies of the group organizer, entrepreneur of collective action. As we have seen, once we consider the heterogeneity of information, we will have bridged collective action theory with public entrepreneurship theory. The different forms that heterogeneity can take is a topic that authors such as Oliver, Ostrom, and their associates – pioneers of this research line – have explored with less of a view to our current topic of interest. Indeed, it is one of our tasks in this book to bridge their critical mass theory of collective action with the theory of entrepreneurship.

c. Group heterogeneity

The argument so far has already made unmistakably clear that in discussing the problem of collective action, the assumption of homogeneity should be the exception, a special case, and not the rule. Exploring the idea of a critical mass draws attention to the existence of in-group heterogeneous interests and resources and the potentially crucial role of these differences between group members. Heterogeneity, however, comes in different forms: heterogeneity of endowments, resources, preferences, and beliefs; heterogeneity of information and expectations in regard to interests, to resources, and to the production function itself; and heterogeneity of coordination, communication, and contractual capabilities. At this juncture, it is important, in order to avoid falling back to a merely individual and psychological perspective, to note that heterogeneity is relative and positional, and that intrinsic feature makes it a social feature rather than merely an individual psychological one.

Following, again, the insights of authors such as Ostrom, Oliver, and their collaborators, one may use interest and resource heterogeneity as explanatory variables of the probability, extent, and effectiveness of group actions in pursuit of a collective good. Indeed, it would be very difficult to explain collective action by appeal to the concept of critical mass if we average or collapse agents' relevant interests into one. Group members have different preferences, resources, and social positions. All these differences matter in collective action situations. In the context of our discussion, these differences predefine ways of creating a critical mass, as well as the role for a public entrepreneur in discovering ways of generating the critical mass. In brief, it looks like we have at hand a strategy for identifying and describing the public entrepreneurial function at work by paying attention to the heterogeneity of the group in interdependent collective action situations. Heterogeneity seems to be the foundation of a solution to collective action and, at the same time, a heuristic instrument that leads to the core of the problem of public entrepreneurship.

Indeed, at a closer look, heterogeneity seems to be intrinsic to the very notion of entrepreneurship. Let us elaborate on this point, using as a vehicle Olson's own initial classic argument. Without appealing to the concept of critical mass, Mancur Olson (1971) implicitly needed the public entrepreneurship function in that the entrepreneur was supposed to distribute selective incentives to members of latent groups, either in the form of punishments for noncontributors or in the reward of private goods for contributors. Surely the entrepreneur was supposed to treat differently those who contribute than those who do not and differentially treat the existing heterogeneity where it existed. Olson used the free rider problem to explain why latent interest groups of individuals remain unorganized. In large groups, since the impact of one's own contribution is negligible but the cost is not, no one contributes. At the same time, Olson had to explain the empirical fact that some large groups are organized. His hypothesis was that large organized interest groups were a byproduct of organizations who had first come into existence by providing selective incentives. Selective incentives came either in the form of coercion or excludable benefits that each member would find individually profitable to purchase.

For example, to explain why members of a professional association such as the American Medical Association (AMA) are successfully lobbying and providing collective goods, Olson believed the AMA had first come into existence by selling non-collective services such as defense in malpractice legal suits or technical information. As members join the AMA for non-collective services and set the AMA in place, the AMA becomes ready to use the revenue to extend its mission. Thus, what Olson's byproduct theory needs for the non-collective contracts to be concluded is some interest over and above the base interest in the collective good. That additional motivation is, in fact, able to explain collective action only because it is something on top of the latent interest level in the collective good. Asymmetries and heterogeneity matter. Entrepreneurship in such circumstances is obviously a creation of – and operates with – heterogeneity. When the relevant heterogeneity is already there, it is the entrepreneur's function to play upon it. When it is not, the function of the entrepreneur is to find ways of generating it.

If one accepts this standpoint, one interesting feature of the Olson-inspired literature becomes striking. In a theoretical model that allows for entrepreneurship, heterogeneity can be zero only if we conceive of the entrepreneur as a nonmember of the interest group. Hence, in this literature, one has built in the implicit notion that entrepreneurial solutions to collective action somehow come from outside the group. Olson's as well as Hardin's research results had impressed a view of groups as incapable of moving on their own endogenously to achieve their purpose. If groups need an exogenous force, then the public entrepreneur must stand outside the interest group. Olson's stationary and roving bandit theory of the state was perhaps strengthening the intuition as the state appeared as the result of an encounter between a group and an outsider.

But the main problem with this view (in addition to the historical and empirical evidence) is Olson's own definition of interest group membership (Olson 1971, 8), according to which having a positive interest in the collective good is sufficient to make one a member of the interest group. But that means that the social actor's particular social position or motivation are irrelevant as long as an interest in the collective good exists. The nature of one's motivation, in itself, the entrepreneur's identifiable conscious contribution to the provision of the collective good, demonstrates an interest in bringing about the collective good. Motivation or the absence of other sociological ties notwithstanding, entrepreneurs are individuals who prefer the state of affairs in which the supply of the public good is provided. Even if they do not wish to consume the collective good themselves, they have a desire to consume whatever good can "only" come packaged with the collective good. An entrepreneur who solves a neighborhood problem may not be a resident. But this is irrelevant, because many of the rank and file members may have their own peculiar motivations. Someone may contribute to a neighborhood solution simply because they like to dress up for local meetings. In brief, the entrepreneur must be part of the group not just because under a critical mass theory of collective action they "can be" so, but because by Olson's definition of group membership, and by the logic of revealed preference, they share an interest in the good. And if they are part of the group but still entrepreneurs, the intensity of their interest must positively diverge from the average. If so, then positive heterogeneity is an intrinsic, necessary feature of collective action and public entrepreneurship.

Hence, a focus on heterogeneity of groups confronted with collective action situations is obviously an important track in our investigations of public entrepreneurship. A simple methodological caveat of major analytical importance could be thus drawn: It is misleading to treat heterogeneous groups as homogenous by examining only the aggregate group interest in the collective good. Again, Oliver, Marwell, and Teixera (1985, 529) offer us a very constructive insight: "If an interest group is heterogeneous, there may be some highly interested or highly resourceful people available for a critical mass even when the mean interest or resource level is rather low. Greater variance and positive skew are the statistical properties of distributions that favor the presence of such persons." It is obvious that we cannot afford working only with aggregate variables.

In this respect, the simplest argument is that heterogeneity of resources obviously should matter. Actors who have more resources than others may also have different cost–benefit assessments of contributions. Hence, they may have a different structure of motivation and may act differently. Since the total level of actual contributions is what matters for the provision of the public good, when initial distribution of resources favors a small number of actors, those actors can make the decisive difference. Because, for a given total level, fewer actors need to actually coordinate efforts, concentration of resources creates the premises for setting into motion the solution to the collective action problem.

That being said, heterogeneity is not limited to endowments or resources but also extends to knowledge and information. When one relaxes the assumption of complete and uniform information about the various intensities of group members' interests, one tacitly bridges the discussion of collective action and that of public entrepreneurship. The idea that some social actors are more knowledgeable about certain circumstances than others are opens the door to the public entrepreneurship action. Once the assumptions of perfect information flow and uniform capacity to conclude contribution contracts are deemed too restrictive and unrealistic, we unavoidably arrive at the domain of entrepreneurship. Already, the discussion of production functions and the tacit knowledge of their existence and approximate shape have merged us into the discussion of heterogeneity.

At the same time, it is not only a matter of information and knowledge but also of framing and perception. Contributors may have different perceptions and views about the production function. Some of those modes of screening and framing may inspire actions leading to collective action solutions. Moreover, in practice, nothing guarantees an objective production function that serves as focal point all the way through the contribution sequence. The role of perceptions, ideas, beliefs, and their variety is even more pervasive. Due to reflexivity, which is the mutual influence of expectations and future events (see the line of research opened by Merton [1948]), someone's biased perceptions manifest in their contribution and shapes other contributions. If, for instance, a contributor believes their contribution makes a greater difference than it does and acts on that perception, this changes subsequent contributors' perceptions about the production function or where they are in the schedule. Not only may they now believe that their own contributions make a greater difference than they thought they would, but they may start appreciating the collective good more. The value of the collective good itself modifies with expectations as manifested in action as we move along. An entrepreneur may speculate all these possibilities, while the researcher may be able to use them as heuristic and analytic instruments in shaping the research strategy.

For instance, as Wagner (1966) observed, if we relax the assumption about the information flow in collective action situations and accept some role for perception and expectations while recalling basic social exchange and social coordination principles, then we only need the entrepreneur to assume the risk and engage in second-order actions such as drafting contracts. To recast the entrepreneurial function in the language of exchange, the entrepreneur may be modeled as engaged in a social exchange process of selling changes in the probability that the collective good is finally provided. But different marginal changes are available at different times for the same dollar contribution. What the entrepreneur must do is engage in selective pricing. From this simple but powerful conceptualization, one may already draw corollaries in further clarification. For instance, one may note that, seen in this light, there are two kinds of entrepreneurial errors. One error is to marginally overprice and risk to achieve overall surplus. Another is to attract and waste someone's contribution to effect a too-high change in probability compared to the change that the buyer would be willing to purchase at that margin. The danger in underpricing is to not reach the overall target contribution since this buyer may not have the resources to contribute again later on in the sequence.

All of the above put us in a position to better understand how the heterogeneity of endowments, preferences, and resources framed by the heterogeneity of knowledge, information, and expectations provide the fuel and the space for the entrepreneur. The path leading to the parameters of public entrepreneurship involves an account of the interdependence, heterogeneity, and production functions that define the operating environment. The entrepreneur is contributing to the succeeding collective action by aligning contributions in the order dictated by the production function and member heterogeneity, operating with this end in view on resources, incentives, perceptions, belief systems, and even values and preferences. The public entrepreneur is, indeed, a real change agent and a driver of governance processes.

At this stage, we are in a position to step back for a second and revisit the broader picture. By developing this analytical discussion of collective action and critical mass, one can see how the *market process* of the standard entrepreneurship theorizing, with its intelligible patterns and theoretical framework, may be substituted with a *collective action process* that has intelligible patterns, too, and that offers a comparable conceptual background for entrepreneurial functions to emerge and be identified. The notion of public entrepreneurship becomes embedded into a conceptual apparatus that gives it both theoretical meaning and analytical traction. Heuristic analogies and research designs and conjectures of empirical relevance may be built up, starting from there.

CONCLUSIONS

This chapter has shown how using the problem of collective action as a key dimension of the conceptual space of public entrepreneurship theorizing, one can build, step-by-step, the elements of a more precise understanding and operationally meaningful approach to the nature of entrepreneurship in nonmarket settings. It has shown how given a collective action situation and a critical mass sufficient to solve the collective action problem, factors such as (1) contribution interdependence, (2) the production function, and (3) heterogeneity create the conditions for the emergence of public entrepreneurship and for its identification and analysis. One may conclude that the polycentricity and collective action arenas, and the situations created by them, are the first-order parameters of such forms of entrepreneurship. As such, they are part of our methodological framework in our empirical research attempting to identify and study public entrepreneurship. They become heuristic instruments, guiding our investigation. Each of them offers some clues, some direction to our efforts to identify and analyze public entrepreneurship cases. At the same time, they offer the basic building blocks of a coherent and systematic theoretical approach to public entrepreneurship, on a par with the more advanced theorizing of entrepreneurship in market settings.

The power of entrepreneurship theorizing in market settings comes from the fact that market process theory offers the background upon which the entrepreneurship function could be identified and defined as part of the broader theoretical structure that is charting the market and its operating patterns in a functionalist way. The notion of market equilibrium is pivotal for identifying, classifying, and analyzing different forms of entrepreneurship, such as the Kirznerian and Schumpeterian ones. Collective action and competitive governance in polycentric structures offer an equivalent background for the public entrepreneurship function. That is to say, the public entrepreneurship function can be identified and defined with greater precision and increased empirical promise when projected on a theoretical structure charting the collective action and its competitive governance operating patterns in the overlapping and competing interplay of collective action polycentric arenas in a public governance system. Various taxonomies and analytical categories may be constructed on par with those generated in market theory. With this comprehensive apparatus, both at the micro and structural levels, we may be able to deal in a more satisfactory way with the challenge posed by the compounded and complex phenomenon defining self-governance systems.

3

Voluntary Actions and Institutions

Charting the Territory

The first two chapters have shown how the notion of public entrepreneurship entails theoretical luggage that, once articulated, illuminates an entire array of structures and processes at the core of self-governance. The domain thus illuminated has as its first dimension the polycentricity and competitive governance conditions. The second dimension reflects the intrinsic connection to the problem of collective action and its solutions. In addition to all of the above, there is yet another element entailed, which has been an underlying implicit presence in the previous chapters. Both dimensions have their roots in and derive their strengths from voluntary action and voluntary organization: the third element of relevance. Following the logic of our approach requires us to make explicit and elaborate it as well.

Underlying the notions and processes discussed so far is the idea that voluntary action and voluntary association are essential. There is a strong link between the concept of public entrepreneurship and the principles of freedom of choice and association. The sphere, scope, degree, and intensity of competitive governance and collective action arenas are defined by the sphere, scope, degree, and intensity of freedom of choice and association. By implication, the sphere, scope, degree, and intensity of public entrepreneurship are defined by the sphere, scope, degree, and intensity of freedom of choice and association. Together, they circumscribe the sphere of self-governance and define the ultimate conditions of the emergence and stability of self-governance systems.

The objective of the chapter is to explore and elaborate the voluntary association facet and its governance and institutional theory implications. In plain terms, the problem starts from simple questions: Where are we more likely to identify the phenomena described by the stylized facts of public entrepreneurship theory? Where are we more likely to see self-

59

governance happening? The answer is: In the social arenas where the principles of voluntary action and association are operating.

The chapter takes a two-step approach. First, a vision and a social philosophy of human cooperation and voluntary arrangements are introduced. The Ostroms' approach to public entrepreneurship and collective action in polycentric competitive governance systems has a history and a context. Behind it, there is a system of thought, a certain vision and intellectual tradition. In this respect, James Buchanan's social philosophy of voluntary governance has a special intellectual relevance given the close association with the Ostroms and their related public choice inspired research programs. The public choice roots of the idea of a "neither markets nor states" institutional diversity that is associated with the Ostroms' view of self-governance is part of the genealogy of the Bloomington School. Revisiting Buchanan's relevant and influential work in this respect helps us put all this in the appropriate context.

The second task of the chapter is to chart the territory of voluntary institutional arrangements through Ostromian lenses. The better one understands the variety of institutional arrangements and action arenas within this heterogeneous domain, the closer one gets to understanding how the public entrepreneurship phenomena are induced, shaped, or determined by them. That domain could be structured along two lines: on the one hand, it could be in settings in which the market and the price system are the basic methods of coordination, and on the other hand, it could be in nonmarket, nonprofit settings. After identifying and elaborating the distinction using the insights of the school that has done the most to advance a precise way of distinguishing the two (i.e., Austrian theory), the chapter focuses on how the Ostroms contributed to the efforts of conceptually mapping the territory of the institutional diversity of "neither markets nor states." Better understanding this complex heterogeneous territory of institutions and collective action arenas helps us to understand the varieties of forms public entrepreneurship can take, as well as the associated forms and facets of self-governance made thus possible. The result will be a more nuanced appreciation of the Ostroms' contribution to the study of public entrepreneurship in all three dimensions: polycentricity/competitive governance, collective action, and voluntary association. Needless to say, that also means a contribution to a better-grounded understanding of the anatomy, physiology, and building blocks of self-governance systems.

ELEMENTS OF A THEORY OF VOLUNTARY ACTION AND INSTITUTIONS

James Buchanan, Nobel Prize winner in economics and a key inspirer of the public choice revolution in political and economic sciences in which the Ostroms were major participants, offers a concise articulation of the emerging perspective that shifts the focus toward a broader theory of voluntary institutional arrangements and human cooperation. Buchanan (1979, 24–25) starts with a criticism of the mainstream neoclassical paradigm. He claims that to view economics as a theory of resource allocation leads to a dead end.

When allocative efficiency becomes the preeminent (sometimes even the unique) conceptual framework to be used as a universal background theory, the result is simply confusing. There are many situations when allocation analysis is warranted, but their relevance and meaning get muddled and lost when there is no demarcation criterion to be applied to them. But even more worrisome is that allocation thinking transforms all problems into merely computational problems. How far can one go in analyzing social order when all explanatory endeavors are about maximizing a more or less simple computational formula? If social science is just that, then it is a mere formal exercise in mathematics and logics followed by attempts to fit the heterogeneity of social life into those formulas more or less convincingly. That is not to say that such an approach is not interesting and is not, in some cases, useful. However, argues Buchanan, it should be recognized as what it is: not social science (of universal aspirations); not political economy, not even economic science, but a branch of applied mathematics or of applied managerial science. To study human cooperation and social association requires more than that.

Buchanan (1979, 27) moves ahead with a radical proposition. He merely proposes "that we cease, forthwith, to talk about economics or political economy," although "the latter is a much superior term." If it would be possible "to wipe the slate clean," he wrote, "I should recommend a wholly different term such as catallactics or symbiotics." This is crucial to our argument. Buchanan defines symbiotics as "the study of the association between dissimilar organisms and the connotation of the term is that the association is mutually beneficial to all parties." The focus should be on "a unique sort of relationship," a relationship "which involves the cooperative association of individuals, one with another, even when individual interests are different."

Important elements of the theory of choice (which underlies the allocative/efficiency perspective) remain part of symbiotics. But a theory of choice is and should be much more than what the neoclassical apparatus advances under that label. The social fact of association requires a special type of behavior based on division of labor, specialization, exchange, agreement, cooperation, and transactions. At the same time, it implies specific social or institutional arrangements, some of them emerging spontaneously and others emerging as a result of choice and deliberation. We are in the domain where a contractarian normative philosophy meets what another Nobel Prize in Economics winner, Vernon Smith (2003), has called "ecological rationality." Both Buchanan and Smith react to the neoclassical strategy as amounting to an ultra-reductionist, analytically dubious, and normatively incapacitating "conversion of individual choice behavior from a social–institutional context to a physical computational one" (Buchanan 1979, 29). Both consider the context of decision and choice as being crucial. As one may note (and as we'll further see in later chapters), the convergence with the Ostroms' approach is palpable on both analytical and normative grounds.

From the perspective of our discussion, it is important to note how Buchanan had a special interest in phenomena in which decision and behavior are based on agreement and that lead to voluntary forms of association. He was interested in the large domain that is "the institutional embodiment of the voluntary exchange process that are entered into by individuals in their several capacities." To study that, one doesn't need to make any special and extensive appeal to maximizing and systemic efficiency computational formulas. People enter into voluntary arrangements. "This is all there is to it. Individuals are observed to cooperate with one another" (Buchanan 1979, 31). It doesn't make too much sense to talk about efficiency in aggregative and composite terms. One may think about efficiency and inefficiency in particular terms as in the survival, or not, of a particular institution. One may evoke, from time to time, systemic allocation and efficiency principles as broad, ideal-type normative benchmarks. But evoking overall systemic efficiency (or optimality) in the grand scheme of general allocation or its methodical application as an analytical formula to all institutional forms are practices that create more confusion than clarity.

The underlying idea is unassuming but consequential: Individuals are confronted with problems, and they try to solve them by cooperative, "symbiotic" means. The result is the emergence of a special class of institutions. Those institutions deserve special attention for both analytical and normative reasons. To illustrate his general argument, Buchanan gives the hypothetical example of a community confronted with a collective problem: draining a swamp. They may try markets, and they may find them working or not working as they wanted them to. The free-riding problem and other social dilemmas may pose difficulties. Individuals may (again, *voluntarily*) decide that they want to transfer, at a community level, some decision-making powers, based on a collective decision-making procedure. They may search voluntarily for more inclusive exchanges and cooperative arrangements that go beyond the market mechanisms or simple cooperative formulas. A more complex institutional arrangement may emerge, involving collective decision-making procedures that might take different forms and may imply different levels of governance arrangements. At one point, the arrangements may even involve collective enforcement and special procedures, social roles, and social functions in this respect, as a legitimate result of a collective arrangement process.

The bottom line is clear: Ultimately, this is a domain of voluntary action toward cooperation in achieving specific objectives. The emphasis shifts to the nature, conditions, and implications of voluntary cooperation. It is something that includes both private and collective organizations, all based on the agreement of the social actors involved in creating and maintaining them. When all is said and done, we are truly dealing here with a general theory of the voluntary sector based on the assumption that we need to concentrate on (a) the nature, structure, and functions of voluntary action and (b) on what emerges from it in terms of social processes and institutions. It is a theory that includes, in an undiluted form, a recognition of the nonmarket, nonprofit aspect of social organization. Its principle is straightforward. We need to

concentrate attention on the institutions, the relationships, among individuals as they participate in voluntary organized activity, in trade or exchange, broadly considered. People may decide (. . .) to do things collectively. Or they may not. The analysis, as such, is neutral in respect to the proper private-sector-public-sector mix. (Buchanan 1979, 36)

This broader vision of the institutional order that has as a focal point the problem of voluntary actions and institutions could be further developed along both analytical and normative lines.

In the symbiotics framework, the central problem is the nature and conditions of cooperation under the assumption of various degrees of freedom of association and exchange. We have seen that social systems and their *aggregated* processes are not about maximizing or optimizing anything. They are not teleological. Instead, they are open systems that allow (in various degrees) individuals to pursue, more or less voluntarily (in function of the incentives, constraints, and rules in place), the things they value and to use or create a variety of association, collaboration, and exchange formulas in this respect. An alternative vision of social order is thus advanced: an open-ended, nondeterministic evolutionary process emerging as an aggregate result of ideas, preferences, and values materialized into the voluntary decisions of the social actors. In such circumstances, entrepreneurship emerges naturally. This change of analytical focus leads to a more nuanced view of the mechanisms at work in the institutional circumstances of cooperation and competition. Notions of polycentricity and collective action help us identify those mechanisms. The questions of interest are increasingly regarding adaptation, learning, and innovation as shaped by the rules, incentives, and beliefs framing different action arenas. Entrepreneurship (in both its private and public forms) emerges as a key feature of the landscape. The very theory of association and voluntary exchange becomes a major exploratory framework used to analyze and understand its nature and functions.

The center stage is taken now by a focus on alternative institutional settings that facilitate or hamper different forms of learning processes and institutional innovation and adaptation and that, thus, are instrumental in the emergence of a variety of organizational forms. The ecology of information, incentives, feedback, and knowledge production and dissemination determines in large part the nature of the arrangements and performance at the individual and organizational levels. Institutions as "orientation schemes" (Lachmann 1971) change in light of learning and, at their turn, change the evolving incentive and information structures. The task is to explore the entire range of feedback and disciplining mechanisms by which one increases the chances that the intentions that fuel these organizations are materialized as envisioned. Once approached from a symbiotics and ecological rationality perspective, this is no longer a matter to be treated just at the individual or organizational level. The issue is also institutional and systemic (or structural).

We are thus reentering familiar territory from a different analytical angle. The functional and performance issues become, in many respects, a matter of the broad institutional framework, of the meta-level setting in which the actors and organizations are operating. As the discussions of polycentricity as a system feature and of public entrepreneurship as a function have shown, the analysis becomes an ongoing interplay between zooming in to the level of individuals and organizations and zooming out to the level of the structure and systemic parameters that are setting the rules of the game and the playing field. The multiple levels of analysis approach pioneered in institutional theory by Ostrom (2011) recommends itself both as a theoretical lens and an important instrument for making possible an approach that combines institutional theory, models of learning and adaptation, and organizational ecology theory insights.

The idea of multiple levels of analysis could be rooted in the distinction between the "order of rules" and the "order of actions"; between the rules of the game and the game itself, as played within those rules – an idea developed by Hayek, Buchanan, and North and elaborated on in more operational terms by the Ostroms. The properties of the order of rules determine the order of actions. Yet, social actors could reflect on and change the rules of the game: a typical constitutional act, but also, in many cases, interpretable as a typical form of public entrepreneurship. The idea has been extensively applied in the study of constitutional structures. The distinction between the constitutive or constitutional aspect of the game and the sub-constitutional level was converted into an important analytical instrument, and an entire field (constitutional political economy) was created around these insights (Buchanan 1990).

The most important point for our discussion is the strong assumption that individuals may exercise their freedom to contract or enter into exchanges and associations at both levels, constitutional and sub-constitutional. Market decisions and actions are a typical example of the sub-constitutional level: voluntary exchange micro-processes taking place within an institutional framework. Yet, gains from voluntary cooperation may be obtained through other forms of voluntary transactions and combinations. Individuals may seek gains that emerge not only from mutually beneficial market transactions but also from deciding collectively to create rules and organizational constraints that will help them be more effective in achieving a large variety of goals. It may be the case that, as Vanberg put it, "people may choose to enter into constitutional contracts the very purpose of which is to jointly restrict their freedom of contract at the sub-constitutional level" (Vanberg 2002, 29). Our attention is thus drawn to the fact that too many times, theorists in economics have focused exclusively on the market (sub-constitutional level) processes, sometimes trying to reduce to just that sphere the entire variety of mutually beneficial forms of social cooperation and exchange. Missing the public entrepreneurship element was part of a larger blind spot.

In light of the discussion so far, it seems logical and natural to extend further the constitutional political economy perspective to a variety of institutional arrangements and levels. Its extension leads, from an additional and new angle, precisely to the notion of a general theory of voluntary action and institutions. The path is relatively straightforward: This type of approach is not limited to two levels, and – as Ostrom's (2011) work has shown – could be easily transformed into a tool of general institutional analysis. The result is that by extending it to a multitude of levels and social circumstances, we in fact extend the domain of the theory of voluntary action and organization both in analytical and in normative terms. With that, the domain of entrepreneurship function is extended. Accordingly, the public entrepreneurship approach could be seen as a facet of the constitutional political economy paradigm advanced by James Buchanan as a natural extension of public choice and the new contractarianism associated with it.

A general theory of voluntary actions and institutions may, thus, be reinforced using tools forged in the contractarian theory tradition. The combination of an analytical and normative contractarian perspective embedded in a broader theory of learning and adaptation, in which choice and human creativity complement the standard decision theory models, leads to a modular theoretical structure, within which entrepreneurship plays a key role. Moreover, this is in earnest a theory of voluntary action and institutions as it pivots on the notion that the choice of the social actors to voluntarily associate could function as a background conceptual benchmark in the double role of analytical assumption and normative ideal.

In brief, we have in public choice constitutional political economy an approach that elaborates the concept of voluntary association, contract, and organization into a powerful analytical engine and a robust normative standard. It is a move that takes seriously the empirical and normative reality of the fact that people try to achieve different goals by creating a variety of voluntary organizational arrangements and that they decide to submit collectively to various constraints established as part of the explicit or tacit agreements they make. At the same time, it is a perspective that captures an important feature of the ethos at the core of the studies of voluntary action and institutions.

As repeatedly noted, this perspective contains both a positive theory and a normative theory. The positive theory suggests the adoption of a comparative institutions analysis approach focused on the knowledge processes among participants in cooperative, symbiotic social coordination endeavors as well as on their incentives to obtain and act on that knowledge in order to coordinate their plans. In it, the attention is shifted from systemic efficiency and aggregative criteria toward learning and creative processes and the continuous institutional adjustments and adaptations resulting from them. The normative theory suggests the primacy of agreement and voluntary cooperative social actions and institutions, and hence, a preeminent role in the normative scheme of things for the independent voluntary sector and the entire variety of institutions and organizations based on voluntary institutions and agreements.

In both its aspects, normatively and positively, it advances a radically pluralist paradigm: As a positive social science framework, it allows for multiple theoretical approaches with a genuine interdisciplinary openness. For instance, it opens the door for engagement with the evolutionary theory of human behavior and social organization. It also has room for approaches focusing on human intentionality, belief systems, and historical interpretation as means of understanding institutional forms and processes in their context and path-dependent development. As a normative framework, it acknowledges a pluralism of values, preferences, and principles of social organization. Individuals decide voluntarily to pursue one form of organization or another, and they may succeed, or they may fail. As long as their enterprise is based on agreement and doesn't impose negative consequences on those who have chosen not to be part of the agreement, it has a place in the normative universe of this theoretical vision. Last but not least, when it comes to the study of phenomena defined by agreements and voluntarism, entrepreneurship, both private and public, comes naturally into play as an important component.

MARKET SETTINGS AND NONMARKET SETTINGS: THE BASIC TYPOLOGY IN THE AUSTRIAN TRADITION

One of the most important contributions of the Ostroms' approach comes from the effort to conceptually chart the heterogeneous landscape of institutional and decision arenas in which voluntary action and association may operate in a modern governance system. As we have noted, to understand public entrepreneurship in its forms and operations, we need to understand its institutionally contingent nature and, hence, the various configurations and institutional levels that shape it in environments in which the principles of voluntary action and association are manifest.

However, before moving to the Ostroms, the first step has to be dedicated to an effort to conceptually disentangle the two defining realms, the two major provinces: On the one hand are the market settings of profit and loss, of pure calculation-based environments. On the other hand are the nonmarket, nonprofit settings, the domain of special interest to the

Ostroms. This plain dichotomy offers the background against which one could project any other typologies of the complex and heterogeneous domain of voluntary action and association. To introduce it, we'll use as a vehicle the Austrian theory – the most apt attempt to analyze this dichotomy. Then, the road will be cleared to move on to the Ostromian approach toward the charting for analytical purposes of the nonmarket, nonprofit territory.

At the center of the Austrian analysis of all forms of social organization is the problem of rational action. In the methodological individualist tradition shared with public choice and the Ostromian institutionalism, social order is seen as the emergent result of purposeful rational decisions taken by myriads of agents. The key to understanding complex, modern social order is the relationship between human action and the problem of rational economic calculation. Calculation has a specific meaning in Austrian theory. It is not a purely mental or technical computation. A social process that produces prices (i.e., the market) allows a special form of rationality (economic rationality) to be used as a powerful instrument of human coordination. Market prices, because they permit systematic comparison between diverse social preferences and alternative uses of scarce resources, make possible a special type of rational decision-making. Prices give a precise and comparative sense of profit and loss and, thus, connect human motivation to an intricate network of calculative interactive decisions. The result is a complex and productive system of order that could be described following the logic of monetary calculation (Mises 1922, 1998).

Without monetary calculation, explained Mises (1922, 101), social actors would be lost "amid the bewildering throng of economic possibilities." Mental operations involving the key notions of "profit" and "loss" would simply not be possible. "In the absence of profit and loss the entrepreneurs would not know what the most urgent needs of the consumers are. If some entrepreneurs were to guess it, they would lack the means to adjust production accordingly" (1998, 297). Mises made very clear that monetary calculation is neither the calculation nor the measurement of value. Monetary calculation creates the conditions for social actors to calculate the benefits from the total costs of their efforts; it allows them an ex post assessment of whether or not their expectations were met as monetary profit or loss. They are the pivotal coordination mechanisms for advanced, complex societies based on an extended division of labor. However, monetary prices and calculation should not be confused with a measure of value or "social" value. Values and their implications for the way social orders and institutions emerge and function have a larger sphere of application and many more dimensions than those revealed by the sphere of monetary calculation.

It is important to stress at this juncture – and as an echo to Buchanan's take on allocation theories and symbiotics – that all these observations have nothing to do with any notion of Pareto optimality or general equilibrium. They are statements about human action and human rationality in social settings. Prices emerge at the intersection of individual subjective preferences, and they provide (by allowing the calculation of profit and loss) a unique social coordination method. One does not need any general equilibrium or maximizing model to describe or analyze all this. The real challenge is this: The sphere of social coordination is larger than that covered by monetary exchange. The problem is what happens outside the sphere of monetary calculus, of profit and loss. The issue is critical for our discussion, because a vast number of voluntary organizational forms are, obviously, operating in large measure outside that sphere.

The first point in this respect is to note with Mises that, when it comes to modern organizations, "whenever the operation of a system is not directed by the profit motive, it must be directed by bureaucratic rules" (Mises 1998, 307). Bureaucratic procedures and bureaucratic rationality come to compensate for the limited or absent monetary calculation economic rationality. Rationality is induced via rules. There are, thus, two types of institutional forms: (i) those that operate under the rationality of economic calculation and (ii) forms that operate under the rationality of rule-guided behavior (or bureaucratic logic). As one may expect, there are also mixed arrangements. Therefore, the challenge is to understand the operating principles of each of these types of organizations. The question is, as Boettke and Coyne (2008, 11) put it, what are the mechanisms, if any, that guide human behavior to ensure social coordination in particular nonmarket settings, thus matching local needs and demands with the available resources as defined in the sphere of monetary calculation?

There are several ways of dealing with this question. For instance, to answer this challenge, Austrians such as Boettke and Prychitko (2004) introduced a distinction between nonprofit organizations and not-for-profit firms. Not-for-profit firms are close to the standard economic model. Their inputs are based on market prices, and their services or products have a price tag, or one could be easily estimated. At one end of the process, their inputs and outputs are market price exposed and operate as a result of the voluntary exchange of providers and recipients. At the other end of the process, the expected residual and the realized residual emerging as an output can be calculated and compared. In brief, these types of organizational forms satisfy some conditions of rationality in or near the sphere of economic calculation. On the other hand, there are voluntary nonprofit organizations and associations. These operate further from the sphere of monetary calculation. They may purchase inputs on the market and orient their decisions using price signals, but they don't price their products or services. At this stage of their operation, they simply make unilateral transfers, providing a service without an exchange with the recipient. The profit and loss element is structurally toned down, blurred from a calculative standpoint (for a related approach, see Boulding 1981). Because there are tangents with the sphere of monetary calculation, they engage in measurements and a rational evaluation of processes, but the general operational principles will bear the mark of the non-calculative aspect of the output end of the operation.

Thus, to call such an organization nonprofit has an even deeper meaning in the Austrian perspective. With such enterprises, there is no calculated monetary profit, because by its very nature, it cannot be calculated. The end side of the process takes place in a non-calculative sphere. "Nonprofit" is not a (legal or accounting) convention; it is a social fact. Calculation – in the strict, economic sense – does not and cannot exist on that end, by definition. As Boettke and Prychitko (2004, 22–23) put it, if we take the ultimate calculation benchmark as a yardstick, "there are no 'proxies for calculation': issues of trust, reputation, satisfaction, and so on might serve as effective guides to action, but they cannot serve as sources for calculation itself – in the strict economic sense of the term." And this is the crucial point, a crucial difference. A guide for action is one thing; allocation by economic calculation is something else.

What does that mean, more precisely, in our case? The idea is simple: the voluntary nonprofit domain is in large part the domain of non-calculative but rational activity. The Austrians are simply restating a robust intuition, backing it with a rather sophisticated exercise. The study of the domain requires us to move from the domain of economics (and calculation) to the domain of the general theory of human action, of what Mises called "praxeology." Boettke and Prychitko (2004, 21) are emphatic that "economic calculation is not *synonymous* with rational human action. It is one terribly important *kind* of rational action that evolves with commercial society, but it would be a great mistake to claim that only calculative action engenders rational, coordinating properties."

The sphere of human coordination based on economic calculation (i.e., the standard domain of economics within which the classical standard entrepreneurship phenomenon was identified) is one member, one sub-class, of a wider family of phenomena. Social coordination can take many forms. The domain of institutions in all its variety is the expression of the variety of social forms of coordination. As Ludwig Lachmann (1971, 49–50) explains, "An institution provides means of orientation to a large number of actors." It is a social instrument that "enables them to coordinate by means of orientation to a common signpost. If a plan is a mental scheme in which the conditions of action are coordinated, we may regard institutions as it were, as orientation schemes of the second order, to which planners orientate their plans as actors orientate their actions to a plan."

To sum up, the Austrian theory inspired exercise in basic typologies reveals the possibility of an approach that encompasses both profit and nonprofit, economic and noneconomic voluntary forms of social coopera-tion. It suggests the expansion of the sphere of its study to an entire realm of institutions that operate in the vicinity of, or away from, the sphere of monetary calculation, but not fully inside it. The Ostroms have taken a step further in precisely that direction. A significant part of the Ostroms' work may be seen as a pioneering contribution to the study of the heterogeneous and complex "neither markets nor states" domain, the domain in which voluntary social action is a constant feature and nonprofit organizational forms are salient. In doing that, the Ostromian approach creates a political economy based framework for the identification and analysis of public entrepreneurship phenomena. It is a background conceptual scheme that highlights the functions and significance of public entrepreneurship. At the same time, it illuminates the complex institutional arrangements that define the structures of self-governance systems. Self-governance as the domain of voluntary action, exchange, and association covers all forms of coordination and calculation. To fully understand this, one has to go beyond the simple cases of the market and of the state. As E. Ostrom put it, we should not be limited to the conceptions of order derived from the insights of Adam Smith and Thomas Hobbes, and we should not limit our analytical and institutional imagination to just the theoretical frameworks of the state and the market.

CHARTING THE PUBLIC ENTREPRENEURSHIP TERRITORY THROUGH OSTROMIAN THEORETICAL LENSES

One of the prevalent ways of cataloging the various approaches to the diverse and complex set of issues associated with the voluntary and non-profit domain is to frame it around three major themes or perspectives

(Anheier 2005, 378). Hence, one of the simplest and most effective ways of introducing the Ostroms' contribution in this respect is to simply follow this threefold framework.

The first perspective is that of political economy. Keeping in mind how their efforts are building and further nuancing the theoretical and taxonomical insights reviewed so far, the approach from this angle builds around the logic of collective action and public choice and explores its implications for public governance. In this light, the voluntary sector is mostly about various functional approaches to public and quasi-public goods and services delivery, mainly in conditions of demand heterogeneity. In this respect, the Ostroms' contribution is massive: they were, in multiple ways, pioneers of the theoretical and empirical study of a wide range of arrangements and processes emerging in conditions in which either the nature of the goods (services) or their institutional and technological circumstances demanded solutions that went outside the standard market or state parameters (Ostrom and Ostrom 1965, 2004; E. Ostrom 1990, 1994; Ostrom and Walker 2003). The Bloomington scholars were not only students but also advocates of such institutional arrangements. As such, their work may be seen as heralding the new public management opening toward nonprofit and hybridity and other applied-level efforts emphasizing the public entrepreneurship element of these approaches.

Second is the institutional diversity – the social and institutional heterogeneity – angle. This perspective is related to the first (they have common roots in the public and quasi-public goods theory). It starts, too, with the problem of heterogeneity of preferences, values, and perspectives and, hence, with the heterogeneity of demand of (quasi)public goods. Yet, the emphasis is not on the details of the institutional arrangements and their governance, considered in isolation, but on the role of institutional diversity itself, seen in the larger picture of both the voluntary sector and the entire spectrum of the complex ecology of for-profit, governmental, and nonprofit organizations. A source of social experimentation, innovation, knowledge processes, learning, and obviously, entrepreneurial action, institutional diversity is accomplishing a social function considered crucial for the resilience, effectiveness, and problem-solving capacity of a society. In this respect, again, the Ostroms were pioneers. Their metropolitan governance studies, started in the 1960s and continued in the 1970s, were exemplary, standing even today as models of robust theoretical and empirical approaches to the issue. Their message was a strong argument in favor of voluntary and hybrid organizations and of public entrepreneurship: Allowing experimentation with nonprofit and hybrid alternatives beyond the market and state ideal models, allowing institutional diversity, coexistence, and competition, is the sole way to produce the much-needed information about viable governance formulas and to encourage the emergence of better-fitted institutional alternatives (Ostrom and Ostrom [1977] in McGinnis 1999; Ostrom, Bish, and Ostrom 1988; Ostrom and Parks 1973; E. Ostrom 1972, 2005a, 2005b).

Last but not least is the formative, integrative, and participatory function of the voluntary sector that is known as the neo-Tocquevillian perspective. With that, we are sliding slowly from an entrepreneurship-centered conceptual space toward a space where the notions of "citizen" and "citizenship" take center stage. In this case, the focus is on civic and associative life and on how independence, self-reliance, foresight, and general self-governance capabilities – viewed as essential for the functioning of the economic and political institutions of modern society – are generated and supported in the voluntary sector. As the foundation or infrastructure for social capital and civil society, nonprofit organizations are laboratories and workshops of good governance and participatory democracy. Because they are formative for the attitudes and behaviors that sustain a free and prosperous social order, they are the basic operating condition of the other sectors of the society. The Ostroms' contributions in this respect are multiple. From Elinor's studies on trust, social capital, and self-regulation to Vincent's attempt to advance the notion of public entrepreneurship or to redefine the theory of democracy by combining Tocquevillian and epistemic-deliberative perspectives, their efforts have consistently conducted toward a more nuanced understanding of the civic and formative facets and functions of the voluntary sector and civil society (V. Ostrom 1997; Ostrom and Walker 2003; E. Ostrom 2000, 2003). As mentioned, once the discussion has reached this juncture, we are sliding toward a conceptual sphere defined by the notions of citizen and citizenship and the associated themes and theories (a topic that will be the object of the next part of the book).

In brief, the Ostroms contributed to all three major areas. Out of the many research avenues and insights opened up by their work, the rest of the chapter will try to infer, reconstruct, and further articulate an Ostromian-theory-informed conceptualization of the sphere of the "neither market nor state" domain, and it will be structured on three levels. We'll start with the microlevel, looking at the Ostroms' institutionalism as constructed on a taxonomical analysis of the nature of goods and services: more precisely, on the investigation of the implications of the heterogeneity of these goods for their own provision, production, and consumption through profit and nonprofit organizational arrangements. We'll continue with a discussion of the mezzo-level contribution: the identification and analysis of the various linkages, clusters, and aggregated structures emerging around public or quasi-public goods produced, provisioned, and consumed by individual, collective, and compounded units of production, provision, and consumption. Finally we'll switch our attention to the macro level and the notion of polycentricity as a meta-level analytical and normative framework that, once applied to the third sector, opens up a new vista to the relationships between the for-profit, nonprofit, and governmental organizations in historical and a macro-sociological perspective and invites an evolutionary view of social order and social change in a pluralist, dynamic institutional environment in which the principles of voluntary action and association are at work. All three are arenas for public entrepreneurship. The diversity of action arenas, the polycentric elements, and the collective action create the conditions for public entrepreneurship to emerge. At the same time, all of them are intrinsic parts of self-governance systems. The analysis and evaluation of self-governance always has to consider the structures and functions of the diverse institutional arrangements operating at all these levels.

THE MICROLEVEL PERSPECTIVE: THE NATURE OF THE GOODS, INSTITUTIONAL THEORY, AND COPRODUCTION

One of the most striking features of the Ostroms' work is the reliance on theories that use the particular characteristics of (quasi)public goods and services as a vehicle in defining the nature of the nonprofit enterprise. The basic idea of this theme recurring in a vast proportion of the pertinent literature (Buchanan 1965; Weisbrod 1975; Hansmann and Powell 1987; Steinberg 2003; Rose-Ackerman 1986) is that of the existence of a link between the characteristics of the goods and the different institutional forms associated with their production, provision, financing, and consumption:

Recognizing that the world is composed of many different goods and services . . . and that such goods come in many different forms, we are confronted with the task of thinking through what patterns of organization might be used to accommodate these difficulties and yield reasonably satisfactory results. Just as we can expect market weakness and failure to occur as a consequence of certain characteristics inherent in a good or service, we can also expect problems of institutional weakness and failure in governmental operations as a consequence of the characteristics of certain goods and services. (Ostrom and Ostrom [1977]in McGinnis 1999, 82)

The typology of goods is, thus, the instrument helping our understanding of institutional diversity and hence of the specificities of the "neither markets nor states" institutions that define the voluntary sector. "Given the heterogeneity of citizen preferences and demands, nonprofit organizations may facilitate the provision and production of a variety of collective goods to more homogenous subgroups of diverse, large populations" (Ostrom and Davis 1993, 23).

The basics of the analytical apparatus are already familiar and require no elaboration: exclusion and jointness of use or consumption put parametric constraints on these social actions meant to deal with goods or services bearing these features. There are some extreme or pure cases: purely private and purely public goods. Yet, most situations are in the gray area, where the two key attributes vary in degree. This is the most interesting domain. A closer look at the various aspects of the production and distribution of such goods reveals a further level of complexity and diversity. For instance, in the case of education, Ostrom and Davis (1993) identify features such as economies of scale, economies of scope, information asymmetries, asset specificity, and team production. Such features (and their combinations) inescapably determine the performance and viability of different organizational and institutional arrangements meant to provide these goods or services.

Very early in their work, the Ostroms noted that, in most cases, the nature of the goods is not an ontological given. Technological and institutional arrangements have an effect on the degree of choice – on excludability or the jointness of consumption – hence on the way the nature of goods is perceived and dealt with (Ostrom and Ostrom [1965] in McGinnis 1999, 80). And thus, very soon, their (quasi)public goods theory turned into an institutionalist approach (E. Ostrom 1991). Even in their very early writings, one may already detect the contours of a potential institutional theory of the voluntary sector. Its microlevel roots are in the interplay between goods, technology, institutions, and belief systems. Technology and institutions, in conjunction with the attributes of the goods or services as framed by beliefs, values, and preferences, determine the profit or nonprofit orientation of an institutional form. The real challenge is not to imagine a theoretical model involving all these factors but to capture them in analytical frameworks both able to travel well from context to context and to be flexible enough in adjusting to the circumstances relevant in each case in point.

A natural extension of this position is the already familiar idea of comparative institutional analysis: Instead of looking at ideal-type models of institutional forms and their optimal performance criteria in absolute terms, the sensible thing to do is to look at the comparative strengths and weaknesses of the specific institutional arrangements of interest. That, we know, is nothing more than the typical heuristic approach used when it comes to the discussion of the comparative advantages (and of the nature of the comparative niches) of third-sector entities: public goods theory, club theory, voluntary failure, trust goods, entrepreneurship theory, stakeholder-based approaches, are all serving as instruments in this effort (Anheier and Ben-Ner 2003; Dollery and Wallis 2003; Clemens 2006; Ben-Ner 1986; Anheier 2005; Powell and Steinberg 2006).

The picture gets even clearer if one shifts the focus from the microlevel to other levels. However, before shifting the discussion in that direction, we need to give special attention to a notable element of originality introduced by the Bloomington scholars at the microlevel: the notion of coproduction, an idea that may be seen as the basis for an original take on many forms or aspects of voluntary organizations.

The Ostroms and their collaborators observed that, in many cases of the public and quasi-public goods they studied, two types of producers were featured, a regular and a consumer producer, who "mix their efforts" (Parks et al. 1981). That is to say, while individuals and groups may be regular producers of goods and services they supply for exchange, these same individuals may also be acting as consumers or groups of consumers who contribute "to the production of some goods and services they consume." In many instances, "consumer production is an essential complement to the efforts of regular producers [and] without the productive activities of consumers nothing of value will result" (Parks et al. 1981, 1001–1002).

The Bloomington scholars documented many situations in which such collaboration was decisive for the production process. Education, for instance, needs the active involvement of the consumer or beneficiary in order to achieve its goal: learning. Passive learning is rarely a productive strategy. The same goes for health care and many other social services. A large number of nonprofit activities bear such features in varying degrees.

The coproduction phenomenon – its function and implications – came as a revelation. Indeed, despite the role that coproduction seemed to have in public service, its significance and implications were missed in the literature. The consumer inputs were given only scant attention, considered to have an insignificant, auxiliary role. But once scholarly attention is focused on the role of consumers as coproducers of the services they receive, the contours of various possible organizational forms affected by that reality become obvious (E. Ostrom 1996; Ostrom and Ostrom [1977] in McGinnis 1999b).

Coproduction doesn't offer itself as a universal explanation of the emergence and nature of the voluntary and nonmarket organizations, but it may be able to explain some of them. Paraphrasing Henry Hansmann's essay in clarification of his own theory of nonprofit organization, one should not take the coproduction proposition as a strong or "super-strong thesis." We should simply limit ourselves to the "weak thesis" that there are reasons to think that certain institutional and organizational forms may serve as a crude but effective device for dealing with coproduction situations (Hansmann in Anheier and Ben-Ner 2003, 116–117).

The basic model of coproduction is rather simple and intuitive. First, one has to keep in mind that the coproduction situation is a result of technological, economic, and institutional factors. As the Ostroms' team put it, technology determines whether the production function involves a mixing of the efforts of regular producers and consumer producers. Economic constraints and incentives determine whether that mixing is efficient or not, given the technical feasibility and the economic trade-offs. Finally, the institutional factors determine if and how the combining takes place (Parks et al. 1981, 389).

When coproduction is technically feasible, one can imagine two theoretical scenarios. In the first scenario, the (a) regular producer inputs and (b) the consumer producer inputs are substitutes. Production may involve only regular producer inputs or only consumer producer inputs. One unit reduction in regular producer inputs is, by the very nature of the case, substitutable by an increase in consumer producer inputs. The relationship is symmetrical, and the substitution may go the other way around. Many public services have this feature. Parks et al. (1981, 389) give the example of trash collection. The service in this case is the removal of trash from households and neighborhoods. Either citizens or trash collectors may take the trash to the curb or collection point. How this service is rendered can vary from setting to setting. That may create a niche for public entrepreneurship, nonprofit organization, and self-governance. One can imagine various possible combinations and arrangements, including citizens organizing to execute parts of the task. Yet, this is not the most interesting situation.

There is a second scenario that generates the more interesting approach, a scenario in which the inputs are interdependent and non-substitutable.

In such cases, because of interdependence and non-substitutability, "no output can be obtained without inputs from both regular and consumer producers." As the Ostroms' team explained, the teacher–student interaction in producing education in the classroom features substantial interdependence. "The amount of additional output from adding a unit of one of the inputs depends upon how much of the other input is supplied. Thus, decisions about adding (or reducing) regular or consumer producer inputs cannot be guided by independent marginal calculations" (Parks et al. 1981, 389). Such situations open the door to an entire set of insights regarding organizational arrangements that operate "under conditions where they have incentives to assist citizens in functioning as essential coproducers" (Ostrom and Ostrom [1977] in McGinnis 1999, 93–94). As one might expect, such circumstances are a nexus of problems that are usually associated: trust, unilateral or bilateral misbehavior, locus of organizational control, stakeholder responsibilities, asymmetric information, etc. Coproduction leads to dilemmas of cooperation, coordination, and communication usually associated with collective action. The role of the public entrepreneurship element becomes salient.

For instance, the coproduction collective action problem should not be confused with the better-known team production problem as described by Alchian and Demsetz (1972). Team production involves cooperation for an external consumer. Coproduction means consumption by members of the production team. When producers are also consumers, they have a direct, unmediated stake in the quality and quantity of the results; they are better motivated and informed. Hence, the key problem of monitoring may get different solutions: In the case of team production, as Alchian and Demsetz showed, hierarchical monitoring and a top-down organization render themselves as the solution to the monitoring problem. In the case of coproduction, the monitoring problem and its corollaries are more effectively solved by what the Ostroms call polycentric and compounded arrangements: overlapping, multiple level, horizontal, hierarchical, and networking structures that entail cross-checking, compounded monitoring, and checks and balances in multiple forms (Aligica and Tarko 2013). Features defining the third sector, such as hybridity and heterogeneity, are the natural outcome of all that. In brief, by unpacking the coproduction situation, one can see how the coproduction model opens an additional window to the multifaceted reality of third-sector phenomena.

Consequently, there are solid arguments in favor of adding coproduction to the list of the pivotal concepts in theorizing the voluntary sector and its institutions. Focusing on it, one could arrive at a multifaceted microlevel composite analysis of the nature and functioning of basic nonprofit structures and processes and, at the same time, build a solid political economy anchor for mezzo- and macro-level approaches. In this respect, it is important to remind that institutional factors are crucial for determining the emergence of viable coproductive arrangements. Understanding the mechanisms by which institutional arrangements foster or inhibit coproduction is of great epistemic import, especially when seen in conjunction with the economic and technological aspects and the belief systems of the social actors.

To sum up, the Ostroms' approach, pivoting on a microlevel theory of goods and their attributes in various provision, production, and consumption situations, provides material for reinforcement of the analysis of the voluntary sector along political economy and institutional theory lines. Moreover, it may even offer a relatively original additional theoretical account of voluntary organizations via the notion of coproduction. The upshot of this is that self-governance may itself be understood and construed as a coproduction process. That being said, we have to keep in mind that one of its most interesting aspects is that the Ostroms' work provides the grounding for an approach that goes beyond the microlevel. It offers the basic elements of an integrated micro–mezzo–macro perspective. Indeed, as noted when the notion of polycentricity was first introduced in this discussion, it may be the case that one of the most significant contributions of the Ostroms is at the macro-level perspective: the vision associated with the broad conceptualization of the domain and its implications for the way we see the complex ecology of the profit, nonprofit, and governmental interrelationships. To get a better sense of that, let us move to the other dimensions of their contributions by shifting the focus from the microlevel toward the mezzo and macro levels.

THE MEZZO-LEVEL PERSPECTIVE: PROVISION–PRODUCTION–CONSUMPTION SEQUENCES, LINKAGES, STRUCTURES, AND CLUSTERS IN PUBLIC ECONOMIES

A good starting point for a discussion of the Ostroms' mezzo-level perspective is the distinction between, on the one hand, the provision, and on the other hand, the production of a (quasi)public good or service (Ostrom and Ostrom [1977] in McGinnis 1999; Aligica and Boettke 2009). The idea that some organizational units (be they governmental, for-profit, or nonprofit) may be involved in the production of a good or service, while another unit (be it governmental, for-profit, or nonprofit) is involved in its provision, thus generating chains of cooperation and interlinked structures, opens up the path to a conceptualization that integrates but surpasses the standard microlevel approach. Following this logic, a rather atomized perspective (mainly centered on individuals and disconnected organizational entities) gives way to a perspective that focuses on networks, linkages, structures, and clusters of organizations. It reveals the possibility of an interorganizational system of division of labor, cooperation, and exchange leading to various configurations and conglomerations of organizational and social entities. Viewed in this light, a governance entity should reveal more structural linkages and features than those illuminated by an atomistic analysis. The very existence of some units may be entirely a function of its position in such structures. Additional theoretical lenses are needed in order to explore such phenomena.

One may postulate that in any social system of a certain degree of complexity, when sufficient institutional differentiation is allowed, multiple collective consumption units and multiple production units will emerge, acting jointly to procure and supply particular types of goods or services that are to be jointly consumed by a community of people. Such units would form a larger, more or less stable system of interrelationships. Cooperative and competitive patterns could emerge, sometimes extending well beyond the boundaries of what we arbitrarily separate for analytical purposes as the nonprofit territory. The merit of the Ostroms' perspective is that they have identified and drawn attention to such aggregative structures and even articulated an attempt to conceptualize and analyze them. In doing so, they have given some substance and form to the middle ground that lays mostly unexplored between general, broad macro conceptualizations as the third sector and the microlevel perspective devoted to individual actions, situations, and their organizations' expressions.

To be more precise, the Bloomington scholars have followed the aggregated logic of governmental and private structures (both for-profit and nonprofit) and explored the many possible functional relationships between them with all their structural outcomes, thus leading to a fresh picture of the domain. For instance, "a governmental unit operating as a collective consumption unit may contract with another governmental agency or a private enterprise to produce public services for its constituents," or "a small collective consumption unit might contract with a large production unit, and each might take advantage of diverse scale considerations in both the consumption and production of a public good or service" (Ostrom and Ostrom [1977] in McGinnis 1999, 95). Incentives and opportunities for public entrepreneurship arise, fueling and changing the dynamics of these systems.

Needless to say, all these mean the emergence of specific trans-organizational or interorganizational structures. In a world of diverse goods subject to joint consumption and production in diverse and changing social environments, one may expect "an array of differently sized collective consumption and production units" to provide opportunities not only to realize diverse economies of scale but all sorts of combinations and organizational arrangements that are not available in simple, cellular organizational settings. Taking the analogy one step further, one might say that we are dealing with a molecular perspective. The attention shifts to the emerging compounded structures: Chains of provision, production, and consumption form and re-form, generating multiple-level interlinked organizational formations. Such structures entail new production, provision, exchange, and consumption possibilities with multiple levels of coordination and cooperation, but also competition. Given this background, it is not difficult to infer that what one calls voluntary organizations of "nonprofit arrangements" may have a natural niche in such chains and structures.

Where high levels of interdependency have developed through cooperative arrangements, collective consumption and production units can be expected to develop routine organizational arrangements to reduce bargaining costs. These arrangements often take the form of a voluntary association with regularly scheduled meetings, with officials to set meeting agendas and to arrange for the organization and presentation of pertinent information. Many of these voluntary associations of collective consumption and production units may be formally organized with bylaws and membership fees or assessments to cover the cost of a small permanent secretariat that organizes information, implements decisions, and engages in entrepreneurial activities on behalf of the association. (Ostrom and Ostrom [1977]in McGinnis 1999, 96)

The point of the current discussion is not to delve into the details of such arrangements but to draw attention to the mezzo-level perspective. Profit and nonprofit, voluntary and non-voluntary organizational arrangements are part of systems of exchange, cooperation, cross-subsidization, and complementarity among entities operating at different levels and in different functional parameters. The public entrepreneurship function along the lines described in Chapter 2 has multiple incentives and opportunities to manifest itself in such circumstances. Needless to say, these operations and processes are the very essence of self-governance systems.

The main challenge is to identify and analyze such structures, many of them rather informal and unstable. It is natural to assume that they depend on their context and that their scale and scope vary from area to area and with the passage of time. It is worthwhile to briefly discuss the efforts to deal with the challenge posed by the phenomenon in any case, just to illustrate what a step further on the path to what may be called a mezzo-level approach might look like. The Ostroms and their collaborators decided to denote, through the concept of public economies, the molecular institutional architectures identified in their work on metropolitan governance. They wanted to use the notion as a vehicle for an alternative conceptualization of the organization of metropolitan governance activities. The effort was part of a debate with those operating in a paradigm centered on "a bureaucratic system of public administration in which all relationships are coordinated through a command structure culminating in a single center of authority," and who wanted to both explain and reform things on such monocentric lines. What did not fit the model was simply considered chaotic and dysfunctional (Ostrom and Ostrom [1977] in McGinnis 1999b, 99). The gist of the Bloomington scholars' argument was in the claim that structures and patterns of order subside, whereas their opponents saw only chaos and dysfunction.

Public economies are not as well understood by economists or political scientists as either market economies or hierarchies. Scholars working within the traditional disciplines of political science and public administration have long been perplexed, for example, by the sheer complexity of the delivery arrangements existing in American metropolitan areas. A frequent view of metropolitan institutions has been that they are chaotic and incomprehensible. Given that scholars studying metropolitan service delivery arrangements could find no order in them, the reaction has been to recommend that metropolitan institutions should be radically consolidated and streamlined. (E. Ostrom 1998, 5)

Local public economies were not markets, but like markets, they operated on the basis of regular relationships among collective consumption and production units "by contractual agreements, cooperative arrangements, competitive rivalry, and mechanisms of conflict resolution." Overlapping and duplication is the natural result of the fact that different services require a different scale for efficient provision. Principles of division of labor, cooperation, and exchange function beyond the strict economic domain. In public economies, "no single center of authority is responsible for coordinating all relationships," yet patterns of coordination and cooperation emerge. (Ostrom and Ostrom [1965] in McGinnis 1999,

107–108; Ostrom and Ostrom [1977] in McGinnis 1999, 99). These patterns take organizational forms. Even if those forms may be deemed as chaotic, in the end, it is necessary to explore them first and establish that empirically, not to simply postulate from the very beginning their "chaotic" nature.

As one might expect, consistent with their method and approach, the Ostroms went on to explore the public economies by pointing out the multiple technical and organizational forms used in establishing collective consumption units (consumer cooperatives, municipal corporations, public service districts, etc.) and the many possible combinations of production, delivery of services, and consumption. Municipalities, they explained, may organize their own school systems, roads, and police departments but may also contract with others (including other levels of government) in order to have such services produced for communities that may be directly paying for services or may have alternative provision arrangements. In reaction to the skeptical, the Ostroms and their team asserted that examples of such units abound: small and large, focused on one good or service or multipurpose, organized on a governmental basis (small suburban municipalities or the national government) or organized as nongovernmental associations (neighborhood organizations, condominiums, churches, voluntary associations). Yet, despite their heterogeneity and apparent arbitrariness, one may always identify underlying structures and processes that link them in patterns of order that invalidate the chaotic systems thesis. The concept of public economies was a good heuristic and analytical device in circumventing the dead end of that thesis.

In brief, although far from generalizable to the entire "neither markets nor states" domain, the notion of public economy is an example of how the structure of a sector that is different from those traditionally conceptualized through the theoretical lenses of mainstream political science and economics could be consistently approached. Their featured method does not operate through simple oppositions to market and state principles or models but by following the intertwined relationships and configurations of realistically depicted organizations and processes as they may be observed aggregating at the mezzo level. The legacy of the Ostroms' work in this respect is rather challenging: The existence of mezzo-level aggregation and clustering offers an important insight about the structure and dynamics of self-governance systems and of the domain of public entrepreneurship in such contexts.

THE MACRO-LEVEL PERSPECTIVE: POLYCENTRICITY AND INSTITUTIONAL DIVERSITY

Further extending the Ostromian micro- and mezzo-level logic and insights to the macro level leads to an original view of the third sector as an intrinsic part of complex social systems operating under multilevel, heterogeneous governance arrangements. Pushed to its macro implications, the logic of the Ostroms' approach integrates the "neither markets nor states" domain into a broader view of a dynamic and complex ecology of for-profit, nonprofit, and government organizational forms. The voluntary element (voluntary action, exchange, and association) is preeminent.

As already noted, the relevance of the concept of public economy for governance studies is not in the reification of the notion but in the logic and research rationale that lie beyond its construction: an attempt to capture the trans-organizational interlinkages, configurations of a heterogeneous, multifunctional, multilevel institutional reality. Looking at metropolitan areas as complex domains combining public, private, for-profit, and non-profit attributes, the Ostroms suggested that the existence of multiple interacting and overlapping agencies is far from a pathological situation. "A system of ordered relationships underlies the fragmentation of author-ity and overlapping jurisdictions" (V. Ostrom [1972] in McGinnis 1999, p. 52). Such systems are more than the sum of their parts. The bottom line is that such organizational arrangements, formal or informal, are part of a broader system, they are embedded in a kaleidoscopic social structure driven by a rather dynamic process. In it, the boundaries between formally defined sectors (market, state, nonprofit) are difficult to draw, but patterns of order emerge and may be theoretically detectable. What applies to the micro and mezzo levels applies to the macro level as well.

As we have already noted, to articulate this systemic view, the Ostroms used as a vehicle Michael Polanyi's (1951) notion of polycentricity. They defined a polycentric system as "a system having many centers of decision-making with overlapping jurisdictions that are formally independent of each other" under an overarching system of rules and that generate in their interplay "a set of ordered relationships that persists through time [and] prevail, perhaps, under an illusion of chaos" (V. Ostrom [1972] in McGinnis 1999, 53). The theoretical lenses provided by this notion allow us to separate from the dazzling multitude of entities and processes a macro-level structure and then describe it.

It is an ingenious attempt to combine the lessons of modern political economy and governance theory in a macro-level theoretical perspective that takes seriously the problem of institutional diversity. If, in addition to institutional theory, one takes seriously institutional diversity, organizational functionalism, public, quasi-public, and club goods theories, then sooner or later, one has to follow their logic and implications to the macro level. A conceptual framework based on polycentricity seems to be the natural outcome; difficult to avoid, but impossible to neglect.

One of the notable outcomes of an approach based on a polycentric vision is that it encourages a research agenda that escapes using the government or the state as key reference points and framers of analysis, thus making a departure from the dominant mainstream mode of analysis in twentieth-century political sciences (and partially in economics) (V. Ostrom 1997, [1973] 2008, 1991, 1993). That doesn't mean that the state-focused perspective is deemed incorrect by definition. It simply means that it is one possible way to approach things and that it may not be very effective when dealing with many phenomena and domains, including, for instance, important aspects of the voluntary sector.

A polycentric vision encourages an approach in which individuals and the forms of self-governance and organization resulting from their interactions take center stage. Government itself, the state, we are reminded, is not a *deus ex machina*, an axiomatic entity. In the end, it should be at least partially a construct of voluntary decisions by individuals. After all, the government and the for-profit and nonprofit forms of collective organizations are all the result of similar or related social and decisional ingredients. There is no reason to give a special ontological or methodological status to any of them. Individuals develop diverse, intricate, and interdependent relationships with other individuals in complex situations or environmental conditions. They make choices, organize, and have to adjust to the preferences and choices of others. Competition, cooperation or coordination, exchange, donative acts, and opportunism problems arise. Various institutional forms emerge at different levels as a result of all of this. Any broad, macro-level description of the aggregated result should agree about at least one thing: that it is not a homogenous or monocentric system.

Put in governance theory terms, as the Ostroms did, a polycentric system is one where "many officials and decision structures are assigned limited and relatively autonomous prerogatives to determine, enforce and alter legal relationships" but in which the elements are allowed to make mutual adjustments to each other "within a general system of rules where each element acts with independence of other elements." In societies whose governance arrangements are strongly polycentric, "individual decision makers will be free to pursue their own interests subject to the constraints inherent in the enforcement of those decision rules" (V. Ostrom [1972] in McGinnis 1999, 55–56; Polanyi 1951). Regarding the performance of such systems, the criteria may be easily extrapolated from the public goods and public economy analyses:

> One may expect that the performance of any particular polycentric system depends on the measure in which the actual arrangements on the ground corresponded to the theoretically specified conditions for efficient performance such as: the correspondence of different units of government to the scales of effects for diverse public goods; the development of cooperative arrangements among governmental units to undertake joint activities of mutual benefit; and the availability of other decision-making arrangements for processing and resolving conflicts among units of government. (V. Ostrom [1972] in McGinnis 1999, 54–56)

Yet another way of framing things is to say that polycentricity may be seen as a macro-structural and constitutive – what Vincent Ostrom (1986) called "constitutional" – condition that induces certain patterns of social order. One may expect, indeed, that a particular type of competition- and cooperation-driven institutional evolution is set into motion in a system that has significant polycentric features, while the evolution in a significantly monocentric one necessarily takes a different direction. This is yet another point where the intrinsic connection to the problem of self-governance becomes perceptible.

The Ostroms remind us that "a predominantly monocentric political system need not preclude the possibility that elements of polycentricism may exist in the organization of such a system," and the other way round (V. Ostrom [1972] in McGinnis 1999, 52). Yet, when it comes to the overall tenor and trends, the differences between a preponderantly monocentric and a preponderantly polycentric system are intuitively clear. More specifically, a certain kind of social order emerges when these polycentricity conditions are applied with a certain strength.

For our present discussion, the key point is that there are good reasons to conjecture that, in a polycentric system, what we call public entrepreneurship and self-governance has a favorable space to grow, multiply, and diversify in various forms and in various hybridized versions. One could even formulate a tentative theoretical proposition: The more polycentrism a system contains and engenders, the stronger, more diverse, and more dynamic the self-governance features of the system will be.

That is not to say that voluntary initiatives and forms of organizations are not possible in a monocentric, hierarchical system. They are, and the forms that they take could be an interesting research subject in itself. Yet, based on the micro- and mezzo-level accounts and insights that we have reviewed so far, it looks like polycentrism is the best way of describing the favorable macro-level, structural, and constitutive conditions for the emergence and growth of self-governance. With that conjecture, we have already entered into deep normative territory. In fact, one of the challenges posed by the concept of polycentricism is that it has not only descriptive and analytical facets but also a normative one.

The nexus of descriptive, analytical, and normative is evident in the traditional Tocqueville-inspired literature that has been so important for the Bloomington scholars. While explaining the meaning and conditions of polycentricity, the Ostroms and their associates realized that what they were calling "polycentricity" has already been discussed in classical social sciences literature (Ostrom 1997; Sproule-Jones, Allen, and Sabetti 2008). Alexis de Tocqueville's work was considered exemplary in this respect (Vincent Ostrom's last and unfinished project was a book on "Tocquevillian analytics"). Tocqueville made his influential observations about the invisible mechanisms of social order and associative life of democratic systems while studying the democracy in America. In doing that, he put forward one of the most compelling descriptions of basic facets of polycentric order at work. In that light, the triadic conceptual and intellectual historical link between the Tocquevillian tradition, the Ostroms' research project, and public entrepreneurship and citizenship theorizing gains new significance.

Hence, one may easily view the notion of polycentricity as a mode of conceptually bolstering the Tocquevillian strand of theorizing about the "neither markets nor states" domain by infusing it with a dose of modern political economy. The conversion into polycentric vocabulary of the normative and analytical Tocquevillian theses runs smoothly: The dispersion of decision-making capabilities associated with polycentricity "allows for substantial . . . freedom to individuals and for effective and regular constraint upon the actions of governmental officials." Polycentricity seems to be an important characteristic of democratic societies. Objectives such as liberty, freedom, and justice may have favorable conditions in polycentric systems, as claimed by the Tocquevillian literature itself (V. Ostrom [1972] in McGinnis 1999). Moreover, further advancing the Tocquevillian analytics, one notes that polycentric arrangements seem to have a built-in mechanism of self-correction:

While all institutions are subject to takeover by opportunistic individuals and to the potential for perverse dynamics, a . . . system that has multiple centers of power at differing scales provides more opportunity for citizens and their officials to

innovate and to intervene so as to correct maldistributions of authority and outcomes. Thus, polycentric systems are more likely than monocentric systems to
provide incentives leading to self-organized, self-corrective institutional change.
(E. Ostrom 1998, 17–18)

To sum up, even a brief outline of the notion reinforces the conclusion that
the macro-level conceptualization developed around the notion of polycentricity offers a fresh view of the complex domain of voluntary institutions and processes and their place in the architecture of social order and
human governance. It is a meta-level perspective on the governance structures, principles, and processes that offer us the possibility of an interdisciplinary exploration into the systemic links between the diverse individual
and collective entities interacting over the entire spectrum of human
organization. It is a truly macro view, a meta-framework involving no
theoretical privilege or discrimination between private, market, state, hierarchical, non-hierarchical, etc. forms of social organization. It illuminates
the structure of self-governance systems, allowing a more precise understanding of the mechanisms and processes supporting them.

In other words, once approached through polycentrism theory lenses,
what we call nonprofit and third-sector entities come to be seen not as
residuals, default second-best solutions, but as intrinsic parts of a loosely
integrated, dynamic system. These entities and their networks are not
a secondary tributary or separated domain brought into the picture by
the failures of the two major players. We may not yet understand very well
their individual and aggregated functions and structures and their place in
the broader architecture and dynamics of things, but definitely, this place is
not residual and accidental. Or, at least, it is not by definition, by theoretical
assumption.

Last but not least, let us note that using the polycentric perspective in
combination with the typical "three sectors" (state, market, and third
sector) theories that provide the mainstream macro conceptualization in
the literature leads to an entire series of stimulating questions regarding the
structure and evolution of modern social order and governance systems.
For instance, the possibility of re-conceptualizing the relationship between
the sectors within a polycentric framework seems to be one of the most
interesting challenges emerging from Ostromian theorizing: Could
a polycentric order, with its complexity, hybridity, functional diversity,
and pluralism, be in fact the dominant proto-organizational substance out
of which the modern market and modern state structures emerged in
a process of social differentiation? Is polycentricity – with its polymor-
phous, multilayered diversity of institutional and organizational forms–

the primeval, original condition of complex social order systems? Did polycentricity precede modern, more differentiated and segmented systems? In what sense may one say that the medieval or antique forms of organization were polycentric? How do we deal with the non-modern, non-primitive, large-scale complex systems when applying comparatively polycentric theoretical lenses? What does that say about what we today call the third sector? What are the implications for governance theories and models?

Or, on the contrary, is it the case that the third sector is, in fact, an upshot of modernity? In other words, are the growth of the market and the state, as major forces in modern social systems, the main drivers in the emergence of the complex class of arrangements that we dub the third sector nowadays? Is, in fact, the voluntary, nonprofit domain as we know it made possible only by the complex forms of organizations of modernity, as driven by the modern state and modern capitalist system? If that is the case, then it is no accident that the Tocquevillian analytics did emerge at a precise moment in history and not earlier. But what does that say about what we call today the third sector and our ways of defining and analyzing it?

Using such questions as a vehicle, we may take even further steps in a macro-level, macro-historical analysis: What does a polycentric theory and political economy approach suggest about the interaction between the state and the market as drivers determining the size, shape, and dynamics of the nonprofit, voluntary sector? Is the growth of the market and the productivity and efficiency induced by that a source and a condition of the growth of the third sector? Is the modern state as a macro-social entity helping or hindering the voluntary sector, and in what way does it do one and/or the other? Is there an optimal balance between the three sectors when it comes to self-governance? What are the operational approaches to such questions, theses, and conjectures within the polycentric paradigm? What kind of predictions could one make based on themes and questions such as the above regarding the capacity, scale, sustainability, and impact of self-governance institutions and systems?

To sum up, by elaborating and theorizing the notion of polycentricity, the Ostroms give us the chance to revisit the problems of self-governance and to ask old questions in novel ways, inspired by a fresh analytical and interpretive framework. We now have available an instrument that allows us to further conceptualize and explore innovative avenues of the relationship between for-profit, nonprofit, voluntary, and non-voluntary organizational forms and structures in the architecture of self-governance. These structures provide various incentives and opportunities for entrepreneurship. The crucial issue is this:

The entrepreneurial forces may be channeled in different directions with different objectives and different consequences. Some of them may be productive and some of them unproductive (Baumol 1990). The Ostroms were fully aware that public entrepreneurship may not always be able to operate in directions consistent with the public interest:

Political entrepreneurs who make it their business to put tougher slates of candidates to win elections and gain control over legislative, executive and judicial offices have interests that are complementary to the organizers of great utility enterprises concerned with rail and highway transportation, water, electrical and gas services. These interests were elements in the structure of incentives that gave rise to the era of machine politics and boss rules. (V. Ostrom 1997, 208–209)

The fact that all social action takes place under the shadow of opportunistic behavior was not missed by the Bloomington scholars. Their take was far from naive idealism. The immediate implication in analytical terms is the need to identify the factors and processes that make a difference one way or another. Public entrepreneurship needs to be further specified, and new elements need to be added to explain (and induce) the publicly constructive entrepreneurial actions of social actors. A specific difference in the case of constructive and productive entrepreneurship comes associated with a certain attitudinal and behavioral profile. And thus, the problem of the citizen emerges as a necessary complement of the basic public entrepreneurship function.

The theoretical apparatus entailed by the type of approach outlined above implies an additional major building block indispensable for a theory of voluntary association and self-governance. It requires a renewed focus on the cognitive and behavioral assumptions at the microlevel; more precisely, operating at the level of the "models of man" and social actor or agent typologies. The key assumption of the symbiotics perspective and its model is that individuals have a rich set of endowments and skills and engage in voluntary cooperation in which they share their capacities (through transactions or association). They have a certain profile – attitudes, beliefs, skills. Thus, they create a large variety of cooperative formulas and institutional arrangements. The sphere of choice is extended exponentially, but that also means that a larger set of mental and behavioral capabilities has to be used in the act of framing and making choices. That creates the basis of a fresh perspective on the micro theory of decision and choice. The very idea of choice calculus changes as the idea of a choice filter discriminating between productive and unproductive becomes crucial. The features of citizenship as a filtering and decision principle materialized into a specific social role and identity. The analytical approach to choice and decision changes as well. The epistemic capabilities and strategies reconsidered as imagining the future and the possible in light of social roles and identity-based expectations becomes a key variable. Recognizing that brings a new understanding of the capabilities involved. As one could note, we are already entering the territory of citizenship theory related to the civic–political capabilities of social actors.

The language of public entrepreneurship is morphing into the language of the role, type, and profile of the citizen. That morphing leaves on the background the complex political economy and institutional theory apparatus. It continues to be institutionally contingent, but the institutional arrangements and processes are now the background on which the contours of the social actor profile emerges to salience and analytical focus. The main emphasis moves on the features and traits of social actors, their beliefs and values, skills, and political and civic capabilities. The language of social roles, epistemic capabilities, and contextual decision-making becomes preeminent.

The three chapters of this section have explored the public entrepreneurship function. At a closer look, public entrepreneurship, seen as a key to self-governance, is intrinsically linked to the notion of citizen. Self-governance requires that public entrepreneurship and citizenship are two facets of the same phenomenon. One of them leads us to an institutionally contingent function or process. The other to a typology or a social actor role with a certain profile, repertoire, and capabilities. To understand one, we need sooner or later to understand the other. Citizenship is the basic notion and the praxeological frame that channels entrepreneurship into publicly constructive directions. We have seen time and again when discussing the public entrepreneurship functions that slowly, and sometimes unexpectedly, in the course of the argument, a discussion of public entrepreneurship turns into a discourse of citizenship and citizens or civic roles and capabilities.

The next part of the book will fully move into the discussion of the problem of citizens and citizenship. The public entrepreneurship aspects (including the institutional and social process dimensions of the phenomena) will continue to operate in the background. Yet the foreground will be taken by notions of citizenship and civic competence. The very logic of self-governance requires that move. To operate in a direction consistent with and supportive of self-governance, public entrepreneurship needs to operate within the logic of citizenship.

PART II

CITIZENSHIP

The previous chapters have shown how the conceptual apparatus entailed by the notion of public entrepreneurship leads necessarily to the question of citizenship. The citizen, an ideal type or a model of social actor, carrier of a bundle of collective action capabilities, is structuring and channeling the entrepreneurial initiative in productive and publicly constructive directions. There is both complementarity and a certain overlap between the two notions. Yet, the differences are evident: Public entrepreneurship implies more of a structural–functional perspective, while citizenship implies more of a social role and capabilities perspective. The first illustrates more the process side; the second illustrates more the social role and repertoire profile. Together, they capture a critical element of self-governance systems.

We have seen in Chapter 3 how, as one advances in articulating and specifying the notion of public entrepreneurship, one slides slowly into the language and conceptual territory of citizenship and political capabilities. The same process would have taken place if the order of introducing the terms was reversed. Sooner or later, in elaborating the notions of citizen and political/civic competence, the discussion would have moved into the territory of public entrepreneurship and the associated conceptual and theoretical notions. It is tempting to push forward in fully disentangling the notions of public entrepreneurship and citizenship. But this strategy has a limit. The two notions capture two facets of a complex social and political reality. There is a lot of ambiguity surrounding the area of their overlap, and one has to learn to live with it. In the end, an instrumentalist, pragmatic approach naturally imposes itself; the aim is to use these notions as heuristic devices. The goal is to understand, explain, and illuminate. When using either of the two sets of notions, we approach the same reality, the same set of institutional phenomena, from different angles, searching for rather different emphases. That, obviously, requires accepting some ambiguity and some redundancies.

Following the logic connecting the two facets (and operating under the above-mentioned heuristic assumptions), the second part of the book shifts the center of gravity of the discussion from public entrepreneurship to citizenship. Chapter 4 will overview the theme of citizenship and civic competence in the Ostroms' work, offering a general sense of the theoretical and thematic landscape surrounding it: a *sui generis* social philosophy and theory of social order and change that illuminates and is illuminated by the problem/concept of the citizen. Public entrepreneurship and the associated institutional theory are, obviously, the main conceptual background for the discussion. The chapter shows how the Ostroms have responded in their work to the need to explain, specify, and develop the theme of citizen and citizenship as part of a theory of self-governance. As already suggested, we'll encounter a familiar landscape in many respects – themes, issues, perspectives already approached from the public entrepreneurship angle. Thus, one can see better how citizenship and public entrepreneurship converge and transmute one into the other, and we start to get a better sense of the complementary epistemic and normative values they bring to the table.

After briefly projecting the Ostromian approach in the context of the political theory literature that deals with the problem of citizenship, two conclusions are derived: The first is that it is very difficult to place that approach squarely in one tradition of citizenship/civics theory or another. Their take on citizenship and civics is sui generis, combining features of different schools and traditions. The second is to note that its truly defining background and its assumed reference point come from the Public Choice institutionalist literature and its intellectual and thematic neighborhoods. While noting the huge potential inherent in a more systematic engagement of the Ostromian perspective with the traditional civics and citizenship political theory debates, the book's argument moves toward the Political Economy, Public Choice, and Institutional Theory dimension.

The next two chapters pick up precisely that task. The logic of an approach anchored in public choice institutionalism defines the agenda: to look at citizenship from the perspective of social agency and political capabilities in collective choice and action. More precisely, to look at the developments in the relevant literature that have bearing upon the citizen-centered approach. First, evolutions that justify, legitimate, and offer intellectual ammunition to that approach, and then, second, evolutions that challenge and undermine it.

Chapter 5 looks at the developments supporting the citizen-centered approach. It reviews the evolution of the relevant literature with a view to the applied-level implications and gives an account of how the problem of social roles – a problem that lies at the foundation of citizen theory – emerges from the research program on institutions and collective action that has revolutionized social sciences in the past forty years. The chapter traces the evolution of a stream of insights and findings that, in the end, require a serious consideration of the problem of social actors as bearers of culture, social norms, and ideology, acting as agents who operate in specific contexts with rules, values, and strategies, assessing facts and evaluating other actors and their actions. The key argument is that the interest in the problem of models of social actors and citizens is not merely an idiosyncratic construct and a normatively induced element from the Ostroms' priors. There are analytical and explanatory reasons to conceptualize social actors along lines that include values, preferences, behaviors, and beliefs and to consider ideal types of citizens. Those reasons have emerged with clarity in the development of the collective action institutionalist research program. That is, indeed, a development that, in both empirical results and theoretical implications, reinforces and justifies this interest in citizenship and its theorizing.

Chapter 6 focuses on the opposite developments: findings, insights, and arguments that challenge the citizen-centered approach and the ideals of self-governance. The chapter revisits the citizen-centered model of governance and its assumptions in light of the significant developments taking place in social and behavioral sciences during the last couple of decades. These developments have profoundly challenged some of the key assumptions regarding the civic and political competence of normal citizens in normal circumstances in a normal democratic-liberal system. The very notion of self-governance may be in question. Alternative governance theories (some of them overtly antidemocratic) based on the assumption of epistemic asymmetries between social actors have been advanced. The chapter charts the nature of those challenges and tries to articulate a response to them from a position inspired by the theoretical and normative stance of the Ostroms.

The three chapters of Part II will, thus, offer three ways of approaching the multifaceted problem of citizenship from an Ostromian perspective. As such, they will give a better sense of its potential and relevance in a manner that is fully anchored in the current developments and debates of the relevant literature.

4

Citizenship, Political Competence, and Civics

The Ostromian Perspective

To understand how entrepreneurial action in public settings takes a turn which is productive and constructive at a collective level as opposed to a privately opportunistic level, one needs a certain model of social action, a certain profile of social actor. Human agency – based on a social actor profile as holder of specific beliefs, capabilities, and motivation – reclaims an essential role. One of the best ways of labeling that profile or social role is introduced by the language of citizenship and civics. The link between the issue of public entrepreneurship and citizenship comes naturally. Citizenship is a necessary counterpart of entrepreneurship in public settings. Indeed, at a closer look, Vincent and Elinor Ostrom's vision of governance is strongly anchored in an incipient theory of citizenship and civic competence. As one may expect, following the logic of their argument and putting the pieces together, one can see that the channeling and conversion of entrepreneurship into the productive-constructive dimensions that are at the foundation of self-governance are the result of modes of action predicated on role expectations and capabilities of a civic nature. Once the themes of political competence and citizenship are recognized and get introduced into the picture, the perspective on the Ostroms' work instantly gains an entirely new dimension (Levine 2011; Sabetti 2011; Sabetti, Allen, and Sproule-Jones 2009; Boyte 2011; Aligica and Boettke 2009).

This chapter will be an attempt to give an overview of the ways the twin theories of citizenship and civic/political capabilities are reflected in the Ostroms' work. The chapter will start with the Ostroms' more visible and relatively better-known views regarding citizenship and civic and political competence. Then, it will focus on the less-known and less-understood dimension that pertains to a deeper and more profound level of their perspective: a possibilist epistemology and ontology of social order and change in which citizenship and the "art and science of association" play a decisive role. Next, the chapter connects the issue of citizenship to the public entrepreneurship perspective, identifying as a potential link and vehicle the notion of ideological entrepreneurship. Ideological entrepreneurship shifts the emphasis from a functional-structural analysis to the social role and social actors' motivations, capabilities, and beliefs – i.e., precisely the move that links the domain of public entrepreneurship theorizing to citizenship theory.

Last but not least, the chapter places the Ostroms' approach in the context of the political theory and philosophy literature dealing with the problem of citizenship and political and civic competence. The Ostroms' approach eludes an easy classification in one strand or another. In fact, its main source of inspiration and area of engagement was more in the political economy, public choice, and institutionalist domains than in political philosophy and theory of citizenship. While noting the huge potential for cross-fertilization at the interface with the political theory and philosophy approach to citizenship and civics, the chapter paves the way for the engagement, in the next chapters, with the political economy and institutional theory approaches and contributions, whose findings and debates address the same core issues related to public entrepreneurship, citizenship, and self-governance. In combination, the arguments advanced in this chapter show, based on verifiable textual evidence, why the Ostroms' interest in citizenship and public entrepreneurship should not be seen as a mere footnote or marginal extension of their main work but as part and parcel of their institutional theory and their core message regarding self-governance. At the same time, they offer a richer and more nuanced view of the way that interest of theirs materialized in more precise conceptual and theoretical terms.

SOCIAL SCIENCES, SELF-GOVERNANCE, CITIZENSHIP, AND THE "ART AND SCIENCE OF ASSOCIATION"

The Ostroms have never been shy about acknowledging that their social scientific work is about the practical intricacies of human governance and, more precisely, about the ways free individuals may be able to better self-govern themselves (E. Ostrom 1990, 2005b; V. Ostrom 1997, 1993). They put at the core of their research program an explicitly assumed normative (political and philosophical) stance of freedom and self-governance.

The condition of freedom requires the courage to assume responsibility for one's own actions and for the way that one makes use of relevant knowledge, skill, and intelligibility to relate to others in mutually productive ways … Self-governing democratic societies can only exist under conditions in which individuals become their own masters and become capable of governing their own affairs and working with others in mutually productive working relationships. (V. Ostrom 1997, 288)

The Ostroms' work has been avowedly meant to contribute to the creation of a collective cumulative knowledge base to be applied by citizens to governance processes. In fact, they saw their efforts as part of "the central tradition of human and social studies."

There is no better testimony for that than the questions that structure our work: How can fallible human beings achieve and sustain self-governing entities and self-governing ways of life? How can individuals influence the rules that structure their lives? Similar questions were asked by Aristotle and other foundational social and political philosophers. These were the concerns of Madison, Hamilton, and de Tocqueville. (E. Ostrom in Aligica and Boettke 2009, 159)

In other words, the Ostroms strived to contribute from today's perspective (i.e., using the intellectual tools of the age and the historical insights gained thus far) to a long tradition of creating relevant knowledge about self-governance, knowledge to be used by individuals organizing and reorganizing their coexistence in human societies. This is not knowledge for knowledge's sake or for reasons having to do with the institutional stringencies of careers in academic settings, but rather is knowledge for improving our ability to organize for self-governance as citizens. As repeatedly noted, the priorities at the Bloomington Workshop organized by the Ostroms was to ensure that the research contributes "to the education of future citizens, entrepreneurs in the public and private spheres, and officials at all levels of government." It assumed a "distinct obligation to participate in this educational process" and create "a cumulative knowledge base" to sustain democratic life (E. Ostrom in Aligica and Boettke 2009, 159). The goal was the "development of a science of citizenship" on foundations implicit in Tocqueville's analysis and further "explore potentials for crafting democratic societies built on principles of self-governance" (V. Ostrom 1997, 30). This effort has both an epistemic and a cultural–educational dimension.

Viable democracies are neither created nor destroyed overnight. Emphasis on form of government and the binding character of legal formulations are not sufficient conditions to meet the requirements of democratic societies. The moral and intellectual conditions of those who constitute democratic societies are of essential importance. This is why building common knowledge, shared communities of understanding, patterns of accountability and mutual trust is as essential as producing stacks and flows of material goods and services. (V. Ostrom 1997, 114)

This position has led the Ostroms to a double criticism of what was seen as the mainstream conventional wisdom on democracy. First is a criticism of an incomplete understanding of the institutional nature of democracy. Second is a criticism of a limited understanding of the role of citizenship and political competence in a democratic system. The Bloomington institutionalists – though fully rooted and engaged in the public choice revolution – have parted ways with their fellow public choice scholars. The latter seemed to increasingly believe that the scientific study of (and accumulation of data about) the workings of the institutions of democracy, and especially elections and bureaucracies, has to be a sufficient knowledge and ideational basis for the operation and improvement of the governance of a social system. But for the Ostroms, the excessive concentration on the formal and standard apparatus of democracy was an error. Vincent Ostrom (1997, 3, 271) was very vocal in this respect: "'One person, one vote, majority rule' is an inadequate and superficial formulation for constituting viable democratic societies." Popular elections are necessary but not sufficient. There are "more fundamental conditions" than that for creating and governing viable democratic societies. In fact, one may have elections, political parties, and governing coalitions, but that may, nonetheless, lead to social strife, chaos, and institutional collapse.

What it means to live in a democratic society is much more demanding than electing representatives who form governments. Not only are democratic societies constructed around the essential place of citizens in those societies, but they cannot be maintained without the knowledge, moral integrity, skill, and intelligibility of citizens in the cultivation of those societies. Calling all persons in all States "citizens" and all States "republics" is a misleading use of language and an erroneous way of conceptualizing political "realities." (V. Ostrom 1997, 3)

The illusion created by a view of social science according to which the specific attitudes and belief systems of the social actors are ultimately of marginal relevance for governance and institutional design has created the conditions for a paradoxical situation. Entire corpora of institutional theory or political science are built on the principles of methodological individualism, but then, in the next breath, decline to consider of interest the individuals' patterns of beliefs, competencies, and attitudes. Yet, it is not controversial that some sets of beliefs and attitudes make for good governance, and some don't. Citizenship – as a coherent nexus or set of such attitudes and beliefs – matters. In an era of scientism, we tend to forget that many institutional pathologies of modern governance may, in fact, be the result of "the superficial way we think about citizenship in democratic societies" (V. Ostrom 1997, 3).

The future of human civilization, writes Vincent Ostrom (1979), "will not just happen"; it "will be constructed and will require attentive care." A focus on citizenship is a focus on a world of possibilities, on the "computational" and "combinatorial" logics of alternative decision paths and alternative institutional constructions (V. Ostrom 1972; 1986). If we agree that the future and the political order of the future are constructed on an ongoing basis, then the problem is in what measure it is constructed by accident and force and in what measure by reflection and choice. Something called "citizenship," or "political and civic competence" should make a difference. Self-governance based on reflection and choice is coextensive with the notion of constructive participation of citizens in the creation and maintenance of social order. In these circumstances, the very idea of a "science of citizenship in democratic systems of order" should be something expected and normal.

Those concerned with the constitution of democratic societies are required to give critical attention to the development of a science of citizenship and civic enlightenment. The idea of self-governance draws attention to the notion of constructive participation of citizens in social order. That science should not be confined to the education of students in schools. It should be a science of association that is studied and applied by all as we assume responsibility for living our lives and learning how to work with others under variable and changing conditions that reach out to global proportions. (V. Ostrom 1992, 271)

These are, in a nutshell, the elements constituting the more visible face of the (otherwise, not much recognized and understood) Ostromian position on civic competence, citizenship, and civic studies. All of the above are intrinsically related, being facets of the same position, connected logically in a coherent viewpoint. The link between public entrepreneurship and citizenship is obvious. We are not talking here about a mere footnote or a marginal extension of the Ostroms' better-known empirical and theoretical work in political economy and institutional theory. We are talking about something at the core of their project and their system of thought. The phenomenon of citizenship (especially when seen in connection with the public entrepreneurship dimension and the political economy processes illuminated by it) is both the fuel and the pivot of a free and democratic social order. Being aware of the citizenship–public entrepreneurship factor and understanding its nature and its ongoing transformation and adjustment in correlation with the evolution of its operating environment are important tasks of institutional analysis as the bedrock of governance theory.

In brief, the Ostroms have articulated a consistent vision in which the problems of governance and an institutional theory of democratic social order cannot be viewed in separation from the problems of citizenship, civic competence, and the science of association understood as a political economy background pivoting on the concepts of polycentricity, public entrepreneurship, and competitive governance. Even if their contribution was limited to that, their place in the genealogy of civic and citizenship studies would be ensured (Levine 2011; Elkin and Soltan 1999; Soltan 2011). However, there is more in the Ostromian position. A closer look at their writings (especially Vincent Ostrom's) reveals the existence of an additional dimension, less visible and even less familiar, that pertains to a deeper and more profound level.

CIVIC COMPETENCE, CITIZENSHIP, AND THE COUNTERVAILING POWERS PRINCIPLE

A closer reading of Vincent Ostrom's discussion of the philosophical principles of self-governance reveals that the Bloomington scholars' recognition of the pivotal role of citizenship and civic competence is ultimately part of a rather sophisticated understanding of a core theme of politics and political theory. Vincent Ostrom joins an entire lineage of eminent political thinkers who consider the issue of governance as, ultimately, a problem of control of power through its separation and checks and balances arrangements. He is, thus, part of the tradition that, from Polybius to the Federalists via Contarini and Montesquieu, recognizes the control rather than the employment of power as the primary problem of politics and subscribes to the doctrine of separation or division of power. "I cannot imagine how democratic societies can be sustained without checks and balances in systems of dispersed authority," writes Vincent Ostrom, adding, "using power to check power is essential to lawful republics." His place in this illustrious tradition is close to Madison's, who in his interpretation, "proposed that a principle of opposite and rival interests could apply to the constitution of order through the whole system of human affairs," which includes "the supreme powers of the State" but, obviously, is not limited to it (Ostrom 1997, 294; 2008; 1973).

That being said, Vincent Ostrom's take on the operation of the principle has a special twist. In his assessment, the mechanics of mere brute counterbalance between the centers of power is not sufficient. Neither is it sufficient to have an overarching set of rules regulating their interactions as a second-order device. The ultimate key essential for the system's functioning is the way social actors behave, or more precisely, their attitudes and strategies within the field of power forces at specific critical junctures. We, thus, get back to citizenship and civic competence.

Behind the checks and balances principle, Ostrom identifies a huge problem: conflict and its escalation. A system based on countervailing powers has built into it, by design, tensions and conflict. Conflict is unavoidable. The solution is not its elimination (which is impossible), but the problem is how it is contained and managed. We need to acknowledge that in some cases, the spontaneous and quasi-mechanical reciprocal checks and balances system is not going to work. Escalation may take place. It is the very nature of escalation that it can take off and amplify from minor tensions. The threat of escalation is real and deadly for social order.

In such circumstances, elaborates Ostrom, there are two scenarios: In the first, citizens are "ignorant of the principles of self-governance"; they lack the political capabilities to manage the challenge. In this scenario, we "would expect the use of power to check power through opposite and rival interests to yield stalemate and then to escalate to a point where the various opposite and rival interests in a society were at war with one another." A different outcome is expected in the second scenario, "when people come to expect that conflicts require recourse to processes of conflict resolution." In this case, "conflict situations become the basis for inquiry about the sources of conflict and how conflict situations have the possibility of being transformed" (V. Ostrom 1997, 294–295; 1979, 14–15).

To be more precise, one may imagine two types of solutions to the problem of escalation. The first is summarized by the notion of threats and counterthreats out of which mutually assured destruction is one extreme variant. The idea is that a reciprocal threat system leads to various forms of equilibrium. The second type of solution is different. It takes as a starting point the threats system but builds on it a process of mutual adjustment via communication and negotiation set up by institutional procedures. It is obvious that this second type of solution pushes the discussion beyond the realm of mere power politics and institutional incentives and their governing rules. Something additional seems to be needed in order to cope with the intrinsic problem of conflict and escalation via this type of approach: an attitude, a know-how, a knowledge base, a culture. We are, thus, again back to the very idea of political competence, citizenship, and civics. Social actors need to be mentally and attitudinally equipped in such ways as to be able to avoid escalation and manage, via a flexible and informed use of institutional procedures, the conflict intrinsic to the system. That attitudinal and mental competence is the foundation upon which citizenship is based.

Despite his reputation as a rational choice institutionalist, Vincent Ostrom (1997, 3, 271–272, 294) was insistent that the system of institutionalized countervailing powers he advocated as being essential to the constitution of order "can only work with the development of a culture of inquiry in which conflict can be addressed in a problem-solving mode of inquiry rather than in a way that provokes fight sets where threats and counterthreats easily escalate into violent confrontations." Vincent Ostrom refers frequently to Montesquieu's view that using power to check power depends on "the virtues of moral communities that seek to use the opportunities associated with conflict as a means of achieving conflict resolution." Successful governance depends on the awareness of this basic reality and on social actors' capabilities for acting on that knowledge, i.e., making it operational. The presence of such mental and attitudinal profiles and capabilities in a society, and the ensuing science and art of association to be practiced by them, do not in any way guarantee success. However, "possibilities of failure can be reduced."

The argument thus places in a clear light both the idea of citizens' competencies and the relevance of the type of knowledge they represent. There is one important thing that should be noted in this respect: the emphasis put on inquiry, on the idea of a "culture of *inquiry*," on people understanding "the utility of forms and procedures in constructing a due process of inquiry bounded by a due process of law" (V. Ostrom 1979, 20). Two things are involved in the fact that inquiry is considered such an important feature. The first is that citizenship could not be associated with mere routines, norms, and simple rule-guided behavior. The second is that citizenship means active, systematic investigation, analysis, and evaluation. It is something that requires both discipline and learning processes. The institutional artifacts related to the checks and balances system, and more so, the nature of its additional supportive elements, notes Vincent Ostrom, do not come naturally, and their role and functioning are not understood spontaneously and naturally by most people. Many things, both in the institutional architecture and the accommodating and facilitating attitudes and ideas needed to master the task successfully, are not intuitive and commonsensical. They need clarification, analysis, and articulation. They need to be explained and disseminated.

Human institutions are, unfortunately, subject to counterintuitive relationships that pose a serious challenge to common sense in a democratic society. If common sense were sufficient to cope with problems in this world, we might expect people intuitively to understand what would be required in coping with any situation. Our common-sense intuitions are clearly unsatisfactory, and we must go to substantial effort to establish counterintuitive relationships that occur in many problematical situations. (V. Ostrom 1979, 15)

Hence, the need for addressing things in a problem-solving mode of inquiry, noting that, in the end, the label does not matter; we could use the notion of civic competence and civic culture to designate the precondition of this substantive effort in clarification. But, irrespective of the label used, the idea and reality, in this case, come to the fore on two levels: First, as an ingredient in the functioning of institutional arrangements – a key component in the cultural and knowledge process mix that supports the management and dynamic adjustment of governance systems. Second, as a meta-level reflexivity function. The human mind can turn on and reflect on its artifacts, such as institutional and governance arrangements, and on itself as designer of those artifacts. Citizenship and civic knowledge represent, thus, an expression of a particular propriety of human systems' ability to contemplate and study themselves and to then transfer the insights thus gained as renewed input into the real-life process. And thus, one can see here the reemerging of the contours of the idea of political knowledge and civic culture, citizenship or civic competence, as part of a larger, adaptive, social learning and collective knowledge process.

That being said, there is an additional element in Ostrom's argument that deserves a special note. The quote above is rather telling. It is tempting to think about civic competence and civic knowledge as something possessing the plain, commonsensical characteristics of any human instrumentality. But Vincent Ostrom warns us that there is something in the problem-solving mode of inquiry that defines citizenship that touches on the counterintuitive and may go against common sense and conventional wisdom. Even when one may see civics as a mere training doctrine or an enterprise aiming at introducing principles and evidence-based social practices, one should not forget that, sooner or later, the solutions or principles may come to clash with conventional wisdom. As such, they presuppose an effort at clarification whose stake is even greater because it may go against popular intuitions and opinions, or even more importantly, against centers of power and dominance.

The significance of any science turns upon its capacity to clarify that which is counterintuitive. This problem is especially great in any system of governance that depends upon the use of power to check power by opposite and rival interests. The equilibrating tendencies in such a system of relationships may be seriously distorted if counterintuitive relationships become manifest in key linkages. Under those circumstances, equilibrating tendencies can be transformed into patterns of dominance that permit some to exploit others. (V. Ostrom 1979, 15)

To sum up, the task of preempting such dysfunctional situations by creating conceptual tools to identify and understand them, and then have the insights thus gained diffused to the citizens, is neither trivial nor easy. To harness for governance purposes the potential of the system of separation of powers and checks and balances, and to deal with the conflict and escalation it engenders as well as the counterintuitive situations it may induce in key linkages, requires a disciplined, systematic way of understanding and analyzing the principles and processes at work in such systems. The ideas, beliefs, and attitudes instrumental for the success of the institutional structures needed to contain and manage power stand at the core of human endeavors for self-governance. This is the point at which the discussion restarts at a deeper level.

INTENTIONALITY, ARTIFACT, CIVIC COMPETENCE, CITIZENSHIP: THE EPISTEMOLOGICAL AND ONTOLOGICAL DIMENSIONS

So far, we have seen how the Ostromian approach to citizenship and civics competence grows out of a theory of politics and institutions that is far from naive and, rather, is realistic in its focus on the problem of power and its control. It is not so much about human flourishing or other maximalist "good society" goals as it is about a minimalist condition of power containment and administration as a prerequisite of any "good society." We have now a more nuanced understanding of the Bloomington scholars' position in this respect. However, the argument has yet another level that grows naturally as an extension or corollary of the positions outlined so far. Its most profound feature is that it brings to the fore the epistemological and ontological dimensions of the problem. Vincent Ostrom follows the logic of citizenship and civic competence beyond the obvious dimension of political theory. He makes explicit what otherwise would have remained hidden and implicit: the ontology and epistemology of social order seen in its relationship to human mind and action.

The context is straightforward: The Ostroms have never been very happy with the epistemological and methodological trends generated in social sciences by positivism (E. Ostrom 1986, 1991; V. Ostrom 1979, 1986,

1990, 2008). Elinor Ostrom, in her edited book on strategies of inquiry (E. Ostrom 1982), discusses under the title "Beyond Positivism" the situation at the beginning of the second half of the twentieth century, when the fashionable positivism-inspired methods were taking social sciences by storm. Thus, in her assessment, many graduate students, lacking proper undergraduate philosophical, logical, or quantitative training, came to "take heavy courseloads in statistics and methods and fewer courses where they might be exposed to the development of systematic substantive theories."

The combined effect of this recruitment process interacting with this type of socialization may have produced a "know nothing" era in the discipline. Many scholars who presumed they were building our new empirical foundation did indeed know very little about substance and about the relationship of the statistical languages they used to the absence of theoretical models to which the language of data analysis should have been related. The criteria for what would be accepted as "facts" became a significant correlation coefficient or a high R2, even when it meant the acceptance of nonsense or the rejection of long-established knowledge. (E. Ostrom 1982, 16–17)

In his turn, Vincent Ostrom (1979, 18–19) identified and criticized a view that was epistemological in nature but that has penetrated "political discourse in the twentieth century." According to this view, systems of governance operate under physical lawlike regularities up to the point that "the method of the natural sciences are applied to the investigation of political phenomena" without any hesitation or second thought. But that, he noted, misses something essential: the special nature of intentionality and its role "in construing the meaning of political experience." Social order is largely artifactual and shaped by intentions. It is a construction based on the activities and ideas of social agents. This is a reality, a fact, and as such, it should make a difference for our research strategies. These research strategies need to consider the sui generis character of the reality they are dealing with. Hence the importance of intentionality and the normative and ideal benchmarks for what one might otherwise take as pure positive analysis. Relying on "brute empiricism" gives us nothing more than meaningless "facts" in the absence of intentions and normative ideals (V. Ostrom 1997, 295; 1979, 20). The "facts" that we observe in human societies, explains Vincent Ostrom (1979, 294–295), following John Searle, are manifestations of institutional facts. They are "artifacts," "patterns of order" having a distinctive ontological status.

If we manage to avoid "brute empiricism," argues Vincent Ostrom, and "if political experience is conceived to be artifactual (i.e., created by reference to human knowledge)," then the focus has to change. Social sciences and the study of governance are not about "covering laws" or "natural regularities but about how intentionality and knowledgeable calculations" generate the "living realities" of the social and political realm. "The whole world in which we function as participants in communities of being begins to take on different potentialities" (V. Ostrom 1997, 295).

In the end, this is not a mere problem of epistemology and methodology. Vincent Ostrom is bold and stubborn enough to follow the argument to its ontological conclusions, despite the unfashionable nature of the exercise. After all, social ontology was one of the last things on the "to explore" list of social scientists in the twentieth century. He is insistent that if the artifactual character of institutions is neglected, then an entire ontological realm, as well as the springs that fuel its existence, would be missed, too. It is a self-reinforcing procedure: missing the ontological reality leads to methodological and epistemological problems that, in their turn, reinforce the ontological blindness. Omitting the choice and cognition aspect leads to missing the key mechanisms or processes by which the social realm and its governance are constituted. At best, they are relegated to the level of derivative or super-structure extensions of more basic forces or variables:

The application of natural science methods to the study of political phenomena during the twentieth century has meant the abandonment of any serious preoccupation with the critical problems of [choice and cognition] that inform the artisanship inherent in the design and alteration of systems of governance as these are constituted and reconstituted. Political science in the twentieth century has become a science without an explicit understanding of the critical role of theory as a system of conceptual-computational logics that applies to the design of different systems of government. (V. Ostrom 1979, 19)

There are two major ideas underlying Ostrom's argument. Both have significant implications for the citizenship, political competence, and civics theme. The first is that the "artifactual" social system is a distinct ontological realm. It emerges out of the biological realm and takes on dynamics of its own, generating, as Filippo Sabetti (2014, 26) puts it, "an artifactual world in history." In it, the specific forms intentionality and computational logics may take matter, and social order and its complex combinations of institutional arrangements grow and evolve out of them.

The earth has been transformed into a human habitat that is a visibly different "reality" than the earth in its "natural" condition. Pierre Thielhard de Chardin characterizes this transformation as a noosphere, a sphere shaped by human knowledge which has its analogue in the biosphere, a sphere shaped by the existence of life. Artifacts cannot be understood as natural occurrences. In explaining artifactual constructions, we are required to account for human artisanship and the conceptual-computational considerations that entered into the design and creation of artifactual constructions. (V. Ostrom 1979, 19)

The second major idea is that the excessive naturalization of social sciences leads to the abandonment of a preoccupation with the constitutive role of choice and cognition. But choice, cognition, and combinatorial logics are exactly the foundations of citizenship and civic competence, and they manifest with particular force and specific results in those systems that experiment with self-governance. On the one hand, it seems rather obvious that the quality and quantity of civic competence should make a difference in the way a governance system is both constituted and administered. On the other hand, when the ontology and epistemology of your paradigm doesn't allow you to conceptualize this properly, when in the underlying philosophy of a social science paradigm, ideas, cognition, and individuals' collective decisions based on various computational logics do not matter, it is difficult, if possible at all, to make sense of phenomena such as civic competence or citizenship.

In conjunction, these two ideas outline the larger context, the appropriate big picture in which we need to place and address the problem of citizenship and civic competence as key ingredients of constitutive arrangements dealing with the control and management of power.

The challenge facing us in exploring the problem of "constitutional rule and shared power" is to reconsider the epistemological and metaphysical grounds on which we stand. Human beings have been agents in an extraordinary transformation of the world of nature into an artifactual realm. This artifactual realm uses the materials and processes of nature and transforms them through the use of human knowledge and artisanship to serve human purposes. (V. Ostrom 1979, 19)

That is to say, human beings and their social order are part of a great evolutionary process generating an entirely new realm. Within this realm created by intentionality, knowledge, and artisanship, citizenship and its corollary, public entrepreneurship, are phenomena that are both a result of the process and a factor pushing the process forward in possible new configurations. It is crucial to remember that the domain of the artifactual world of the noosphere is vast and diverse. In the interplay between human intentionality and cognition and the environment in its evolution, there are many possible combinations, and they may generate a variety of forms of order and governance systems.

The key difference, explains Ostrom, is the difference between, on the one side, those systems of governance based on citizenship aiming at self-governance and, on the other side, the systems in which "governments exercise tutelage over Societies and steer and direct those Societies." The two ideal types defining the polar model of order should be the basic lenses for assessing the nature and evolution of the realm of the artifactual. Approaching them, the logic of the analysis leads, sooner or later, back to the computational logic of the actors involved in its generation. Ultimately, when it comes to such macro-level structural and ontological dimensions, these dimensions are a matter of how individuals think and act in constructing the social order surrounding them. How do they conceive governance? Do they see and think like a state? Or do they see and think like a citizen? (Scott 1998; Levine 2011). This is the key question.

When Tocqueville wrote *Democracy in America,* he recognized that a new conceptual-computational logic was required for the constitution of democratic societies if human beings under conditions of increasing equality were to achieve and maintain substantial freedom in their relationships with one another. He was persuaded that alternatives were available so long as human beings might have recourse to a science of association in the conceptualization and design of human institutions. (V. Ostrom 1979, 20)

To sum up, Vincent Ostrom notes, along with Tocqueville, that a certain conceptual-computational logic, i.e., the logic of citizenship, leads to a certain form of social order or governance. The emergence of that logic on a larger scale and its related impact are something relatively novel in history. With it, an alternative to other modes of governance is increasingly becoming possible, and a new reality of the noosphere may be created. Citizenship implies an entirely new world of possibilities growing out of its specific computational and combinatorial logics (Ostrom 1972, 1986).

At this juncture, the intricacies of the multifaceted convergence between the themes of entrepreneurship and citizenship have become evident. The logic of citizenship – a model of social agency operating with a set of values, beliefs, knowledge, and capabilities – is, in the end, linked naturally with the logic of public entrepreneurship. The logic of combinations and coordination fueled by the problem-solving mode of inquiry in collective settings of competition, cooperation, and conflict sounds, indeed, exactly like the logic of public entrepreneurship that we have already outlined in the previous chapters. One can now see even more clearly how the concept of citizen morphs into the concept of public entrepreneurship. Yet now, the emphasis has shifted from the functional-structural dimension to the typological and social role.

A CONCEPTUAL LINK: IDEOLOGICAL ENTREPRENEURSHIP

Probably the best way to capture and illustrate this subtle but important transition or transformation point is to use as a vehicle the notion of ideological entrepreneurship, the missing link, so to speak, that helps us illuminate the structure of the conceptual transformation. The notion of ideological entrepreneurship has emerged as part of the effort to explain the creation and functioning of nonprofit organizations (NPOs) and in the context of the neo-institutionalist literature and its elaboration on Austrian theory lines (Storr 2008). In articulating the nature of ideological entrepreneurship, the institutionalist Austrian literature has focused on the dynamics of institutional change: Ideological change must "accompany institutional change if the new institutional structure is to stick; an ideological shift must follow, co-evolve with, or precipitate institutional change" (Storr 2008, 103). Hence the focus on the prime mover of belief systems and operational codes. The NPOs literature has focused on the motivational and preferences dimension of the social actor. It is precisely the kind of move that leads to the concept of citizen in the theoretical framework of Ostromian inspiration that we are developing here. A closer look at how the concept of ideological entrepreneurship is configured mirrors the configuration of the concept of citizenship. The approach is simple: In going through the overview of ideological entrepreneurship, all we have to do is to substitute NPOs with a larger class of governance organizations within which the public entrepreneurship and civic action take shape.

The starting point is the familiar observation that those who create and engage in nonprofit enterprises – broadly defined – have to overcome nontrivial and specific environmental constraints in addition to incentive and knowledge problems unique to nonprofit forms of organizing. Why, asks the ideological entrepreneurship literature, would people engage in enterprises in which the profit motive, at least as it is usually understood in standard financial and monetary cost–benefit analysis, is at best ambiguous? But this, at a closer look, is exactly the same issue as the one at the core of the citizenship issue: Why would people engage in public and collective enterprises that are vulnerable to so many incentive alignment and information problems? Why would the citizen engage in matters plagued by such profound collective action and free-riding problems?

As one may expect, the conjecture that a significant part of the explanation may relate to the ideological commitment that nonprofit entrepreneurs have to their strong belief systems and values comes to the forefront. Belief systems matter. The configurations of the social role, as defined and perceived by the social actor, matter. When it comes to the specific cases of NPOs, ideologically motivated entrepreneurs may prefer the nonprofit form of organization, while customers prefer, for economic or ideological reasons, the services provided by them. Citizens function within similar parameters. Cooperation becomes possible because of the beliefs and values shaping the preference functions.

As Rose-Ackerman (1997, 125–126), the scholar who is credited with being crucial in initiating the economic approach to this theme, has put it, the ideological entrepreneur "is a person with strong beliefs about the proper way to provide a particular service." This is a type of entrepreneur who "espouses an educational philosophy, holds religious beliefs that imply certain forms of service delivery, or subscribes to a particular aesthetic or psychological theory." Nonprofit entrepreneurship "is motivated by ideas rather than [monetary] profit." The calculus of decision-making thus takes particular forms. That means, for instance, that "relatively modest tax or regulatory benefits would push the founder in the nonprofit direction." The structural and legal features of the nonprofit firm may offer an advantage when the goal is promoting an idea, belief, or value and not selling a product. Hence, an additional conjecture: Within any given service sector, one "would expect that nonprofit providers would include more ideologues than the competing for-profit firms" (Rose-Ackerman 1997, 125–126).

The ideological entrepreneurship literature is very relevant for the purposes of our argument because it illuminates some essential elements that also pertain to the citizenship model in larger governance and collective action situations. At the same time, it shows with greater precision the convergence area between the public entrepreneurship and citizenship theoretical apparatus. Ideological entrepreneurship illuminates in numerous ways the multiple aspects of citizenship and civic behavior.

For instance, there is an entire line of empirical work trying to assess the degree to which nonprofit entrepreneurship is ideological, and that very effort reveals a lot about the relevant phenomena (James 1989, 1990). Studies of service sectors in which identity and beliefs matter, such as education, have shown that religious and linguistic identities are robustly correlated to the number of nonprofit schools. There is a demand for schools that have a religious and ethnic dimension, and there are entrepreneurs ready to supply them. The literature has gone even further, exploring in more depth the question of why customers patronize firms run by people who offer "services that satisfy their own idiosyncratic beliefs or express their religious faith" instead of patronizing "a for-profit firm motivated to satisfy consumer tastes" (Rose-Ackerman 1997, 124).

Following the line of inquiry opened by Rose-Ackerman, one could look at institutional and organizational aspects in operational details. Ackerman notes that scholars have narrowed down their analyses around two organizational features of special relevance: the quality control advantage of NPOs and the product differentiation advantage. An entrepreneur motivated primarily by ideology will strongly prefer to work with managers and employees who hold similar views, values, and visions. The link between producers' values and the product is stronger in such enterprises. Such entrepreneurs rely much more than the normal practice on employees who share their values.

This convergence around values reduces monitoring costs, savings that can make up for the loss of the profit motive. The quality of service is ensured in more cost-effective ways. The lack of equity holders signals to both employees and consumers that they are not working for someone's enrichment. Lower levels of pay and greater motivation fueled by the satisfaction and certainty that one is working to achieve altruistic goals come from this dedication, reinforced by the organizational structure. A nonprofit may, thus, have not only a quality advantage but also a quantitative economic advantage over a for-profit in certain fields.

In addition, NPOs may have a product differentiation advantage. There are domains and service sectors (education, arts, culture, social beliefs, or lifestyle) in which customers do not have well-formed tastes. The preference formation function is obviously crucial in this respect. Entrepreneurship has to play a major role in this. Yet one notes immediately that this is a typical "experience good" situation. The quality cannot be evaluated confidently in the absence of the direct experience of the good. Hence, consumers rely on ideological signaling. "When customer information is poor, firms may be unable to convince customers that their intentions are not mercenary unless they actually renounce private profits by organizing as a nonprofit" (Rose-Ackerman 1997, 128). The elimination of residual profit from the organizational mission strengthens the credibility of an entrepreneur by eliminating a (real or perceived) incentive compatibility problem.

Poorly informed customers or their relatives may want to rely on experts or specialists. However, they may fear exploitation. They seek providers with a clear service philosophy, but patrons differ on what set of principles they want embodied in schools and psychological care. The commitment of the provider to Dewey, Montessori, Freud or the Roman Catholic Church acts as a signaling device. Customers are buying reified ideology. (Rose-Ackerman 1997, 127–128)

To sum up, the literature shows that ideological entrepreneurs not only are viable but also are not necessarily at a disadvantage in their mission and relationship to their consumers and stakeholders. The notion of ideological entrepreneurship is thus established as a consistent and productive component of our theoretical apparatus in studying NPOs. It is clearly conceptually articulated and also well grounded in empirical insights and commonsense observations. Its key point is that ideology, beliefs, and values are a crucial factor in creating and operating NPOs. Although not the sole factor, the "ideological" variable is, nonetheless, a significant one. Explaining and understanding NPOs require a serious engagement with it.

But as we have already seen, NPOs are part and parcel of the governance system of polycentric systems. Polycentric governance requires and is based on various forms of entrepreneurial decisions and actions. Ideological entrepreneurship indicates with precision how a model of citizenship can be construed by extension and elaboration. In conditions of competitive governance, there are vast domains in which the two are practically and functionally indistinguishable.

POLITICAL THEORY AND INSTITUTIONAL THEORY PERSPECTIVES

On closer examination, the Ostromian perspective on the problem of citizenship, political capabilities, and civic competence is far from being a mere corollary or footnote to their system. It is, in fact, part and parcel of their basic vision, a well-rounded perspective intrinsically linked to public entrepreneurship and governance theorizing. As such, it encompasses an epistemological position, a political and institutional theory, a normative political economy, and even an ontological perspective. That being said, it would be a mistake to claim that their system could or should be read only in this light or could be reduced to an approach that pivots exclusively around it. However, to neglect the important positions public entrepreneurship, citizenship, civics, and political competence have in their system would be an equally erroneous approach. As this chapter has tried to show, the elements of citizenship and civics are important underlying themes in their work; they have an underlying inherent connection to the public entrepreneurship theme. Focusing on that opens up interesting, novel, and potentially productive avenues.

At the same time, now that we are more familiar with it, it is noteworthy how hard it is to place the Ostroms' approach in the larger picture of the political theory literature on citizenship. It eludes the standard linear association with any one school of thought or another. Let's take a brief look at this and illustrate the point. First is the classical liberal checks and balances element in their approach. Classical liberalism emphasizes that when it comes to governance, the main priority is institutional design in the management of power. Usually, it is considered that, in this tradition, the separation of power and procedural institutionalism mechanisms to balance self-interests is more important than citizens' virtues. Yet the Ostroms insist on defining their notion of citizenship, which intrinsically relies on capabilities and virtues, in relationship to precisely those power management institutional mechanisms. So, from the very beginning, the Ostrom approach is difficult to fit into one clear-cut tradition.

Things are even more complicated if one tries to find its place in the diverse landscape of the typical hard-core citizenship literature. There are various approaches to the notion and theory of citizenship in terms of how one defines the main arena of learning and participation: Obviously, and closer to the classical liberal tradition, the domain of exchange and market experience is one of those arenas. Individuals learn the basics of social cooperation in the settings of economic processes. Those skills in coordination, credible commitment, self-regulation, etc. are then transferable to the political arenas.

Then, directly related to politics, is the participatory democracy tradition (Mill, Rousseau) – empowerment via dispersion of power through local governance, learning through participation in various communities, and lower-level decision arenas. Civil society theories are another strand of citizen-centered approaches, strongly related but still different from participatory democracy models. Learning takes place in voluntary and intermediate organizations and is the seedbed of citizenship. Personal responsibility, mutual obligations, rule-guided behavior, and procedural approaches to collective action are learned in those circumstances. The emphasis is on the voluntary organizations – churches, families, neighborhoods. This strand is related to older pluralist traditions (see Levy 2015) bolstered by communitarian elements (Walzer 1983; Nisbet 1953).

Next is civic republicanism (Skinner 1998; Pocock 2016), emphasizing the intrinsic value of political participation as a superior form of life – qualitatively different from private life. Citizenship takes on additional meaning in this context. The fulfillment of a human being requires public participation. Then there is the "liberal virtue theory" perspective. It is an attempt within the liberal paradigm to shift attention from rights to responsibilities (Gutmann 1980; Macedo 1990; Galston 1991). Hence, the virtues requested of responsible liberal citizens are brought to the forefront: law-abidingness, loyalty, independence, open-mindedness, work ethic, delay of self-gratification, etc. (Galston 1991, 221–224). The key assumption is that these virtues are produced in the arenas of the education system. Hence an emphasis on educational institutions and organizations as the main arenas of learning.

Last but not least is the separate but related line of the capabilities approach associated with Amartya Sen's work. The link between the Ostroms and Sen represents an entire agenda in itself. The elements of their convergence are all there. And yet, as Johnson and Orr (2017) have noted in their excellent discussion of the puzzle, the convergence hasn't taken place yet despite the huge potential for these complementary and perhaps reciprocally supporting theories. For our purposes, at this juncture, we just need to note the affinities and the huge potential of the concrete work of building a synthesis between the two.

Even a superficial survey of the basic strands of the political theory literature on citizenship, such as the one attempted above, helps us to (a) better locate the parameters of the Ostromian approach and (b) understand how difficult, in fact, it is to place it in one definite tradition or another. In the end, one has to stick to the observation that its distinctive feature is that it is revisiting, reconstructing, and reinventing some of these political theory themes on a track that is not so much shaped by the tradition of political theory or political philosophy but by developments emerging from political economy and institutional theory roots, even more specifically, institutionalism in the public choice tradition, including its normative corollaries and extensions.

One could, obviously, further nuance and elaborate the contours of the Ostroms' views in the context of the various schools of political theory noted above. And that is a task ahead for an entirely separate project. Indeed, elaborating on the Ostromian approach, nuancing it in light of the most interesting recent developments in each of these lines of literature is a fascinating and potentially fruitful task. However, for the purposes of the present project, we'll take a different direction. We'll try to further engage the Ostromian project on citizenship following mostly the political economy, public choice, and institutional theory dimension. We have established that institutional theory, political economy, and public choice (and, at the applied level, institutional design and governance theory) are the main reference points, sources of inspiration, and sources of challenge in relation to which the Ostroms developed their ideas of citizenship. The following chapters will address the problem of citizenship against the background of precisely that type of literature.

The next chapter, Chapter 5, will show in some detail why and how these themes and analytical interests are not an arbitrary normatively induced construct of Ostromian thinking. The problem of a model of human agency endowed with capabilities and having specific belief systems and values emerges naturally and independently of any public entrepreneurship and citizenship normative musings if one follows to the logical and empirical conclusions the investigative line advanced in institutional theory and collective action studies during the last thirty years or so. The chapter will focus on how the citizen-centered approach is supported by some key developments in social sciences. Then, Chapter 6 looks at the opposite developments in social sciences and philosophy that undermine the citizen-centered approach and, by implication, the self-governance paradigm. At the end of this part of the book, one can get a better sense not only of the Ostromian approach to citizenship and its political economy and institutional theory foundations and ramifications but also of what is at stake – both for political theory and on an applied level – in the debates surrounding citizenship, public entrepreneurship, and self-governance in light of recent developments in social research and public discourse.

5

From Institutionalism to Models of Social Agents

Citizenship in the Institutionalist Context

As noted in Chapter 4, the distinctiveness of the Ostromian take on citizenship comes from the fact that it has its roots in the framework of political economy and institutional theory. They engage and project a notion typical for political theory and philosophy but anchor and employ it in a theory of governance and institutional analysis based on an applied-level perspective with a special emphasis on the problem of collective action. This chapter will show that linking the problem of citizenship to the political economy and institutionalist literature is not an artificial construct but an analytical necessity bolstered by empirical analysis. It is true that the notion of citizenship may be seen as a construct exogenous to the logic of political economy and its tradition. Yet, as we'll see, the problem of human agency underlying the theme of citizenship (as defined by a certain set of beliefs, values, capabilities, and motives) emerges naturally from the development of this research tradition. The necessity of building and using a social actor profile that incorporates the strengths of the basic rational choice models, but goes beyond that, is indispensable for analytical reasons.

This chapter will illustrate, step-by-step, how a major research program in contemporary social sciences, focused on institutions and collective action, comes to gradually identify and illuminate the need for thinking more substantively about social agents and the various ideal types and models dealing with them. The more the analytical attention moves to the heterogeneous set of informal institutions, social norms, values, beliefs, rules, and cultural and contextual factors, the more the need for a social agency model able to meaningfully operate in the complex environment such defined becomes apparent. The normative dimension is even more momentous. We are operating in a world of multiple combinations, "a world of possibilities rather than necessity" in which agency matters.

We are not trapped in deterministic, closed systems, but in open and dynamic situations. Not everything is possible. But some things are. There is freedom of choice, and that creates a space for responsibility. One needs to capture that reality for both analytical and normative reasons, and thus, the notions of social role and agency become salient. The necessity for ideal types and social roles such as those referring to the citizen and citizenship becomes unmistakable.

Out of the vast relevant literature, this chapter will look specifically at the contribution made by the family of research programs broadly associated with the "new institutionalist turn" or "revolution" that has reshaped the social sciences landscape during the last four decades or so. There are three major reasons for this choice. First, it is because of their massive impact on contemporary social scientific thinking. Arguably the institutionalist revolution was the defining mark of recent social sciences, and it was responsible for some of the most relevant social scientific developments for our subject. Second, it is because of its assumed stance as an applied-level oriented scholarly enterprise. In this respect, it is, by its very nature, the preeminent domain of governance, institutional design, and institutional feasibility research. Finally, it is because the Ostroms' work on collective action (the phenomenon and its theorizing) has been, in multiple ways, associated with it and its agenda, being in numerous senses and in different guises at the center of their investigations. Placing their work in the context of the institutionalist program is one of the most effective ways of showing that *the problem of citizenship and the model of social agency it tries to capture are not outliers driven by the Ostroms' normative priors fueled by their interest in self-governance but part of a pattern intrinsic to the broader institutionalist research agenda.*

One of the most interesting aspects of the institutionalist research is the fact that, without intention or plan, it has amply illuminated the surprisingly pivotal position an entire set of informal and contextual factors and variables have in both institutional order and in its change (including deliberate change via institutional design and public policy). Thus, an unintended, unexpected, and still neglected result of the so-called institutionalist revolution in social sciences has been the emergence to salience of the informal dimension and the related contextual analysis. This chapter will show that far from being just one of the typical, normal science growths of knowledge by variable addition schemes, the reorientation of focus signals a larger shift of methodological, theoretical, and epistemological perspectives of rather profound significance. Such a shift has the potential to alter the ways we understand structure, change, prediction, and control in social settings and, hence, is intrinsically related to the twin problems of human agency and institutional feasibility (two foundational problems of applied theory and governance studies). We'll see how the problems of political capabilities and the issue of citizen as a social role or social actor profile emerge as focal points of epistemic and normative significance. In brief, this chapter illustrates how clarifying the nature and functions of the heterogeneous domain of the informal and the contextual nature of decision-making leads, step-by-step, with logical and empirical necessity to the conceptualization of human agency along lines that incorporate but go beyond the standard basic rational choice models. When it comes to theories of governance and collective choice, and even more specifically, to democratic self-governance, a serious engagement with richer notions of agency conceptualized as, for instance, citizen and citizenship is mandatory.

THE INSTITUTIONALIST REVOLUTION AND THE DOMAIN OF THE INFORMAL

Revisiting the relevant literature on the social, political, and economic analysis of institutions offers a fascinating view of how the problem of the informal, of contextual configuration and processes, came to occupy a pivotal place in the larger picture of institutional order and change emerging from the research done during the last decades. From there, it is only one logical and analytically necessary step to the problem of the human agency operating contextually and employing capabilities and local and personal knowledge. In following those developments, let us start with the initial broad category of "institution."

Institutions, broadly defined as "rules of the game" or "constraints" or "constitutive parameters" of individual and collective action, were always recognized as important explanatory variables and, in applied theory, as key instrumental or target policy variables. The last decades – under the impact of what was called the institutionalist revolution in social sciences – have brought, however, a more nuanced understanding of the phenomena under discussion and of the processes at work. Leading this trend, D. C. North noted the problem:

Curiously enough, institutions are front and center in all current explanations of growth or lack of it in third world or transition economies; but the explanations lack both analytical content and an understanding of the nature of institutions or the way they evolve. The implication is that they can be created at will or frequently that they are a dependent variable to getting the prices right. (North 1997, 2)

The first step in providing the lacking analytical content was the de-homogenization and firmer conceptualization of the large class of phenomena and variables identified under the label of "institutions." One of the outcomes of that move was a gradual but decisive shift of emphasis. The more the empirical and applied-level literature have advanced along this line, the more the problem of the distinction between formal and informal institutions has become salient. The interplay between formal institutions (economic, political, legal) and the realm of the informal (social norms, tacit, implicit, non-legally binding, customary practices, etc.) has slowly taken center stage.

The variety of definitions of the formal–informal dichotomy and the different paths to conceptualization illuminate the heterogeneity of the informal. For instance, Brennan et al. (2013) illustrate how one could create operational distinction within a subset of this class. On the one hand, formal institutions are clusters of primary rules that "enjoin us to perform or refrain from performing this or that action" and that are supplemented with "secondary rules," rules that lay down the criterion of rule recognition, rule change, rule interpretation and adjudication. Formal institutions are thus backed by a network of secondary norms that "create a structure of formal mechanisms for the creation, modification, application and interpretation of the norms that belong to the relevant network" as well as by "formal mechanisms of enforcement" (Brennan et al. 2013, 41–42). On the other hand are the social norms: the primary rules lacking a secondary-level structure of support. Within this context, social norms are seen, first and foremost, as a social fact, accepted rules, or normative principles, not made, interpreted, or enforced by central authorities: a socio-empirical phenomenon of psychological, behavioral, and cognitive dimensions. Although they overlap in many cases with moral norms, and in many cases, they derive normative strengths from morality, their sphere is substantially larger than that of typical moral norms. The literature further introduces many important distinctions and typologies of social norms (nuancing differences between diverse classes and subclasses in accordance with structure, function, origins, operating principles, the role of rationality and irrationality in their emergence and resilience, etc.). Such distinctions are important in the function of analytical context, particular case, and specific policy target, but for the current purposes, the point is to first illustrate the heterogeneity of the class of the informal, with its social, psychological, behavioral, and cognitive dimensions. Second is to demonstrate the fact that the heterogeneity is, nonetheless, amenable to rather precise descriptions and taxonomies.

Awareness of the role of the informal dimensions has always existed, but the detailed studies of a variety of policy-related issues such as policy implementation, transition economics, legal pluralism, shadow economies, corruption, Asian business systems, informal markets in the Soviet system, etc. have put their key role in a new light (Helmke and Levitsky 2004). Increasingly, the old policy theory assumption that incentives and expectations could be shaped mainly, if not exclusively, by formal rules and institutions was deemed naive. Even more interesting – although rarely acknowledged explicitly in its implications – the realm of the informal was increasingly assumed to have a decisive causal weight in explanation and analysis. Helmke and Levitsky (2004) synthesized what, by the end of the 1990s, was common knowledge:

> Good institutional analysis requires rigorous attention to both formal and informal rules. Careful attention to informal institutions is critical to understanding the incentives that enable and constrain political behavior. Political actors respond to a mix of formal and informal incentives ... and in some instances, informal incentives trump the formal ones. (Helmke and Levitsky 2004, 22)

The implications for the study of institutional performance are profound, as Elinor Ostrom, writing at about the same time, has explained:

> The differential political and economic performance across nations and communities, for example, could not be answered satisfactorily without seriously studying the omitted factors: trust and norms of reciprocity, networks and forms of civic engagement, and both formal and informal institutions. (E. Ostrom 2007, 2)

The studies invoked by Elinor Ostrom have long moved beyond the older, common practice of using informal institutions as a residual category brought forth (sometimes in conjunction with – or as a substitute for – culture) as a last resort, somewhat improvised explanatory variable in analyses faced with the exhaustion of the potential of other more formal variables. And thus, the literature has entered with increased focus and some precision into that deep area of fuzzy contours but strong explanatory and policy weight. And this is exactly the domain that has been pushed to the forefront by the institutionalist turn in social sciences, sometimes as an unintended consequence of it: a revolution within the institutionalist revolution.

Examples abound in fields that are directly relevant for public policy and institutional design. A brief overview of some of the most salient will help us to get a sense of their concurrence and, at the same time, will provide the grounding for a series of important observations. At the core of the field of policy studies itself, the line of research on policy implementation in advanced Western democracies inaugurated by Pressman and Wildavsky (1973) had been an uninterrupted source of insights. The analysis of the processes associated with implementation success or failure brought a wealth of evidence regarding the role of the informal and contextual residuals: institutional, social, and cultural factors. However, the institutionalist turn in social sciences has brought a new range of perspectives to the table, mutually reinforcing each other and converging in their conclusions.

In analyzing the institutional foundations of economic performance, D. C. North, perhaps the best known advocate of neo-institutionalism, concluded that to successfully restructure an economy, one needs more than the restructuring of property rights to provide the "correct" incentives while supporting a judicial system that will enforce such rules. Social rules, the culture, and the mental models of actors matter (North 1993). The universality of the problem that cuts across the modern–premodern divide was well captured in Raiser's observation that while there is a tendency for some informal institutions (such as social monitoring through reputational mechanisms), to be replaced by formal rules as the division of labor becomes more complex, informal institutions continue to exert a strong impact on institutional performance (Raiser 2001, 220–221).

Elinor Ostrom's work on social norms and social capital has been exemplary in this respect. As she explained, the use of the concept of social capital as "an attribute of individuals and of their relationships that enhances their ability to solve collective action problems" opens a more nuanced insight on the nature and conditions of collective action, the foundation of policy analysis and design. Incorporating forms of social capital such as trustworthiness, networks, and institutions into a collective action framework has become one of the sources of what she called the second-generation theories of collective action (E. Ostrom 2007). By the 1990s, one had witnessed the emergence of an entire subfield dedicated to the study of social capital, "features of social organization, such as trust, norms, and networks that can improve the efficiency of society by facilitating coordinated actions" (Putnam, Leonardi, and Nanetti 1994, 167). Keefer and Knack, in an overview for the *Handbook of New Institutional Economics* of the literature on social capital and social norms fueled by the new institutional economics note that "substantial evidence demonstrates that social norms prescribing cooperative or trustworthy behavior have a significant impact on whether societies can overcome obstacles to contracting and collective action that would otherwise hinder their development" (Keefer and Knack 2008, 701).

The study of the conditions, policies, and strategies of economic development has been another important arena for these intellectual evolutions.
The work of J. P. Platteau (2000, 2006, 1996) on institutions, social norms,
and economic development is highly illustrative in that it explains in great
empirical and analytical detail, based on fieldwork, how informal social
norms operate to support or hinder development in non-Western societies. For instance, it has shown how norms regarding the allocation of
locally controlled natural resources such as land, forest, pastures, and water
could be viable and effective, but also how they respond to the pressure of
market integration and the emergence of alternative economic and political institutions. Building on this vein, William Easterly (2008) has
become the flag bearer of the scholars challenging the traditional approach
to aid and international development.

Similar ideas have emerged in the study of comparative economic
systems. The study of Soviet and transitional economies has revealed the
surprising impact on formal institutions of the informal domain of social
norms, culture, and belief systems. First, the complex institutional arrangements defining the Soviet systems proved to be themselves unintelligible if
one did not go well beyond the formal and official blueprint of the planned
economy. Hence, not the official description of the economy but the
arrangements combining official and informal institutions became the
main object of interest. Second, the post-communist transition, seen as
a large natural experiment in institutional change and design, was a huge
source of case studies not only supporting the notion that "institutions
matter" (which has become a mantra of transition) but also illuminating
"one subset of institutional phenomena, namely the role of informal
institutions in economic transition" (Raiser 2001, 220). Informal institutions understood as "the collection of social norms, conventions and moral
values that constrain individuals and organizations in pursuit of their
goals" have taken center stage in the analysis of most areas of transition.
"Any process of rapid formal institutional change such as currently
observed in the transition economies," wrote Raiser, "must contend with
the legacy of an inherited set of informal institutions that may or may not
be efficient under a changing economic and social environment" (Raiser
2001, 220–221).

It is important to note how the shift of the center of gravity toward the
vast and heterogeneous informal domain has led to a renewed understanding of institutional linkages and complementarities and of the functional relationships in institutional systems. As Frederic Pryor, one of the
leading   scholars   of   comparative   economic   systems,   reminded,

"institutional coherence is inescapable and we could not simply pick and choose particular institutions that appeal to us and combine them in an economic system" (Pryor 2005, 4). Again, the conclusions point in the same direction: "In considering why certain economies perform better than others, many have focused their attention on key institutions. If the logic of institutions holds, however, such institutions are related to others so that the question is whether it is the impact of the key institution alone or together with related institutions that provides the crucial explanation" (Pryor 2005, 271). Institutions – formal and informal – operate in conjunction, united by multiple links at multiple levels. The logic of institutions, "that is the complementarities and coherence in a configuration of economic institutions of society" (Pryor 2005, 270), is an essential determinant of economic system reform and change. However, to follow the logic of these institutional concatenations, one has to sooner or later deal with the problem of the informal domain that provides the functional link between the more visible formal institutional arrangements relying on and expressing in a direct, unmediated way the basic social forces, behaviors, and attitudes in a social system. They are the foundations on which the architecture of formal institutional arrangements grows and the cement that keeps it together (Elster 1989).

To sum up, a review of the literature along the lines presented above would underscore the broad concurrence between the diverse streams of the institutionalist literature when it comes to the informal dimension of institutional order and change. Even a brief survey such as the one attempted above illustrates the universality of the problem: first world, developing world, transition countries; it is not even a matter of modernization stage or complexity of the system. The conclusion emerges naturally: The heterogeneous domain of the informal has such a position in the architecture of social order that concentrating on it gives a privileged vantage point in institutional analysis, institutional design, and public policy.

Henceforth, the following two sets of observations, far from being a mere exercise in speculative social philosophy, are strongly based on the main insights of the literature. That is to say, the analytical significance and applied legitimacy of these observations are well grounded in multiple research agendas and the corroboration of their findings. As such, puzzling, counterintuitive, and controversial as some of them may seem to us prima facie, they legitimately deserve our entire attention.

TWO IMPORTANT IMPLICATIONS

Without intending it, and even without fully acknowledging it, the institutionalist program has created an inescapable shift of emphasis, when it comes to causal weight and relevance, toward the informal sector. It has established that the domain of the attitudes, values, and beliefs of the norm, as well as the practices surrounding them, have a larger causal weight than previous scholarship was prepared to consider. Despite the understated tone in which this finding is usually stated, its radical corollary is unmistakable: The downgrading of the preeminent causal and functional role of formal institutions as assumed or as presented in most textbooks and primers of economic and political analysis. Hence, we arrive at the first major implication:

(1) From background conditions to foreground. Informal norms shape the performance of formal institutions in so many ways, and the very compliance with formal rules may depend in large measure on them, that it makes sense to reconsider some of our most cherished notions about the nature and efficacy of the formal realm. The very constraining and coordinating capacity attributed to formal institutions may, in fact, have its source, its driving force, outside the formal realm. The entire apparatus of formal institutions operates using, so to speak, the social capital, the energy or the fuel generated in a differed dimension of the social system and processes. Formal institutions remain essential, but to understand them and the sources of their efficacy, one needs to look beyond them.

At stake is not just a shift of causal weight between variables. An entire change of fundamental perspective is entailed. As such, it is an issue with a significance that touches the foundational philosophical domain. It is a case of what Schumpeter called "pre-analytical vision," the fact that "in order to be able to posit to ourselves any problems at all, we should first have to visualize a distinct set of coherent phenomena as a worthwhile object of our analytic effort" (Schumpeter 1954, 41). Each analytic effort, argues Schumpeter, "is of necessity preceded by a pre-analytic cognitive act that supplies the raw material for the analytic effort" (Schumpeter 1954, 39). Schumpeter shows that in all social scientific theorizing and modeling, there is such an element, a "preanalytic cognitive act," which he calls a "vision." A vision of this kind, he explained, not only must precede the emergence of analytic effort, but also may operate each time somebody teaches us to *see* things in a certain theoretical light (Schumpeter 1954). This is exactly where the gradual accumulation of factual observations regarding the informal has led.

Indeed, once the role of the heterogeneous domain of the informal in social systems is reframed, a new view opens up: the entire architecture of formal institutions that otherwise are center stage in our analysis recede to the background. The logic of R. Wagner's discussion about background and foreground in equilibrium and disequilibrium analysis applies perfectly in this case. Wagner draws attention to two types of theorizing in economics: theorizing in which equilibrium is in the foreground, while the disequilibrium condition of the system is projected on the background; and theorizing in which the dynamics of disequilibrium are in the foreground, while equilibrium is a background framework that plays a supporting role to disequilibrium analysis. He shows that although the equilibrium and disequilibrium theoretical apparatus remains unchanged in all cases, there are major differences of approach and insight once one places processes of development or emergence in the analytical foreground and puts equilibrium states or conditions in the background (and the other way around) (Wagner 2016).

Mutatis mutandis, the institutionalist research seems to lead to an approach in which the informal, the domain of norms, beliefs, values, etc., takes the foreground, while the formal institutional arrangements – traditionally salient in the spotlight – take more of a background position. Two entangled realms of institutional processes emerge, each with intertwined but different dynamics. One of them seems in a sense more basic: A network of information, values, beliefs, and their associated processes, bolstering (or undermining) in specific critical points the formal domain. The shift of focus doesn't mean the neglect of the formal domain. It means that the very way one conceptualizes the entire institutional system has to be reconstructed. This shift, therefore, means an entire social ontology reconceptualization. The pre-analytical vision and meta-model of institutional reality get reformed. The ways we conceptualize its causal structure and functional relationships changes, and with that, our understanding of what is possible, feasible within such systems, has to adjust as well. With that, we have reached the second observation.

(2) Combinatorics and contextual analysis. This shift in social ontology comes in its turn with noteworthy methodological and analytical strings attached. The reassessment of causal vectors and functional structures has to be seen as part of the complex, contextual combinations of formal and informal, first-order and second-order variables. The full combinatorial

and stochastic dimensions entailed become clearer as soon as we look at collective action not just as a game-theoretical matter but as a large numbers phenomenon. Social norms are the quintessence of this type of phenomena ("When enough individuals perceive that enough individuals are no longer behaving in accordance with a social norm, the social norm ceases to exist" [Brennan et al. 2013, 113]). It is not only that, as a rule, such collective phenomena involve a large number of agents, interacting social actors, making interdependent decisions. It is also a matter of a large number of variables defining various facets of the actors, their decision arenas, and their environments, all bringing into the picture vast combinatorial possibilities. If one also introduces the permutation aspects in which the order of variables, interactions, and factors matters (as in the policy sequencing problem, see the "democratization first" versus "marketization first" debate), the space of possible configuration of variables becomes a large number; a complex, dynamic situation.

The main point is that once institutional structure and performance are understood as a combinatorial causal configuration in which the heterogeneous and elusive informal has, at minimum, an equal status with the formal, the pressure to reconsider the epistemological and methodological apparatus involved reaches a critical threshold. It is not only the increase of the number of variables but also the way they are weighted in various combinations generated by large numbers, repeated interactions, and multiple nested levels. Methods, approaches, and techniques aiming to capture these nested collective, threshold, and critical mass phenomena have come to the fore.

Indeed, if one revisits the new wave of social science of the last decades, an important part of it – probably the most important – has been the institutional theory fueled by (evolutionary) game theory, decision theory, and the statistical analysis of complexity and emergence. At the core of it: The analysis of how macro-level, formal institutional arrangements come into being and endure through the micro-dynamics of the social mechanisms and processes emerging out of individual social agents' interactions (Lewis 2011; Harper and Lewis 2012). One has witnessed the growth of an apparatus aiming to capture the combinatorics and the behind-the-scenes interplay of individuals and collectives, rule-guided and strategic behavior, of rationality and irrationality that fuels and shapes the otherwise more salient institutional architecture. Yet, that, as we shall see, has led in a perhaps startling way to a necessary reassertion of the role of human judgment and decision. Human agency operating in an environmentally and institutionally contingent decision space of the possible has reemerged as a crucial variable.

In brief, a focus on the domain of the informal leads to a specific understanding of causal configurations that, in turn, entails a methodological and epistemological shift to a contextual analysis (Goodin and Tilly 2008). One may find this at work throughout the entire literature. Analytical contextualization is invariably associated with the focus on the informal. When we have one, the other is not far behind. A focus on the informal seems to lead to rethinking and reframing of the approach and methodology, and the other way around. In fact, it looks like the two reinforce and illuminate each other. Progress in refining our understanding of one side leads to better understanding and refining of the other. A better tuned analytical apparatus leads to a better understanding of social norms. A more nuanced perception of the nature and function of the heterogeneous set of norms, beliefs, rules, values, etc. operating under the label of the informal leads to an adjustment and a better tuned analytical apparatus. And that, obviously, has important ramifications.

All things considered, the foreground–background switch and the contextual and combinatorial analytical perspective that both emerge distinctly from the institutionalist program are much more consequential than we are led to believe by the low-key, restrained ways they are presented by scholars in the field. Given a set of structural constraints that determine the possibility set, the actual evolutions may be decisively determined in the end by specific actions coming from social actors with particular positions and endowments. The surprising result is the emergence of human agency and of the model of man to newly bolstered salience. To understand the problem of social change, the scope and limits of our institutional change capabilities, the feasibility of our design plans require sooner rather than later *a model of agency and a model of man*. To further articulate this point, let us use as a vehicle the standard case of policy intervention.

SOCIAL NORMS, CONTEXTUAL ANALYSIS, AND POLICY INTERVENTION

The foreground–background issue and the contextual–combinatorial analytical approach give us a fresh perspective on the problems of social change, particularly the potential and the limits of deliberated policy change and institutional design. At the core of the public policy approach is the problem of social intervention, of action based on public and private deliberation and choice aiming to change or preserve a social–institutional state of things. The public policy literature describes the parameters of the task via the notion of "policy theory." Any intervention, policy, or institutional design operates under what the public policy literature calls "policy or program theory": assumptions about "the change process actuated by the program and the improved conditions that are expected to result" (Rossi, Lipsey, and Freeman 2004, 101). As Rossi, Lipsey, and Freeman put it in their influential textbook, "When a program's theory is spelled out in program documents and well understood by staff and stakeholders, the program is said to be based on articulated program theory [as opposed to implicit program theory]" (Rossi, Lipsey, and Freeman 2004, 101–102). The clearer and more explicitly the policy theory is articulated, the more chances one has to rationally evaluate the policy in its implementation, effectiveness, and consequences.

Inherent in that is an idea of an operating causal structure, a presumed cause and effect sequence, and a series of key variables that are deemed to be crucial in that respect (including, in most cases, some normative assumptions and standards). For the purposes of our discussion, the main point is that any policy theory needs to deal satisfactorily with three problems: (i) the causal weight of a variable in a configuration of factors determining a policy problem; (ii) the malleability of that variable; and (iii) the external validity of the designs and principles involving the variable in question. In brief: causality, malleability, and validity. Moving the domain of the informal to the forefront requires a reassessment of what that entails for policy theory, in all three dimensions.

The most striking problem posed by the informal domain when it comes to deliberate social change is in terms of malleability. Malleability is the crucial issue in policy design, and it is basically an attempt to orient courses of action and to change structures and processes. A variable that has strong causal impact in a policy configuration may, nonetheless, have very limited malleability. For policy purposes, malleability is what truly counts. Hence, there is a search for those aspects of the social reality that are open to influence and intervention, i.e., are malleable. And that is precisely the problem, for instance, with social norms in the policy design equation. Social norms are not very elastic, malleable variables. The institutionalist research has provided considerable empirical evidence about that. "At a practical level, whether informal institutions are considered to be constraints or parts of a society's opportunity set is probably less important than the recognition that informal institutions fundamentally influence human behavior while not being directly amenable to policy" (Raiser 1997, 2).

There are multiple reasons for that. We have limited knowledge about the changes in informal norms and even less control of that process. The phenomena in this case should be understood in many respects as a matter of collective behavior. One needs to get enough people in a group to accept, recognize, and enforce a norm. It is a collective action, a critical mass phenomenon. Once a social norm is put in place, once the critical mass is reached, then a series of factors set in, systematically diminishing its malleability. There are perceptible costs of coordination and cooperation to change and replace a social norm. The problem is not just the costs directly related to the norm in question, but the cascading costs related to all other behaviors and institutions organized around or linked to that social norm. A certain locked-in and path-dependent transition cost reinforced situation sets in. Brennan et al. (2013) expound upon several other reasons: interests mobilization, loss aversion, self-fulfilling expectations, and absorbing Markov chains. For the purposes of our discussion, all represent an extension and elaboration of the basic transition cost locked-in point. Similar arguments may be advanced from complementary perspectives. D. C. North summarizes it all around the twin notions of time and uncertainty: "It takes much longer to evolve norms of behavior than it does to create formal rules," and when such norms are lacking in a society, "the reconstruction process is necessarily going to be long and the outcome very uncertain" (North 1993, 21). Critical mass thresholds could be engineered and reached by endogenous agents operating in context and making use of local and personal knowledge and resources. The bottom line is evident: Social norms make for an excellent casual explanation, but they are a very tricky policy variable (Brennan et al. 2013). Moving them to the foreground gives from the very beginning a more realistic sense of the challenges confronting institutional design and public policy interventions. Malleability is surrounded by multiple layers of ignorance and uncertainty.

At the same time, it helps us to understand that the success of an institutional design or policy change depends very much on the skills and local and personal knowledge of the social actors directly involved on the ground, in the concrete actions. This is the point where the theory of public entrepreneurship as it operates in collective action situations becomes extremely relevant. We have seen in very precise terms how human agency with specific endowments and capacities may make or break such situations. The bottom line is this: There is, indeed, a rather constraining structural context determined by collective, aggregated factors. There may not be many degrees of freedom there. Yet there are also some chances to have local knowledge and local resources and strategies mobilized to perhaps increase the malleability factor. Public entrepreneurship, when one has social actors motivated and endowed in certain ways, may be the decisive factor.

The same is true for the circularity problem. The conjunction of the malleability problem with the causality problem sets the stage for the circularity problem. To produce a policy change when a change in a social norm is deemed as instrumental in the change equation, one needs to use the system of formal institutions. But in many cases, the very formal institutional arrangement is not functional as an instrument precisely because of informal institutions and social norms. Even more precisely, the social norm in point may have a key role in a causal chain undermining the effectiveness of the formal institutional arrangements to be used in the case in point. The result is a catch-22 situation, and the applied literature abounds with examples: Again and again, legislative and administrative measures aimed at cutting red tape are ineffective because social norms undermine the very process of implementing those measures. A vicious circle is created. Layers of administrative measures and legislation are added to break the cycle. But the inflation of the formal institution's domain and its ineffectiveness undermine the very credibility of that approach. The informal gets reinforced each time, having their resilience and effectiveness demonstrated again and again after each such new wave of reforms. Irrespective of the specific form and shape, taken in context, the underlying logic is the same: the effectiveness of a policy intervention is trapped and undermined by the circularity of the formal institutions–social norms–formal institutions pattern.

We see now how the circularity problem reinforces the agnostic stance on intervention. At the same time, it illuminates again the constrained but decisive role that actors on the ground, operating with local knowledge and using the context to mobilize collective action, may have in solving those patterns. In the interplay between the formal and informal, some things may not be possible given the structure of the action arena. But some may be. There is no scientific method or formula to determine or point-predict that. And what and how it may be possible depends more on the profile, behavior, and capabilities of social actors on the ground than it may depend on exogenous shocks.

All of the above can be generalized from the angle of the validity problem. Establishing a policy theory to be used as a guide for intervention raises issues of its applicability. How could one be sure of the soundness of the causal conjecture? How valid could it be given the circumstances? There are, in fact, two aspects of the validity problem. First is internal validity: Establishing ex post that in case A, a causality structure (the one assumed by the policy theory ex ante the intervention) was in truth operating and producing the targeted consequences. As we have seen, given the combinatorial and stochastic nature of phenomena in point, internal validity is not easy to establish even with the most advanced methods and tools. But even establishing that policy P worked in case A does not lead automatically to the conclusion that the same policy (with its causal process outlined in the policy theory) will work in other cases. That is the external validity problem. The field of public policy and institutional design is filled with case studies of failed attempts at institutional implants. They all illustrate how formal institutions and their design fail when clashing with the local social norms and institutional arrangements. The cases of the attempts to export and implant the American constitution are the most spectacular of all.

Irrespective of how solid the empirical evidence establishing the efficacy of P in case A, that evidence is only of limited value in extending it to case B and other cases. Cartwright and Hardie (2012) have amply proved this point using the hard evidence of random control trials (RCT), considered today the gold standard of evidence-based policy. In fact, an RCT, they demonstrate, establishes only the truth level of one single element in the broader equation of a policy decision: "it worked someplace." From that to "it will work in general" or "it will work in this different specific case" is a long way, and the RCT evidence has no traction on that. We are at the core of the feasibility issue. Malleability, circularity, and validity predefine the feasibility space of any institutional design. And feasibility as a practical, applied-level position requires, sooner or later, acknowledging the key role of social actors operating in context with the specific knowledge, skills, capabilities, and values. One could increase the probability of success (both in implementation and prediction) if we understand the measure in which the actors on the ground will follow certain norms, beliefs, and behavioral rules in their actions and decisions. Also, the capacity to imagine and improvise, to take risks and assume responsibilities, is an important factor (Cartwright and Hardie 2012).

To sum up, using the phenomenon of policy intervention (or, more precisely, its operational anatomy) as a vehicle, we have seen how moving the informal to the foreground offers a much more realistic view of the task of institutional design and policy intervention. Context matters, and the ways the vast range of possibilities in which the relevant variables (with their different causality impacts and malleability coefficients and out of which social norms, with their low malleability and high causality coefficients, are so salient) may combine should be a serious matter of analytical concern. Yet, trying to build out this general institutional design or policy formula is a daunting task. One may see how various combinations are possible, and how the heuristic toolkit delineated above allows focusing and calibration of the intervention. At the same time, one realizes the incertitude and complexity surrounding each such policy design, the essentially contextual nature of such an exercise. We start to better circumscribe the crucial role that human agency – with specific configurations of abilities, skills, knowledge, etc. – may have in such circumstances.

CONTEXTUAL ANALYSIS, FEASIBILITY INDEXING, AND POSSIBILISM

The previous sections have not just asserted, but have shown, how the research program associated with the institutionalist turn in policy sciences and governance studies is leading to (i) a shift of the domain of the informal to the forefront of the pre-analytic vision in institutional theory; (ii) the consolidation of the contextual analysis approach; and (iii) an increasingly sharper reemergence to salience of the essential role of human agency, of models of social action with specific profiles of resources and capabilities operating in institutionally contingent circumstances. Let us look now at the deeper methodological, epistemological, and social philosophical implications of all of the above as synthesized from an Ostromian position.

In reviewing the developments in this research field over time and looking back at her own work, Elinor Ostrom concluded that the collective action situations we usually associate with the emergence and functioning of institutional arrangements, social norms, and social capital are, in most cases, domains in which "it is not possible to relate all structural variables in one large causal model, given the number of important variables" (E. Ostrom 1998, 14). Elinor Ostrom notes that "an immense number of contextual variables" have been identified by empirical researchers' literature as "conducive or detrimental to endogenous collective action" (E. Ostrom 2000, 148). She lists some of them, and the catalogue is daunting: From the size of the group involved and the type of production and allocation functions to the heterogeneity of the group and the relative scarcity of the goods; from the common understanding of the group, the size of the total collective benefit, and the marginal contribution by one person to the presence of leadership, past experience, and level of social capital and the autonomy to make binding rules; all these and others – in endless combinations and permutations – could make a difference. She also notes the disagreement over the impact of contextual variables. For instance, "the size of a group and internal heterogeneity are frequently considered important contextual variables, but the direction of their impact and how they operate is strongly contested" (E. Ostrom 2014, 238–239).

Marwell and Oliver, working along similar lines, remarked that "today, scholars have concluded that there are many different issues and many different kinds of collective action and that one can shade into the other depending upon the structural characteristics of the situation" (Marwell and Oliver 1993, 25). Hence, a rather radical conclusion is drawn: There is no theory of collective action because there is no single problem of collective action, and consequently, there is no single, universal solution to the problem of collective action. That is not only a matter of configurational heterogeneity but also a matter of dynamics. As Ostrom put it, "changes in one structural variable can lead to a cascade of changes in the others" (E. Ostrom 1998, 15). A small change "may suffice to reverse the predicted outcome." Context matters enormously, and causal weight is thus relative. Social and institutional arrangements are "complexly organized" and "we will rarely be able to state that one variable is always positively or negatively related to a dependent variable" (E. Ostrom 1998, 16). Therefore, it should be no surprise that "the kind of theory that emerges from such an enterprise does not lead to the global bivariate (or even multivariate) predictions that have been the ideal to which many scholars have aspired" (E. Ostrom 1998, 16). The initial search for the theory of collective action seems naive now from a retrospective perspective. The theoretical and methodological apparatus and the epistemological assumptions stimulating that initial search starting in the 1960s seem obsolete as well.

Irrespective of the epistemological or methodological priors one may entertain, it is obvious that the evolution of this vast, systematic, robust, and well-funded family of research programs – broadly labeled as new institutionalist – has led to a point that necessitates a departure from the familiar, well-traveled path of the methods and approaches textbooks. Trying to respond to this challenge, Oliver and Marwell advance the notion of "response surface" as a tool aimed at helping us to think "about the complexities involved in collective action" (Oliver and Marwell 2001, 308).

A response surface is "a k-dimensional graph of an outcome variable as predicted by k − 1 independent variables." In a similar vein, Elinor Ostrom introduced the notion of theoretical scenarios. A possible solution, she suggested, may be to build scenarios of how "exogenous variables combine to affect endogenous structural variables." That may make it possible to "produce coherent, cumulative, theoretical scenarios that start with relatively simple baseline models. One can then begin the systematic exploration of what happens as one variable is changed." Again, one can see how the logic of combinations and permutations becomes the background of the analytical exercise. The analytical path of formal institutions–social norms–collective action is permeated by it.

The very nature of collective modes of behavior arising from local interactions of many individual elements, the impact of the setting, and the interaction effects between the heterogeneity of the setting and that of the agents forces us, at the level of general theorizing, to plunge into the combinatorial and statistical universe that best captures the features of these phenomena. It is difficult to think in terms of covering laws and, based on them, making predictions leading to control when context and circumstances matter and change takes place sometimes as a result of endogenous processes having to do with scale and critical mass. And thus, the institutionalist revolution has inspired a new, updated avatar of older concerns regarding blind spots and naiveties about prediction and control in social systems. As Elinor Ostrom suggested, once one takes that turn, analysis has to increasingly take the form of scenarios. The assumption of the symmetry between prediction and explanation – with its positivist origin – loses its grip: In the new analytical universe, the question to ask is not so much what people will do but, instead, what people would do assuming a certain motivation, a certain endowment of skills and knowledge, a certain set of constraints, and a certain set of parameters of their interactions. Such scenarios become pragmatic instruments for applied decision-making.

Elinor Ostrom has recognized the crux of it all. This puzzling condition has to be assumed as such. There is no going back to the comfort of the epistemology and methodology of the positivist mindset era. But that doesn't mean that we should resign ourselves to the forces of large numbers or capitulate to environmental–contextual determinism. In fact, there seems to be only one way moving forward: to recognize that this condition leads us toward thinking in terms of "a world of possibility rather than of necessity." That is to say, "we are neither trapped in inexorable tragedies nor free of moral responsibility for creating and sustaining incentives that facilitate our own achievement of mutually productive outcomes" (E. Ostrom 1998, 15–16).

One of the major merits of Ostrom's take is that among new institutionalist scholars, she was the one clearly identifying and articulating the philosophical ramifications in this respect of the research on institutional change and institutional design. Whether we like it or not, she noted, we are inescapably operating deep in the territory of possibilism – not just a matter of a combinatorial theory of multiple variables and forces but also a matter of human deliberation, decision, and responsibility. When it comes to social structures and institutions, and we recognize that they are largely based in collective and evolutionary–contextual behavior, we even more sharply understand that not all things are possible. Yet some are. And to determine what is possible and what is not, what is desirable and what is feasible, requires an intellectual and normative engagement that goes way beyond what empirical analysis could provide. This engagement implies a perspective on social order, social change, and social causality as well as an interpretation of the function of human deliberation and choice – social reflexivity. There is no method or algorithm, no operations research, systemic thinking, or expert system that could save us from the troubles of judgment, analysis, and responsibility. Human judgment and human agency matters. Judging in context and assuming responsibility for decisions is, in the end, essential. One cannot understand institutional order and change and could not think in practical–normative terms about collective action problems without fully acknowledging and taking into account this basic reality.

The space of possibilism, as rediscovered at the end of the institutionalist journey, entails many possible scenarios of institutional configurations and their evolution. Each of them entails, in its turn, specific social actor profiles, specific models of agency and of judgment and decision-making. And thus, a discussion of institutionalist arguments and collective action from an applied perspective that uses as a vehicle the results of the institutionalist research program leads us consistently, via so many pathways, to the engagement with the complex domain where a meta-theoretical philosophical apparatus meets the policy theory and the social science dimensions. All are pointing to the problem of the social actors and their capabilities, beliefs, knowledge, and behaviors.

The institutionalist program started with a basic model of man and rational choice. This basic conceptual and heuristic instrument is still there, in the theoretical toolkit. But in the end, as one moves ahead to specific areas of analysis of governance and particular institutional arenas, to specific cases and circumstances, a new stage or level has been reached. Revisiting and revising the problem of the models of man, of the stylized facts defining the relevant social actor in place, becomes unavoidable. As Vincent Ostrom noted, "While customs, norms and rules can be presumed to exist as features or attributes of a community, they also exist in each individual's mind and become habituated in the ways that people relate to one another" (V. Ostrom 1998, 286). The customs, norms, and rules may vary with circumstances, and each individual's mind has its own ways. Yet in the end, "the condition of freedom requires the courage to assume responsibility for one's own actions." Self-governing democratic societies "can only exist under conditions in which individuals become capable of governing their own affairs to relate to others in mutually productive ways" (V. Ostrom 1998, 288).

One may be weary of terms like "public entrepreneurship," "citizen," or "citizenship" and the ways they are conceptualized and theorized. Yet it is important, both for analytical and normative purposes, to conceptualize the reality described by Vincent Ostrom. These terms are attempts to respond to the aspects of reality that were gradually focalized and illuminated by the logic of the institutionalist research at the interface between the space of the possible and the space of the structurally determined. More precisely, they are constructs aimed at specific sets of problems and phenomena. To understand governance systems and, even more importantly, democratic governance systems, and to engage normatively with their structure and change, one has to rely on more specific models of social actors.

Social reflexivity is a basic reality in the construction, maintenance, and change of governance systems. Governance systems are spaces in which self-fulfilling and self-defeating predictions or prophecies are operating continuously. Self-governance, as a normative ideal, cannot be understood or advanced other than through a specific form of social agency operating with certain beliefs, values, and motivations. The model of "citizen" is an attempt to capture this reality. In conjunction with the notion of public entrepreneurship and the theoretical apparatus implied by it, they offer a set of theoretical lenses to approach an otherwise dauntingly complex and confounding domain. Indeed it is a messy area in which philosophical and theoretical matters overlap and combine with empirical and operational aspects, intertwining in complex ways on multiple levels (Gaus 2016, 1–2), and yet, one has no alternative but to engage it frontally.

We are now in a better position to understand Vincent Ostrom's point (1979) that the future of human civilization "will not just happen"; it "will be constructed and will require attentive care." At stake, as he has repeatedly explained, following and quoting Tocqueville, are not only institutional features of societies but "the whole moral and intellectual condition of a people" that constitutes "their character of mind" (V. Ostrom 1997, 284). In the end, what the Ostroms have done is to draw attention to the institutional relationship between a certain form of institutional configuration, a certain system of governance – democratic governance or self-governance – and a certain type of social agency, a certain type of social actor, "the citizen."

What it means to live in a democratic society is much more demanding than electing representatives who form governments. Not only are democratic societies constructed around the essential place of citizens in those societies, but they cannot be maintained without the knowledge, moral integrity, skill, and intelligibility of citizens in the cultivation of those societies. (V. Ostrom 1997, 3)

6

Citizens' Competence, Self-Governance, and the New Epistocratic Paternalism

During our discussion of the multifaceted theme of citizenship as outlined in the previous chapters and as seen in conjunction with the notion of public entrepreneurship and the associated theoretical apparatus, we have been constantly reminded that the theme is part of a larger theory of governance, or more precisely, of self-governance. We have seen how the discussion on public entrepreneurship and citizenship slides again and again into the territory of governance systems and processes. On the one hand, the social role of citizen is a function of the nature and structure of the governance system. The degree of self-governance allowed by the system gives the strengths, scale, and scope of citizenship. On the other hand, the theory and the ideal of self-governance are, obviously, predicated on the assumption that rule by the citizens is both desirable and feasible, while feasibility means that the citizen has the necessary knowledge, skills, and values, as well as the capability of employing them in practice. Yet, this position is far from being uncontroversial. We turn now to this issue that is crucial for the problems of both citizenship and self-governance.

One of the most relevant developments in political economy and public choice institutionalism in recent years has been regarding the very problem of citizens' competence. Significant developments in behavioral sciences and political theory related evolutions have profoundly challenged some of the key assumptions regarding the civic and political competence of normal citizens in normal circumstances in a normal democratic-liberal system. Once this basic observation is put forward, one needs to acknowledge that to further elaborate, advance, and refine the Ostromian position and its governance vision in which citizenship and public entrepreneurship are central, one has to first revisit the citizen-centered model of governance and its assumptions in light of these developments.

Chapter 5 charted developments that bolstered the Ostromian position, giving theoretical and empirical ammunition to the citizen and public entrepreneurship centered approach. This chapter charts some important contrary developments that challenge and question that type of approach and the governance theory they inspire. It is only by responding to these challenges that we can proceed to further elaborate and advance the citizen–public entrepreneurship centered approach to governance. The second part of this chapter will attempt to outline the direction of the Ostroms-inspired response and also a reconstruction of the citizen-based governance theory that takes into account the challenges of behavioral economics, social choice, public choice, and electoral behavior literature.

In the end, the chapter will also illustrate how difficult it is to draw a line between the three key phenomena of interest in this book: public entrepreneurship, citizenship, and self-governance. A discussion starting around the notion of citizenship and its political competencies slides naturally into a discussion about governance systems. In this respect, this chapter can also be seen as a transition between the second part and the third part of the book.

THE SELF-GOVERNANCE PERSPECTIVE: WHAT IS AT STAKE

Any discussion about democratic self-governance is, obviously, predicated on the idea of a strong element of civic/political competence on behalf of the citizens (Elkin and Soltan 1999; Levine 2014). And any discussion of civic and political competence inherently leads to the problem of self-governance (V. Ostrom 1997, 271; Levine and Soltan 2014). Civic competence and self-governance are two faces of the same coin, two ways of approaching a complex phenomenon of an artifactual social order created by fallible but capable human beings. Before moving ahead, it is important to revisit and further elaborate on what is meant by the citizen-centered perspective that we have built up from various angles over the previous chapters. By more exactly articulating the substance of it, what is at stake in the discussion at this stage becomes fully illuminated.

Let us take as a starting point the already familiar Vincent Ostrom argument in favor of democracy, an argument that starts with a caveat: There is a basic difference between, on the one hand, those systems based on citizenship aiming at self-governance and, on the other, those systems in which governments "exercise tutelage over Societies and steer and direct those Societies." A democratic society is more than merely a system of "electing representatives who form governments." Democratic societies are "constructed around the essential place of citizens in those societies" and are maintained through "the knowledge, moral integrity, skill, and intelligibility of citizens in the cultivation of those societies" (V. Ostrom 1997, 3).

Obviously, there are multiple ways in which political reality could be conceptually framed and normatively assessed. The label is unimportant. But the conceptual framing matters. Various authors designate, in different ways, pretty much the same type of approach. Vincent Ostrom, for instance, talked about "democratic governance." But his definition of "democracy" always came with a set of qualifications and elaborations on the lines quoted above. Labels notwithstanding, we are talking about a specific perspective with distinctive features, about a particular system of concepts and theories used to frame reality. This system carries with it a set of normative assumptions and implications. We have already seen that Vincent Ostrom, echoing Tocqueville, associates these notions with "the science of association," a science of citizenship and civic enlightenment, a doctrine of direct practical relevance: "The idea of self-governance, he explained, draws attention to the notion of constructive participation of citizens in social order." Citizens need to be familiar with a science of association "studied and applied by all as we assume responsibility for living our lives and learning how to work with others under variable and changing conditions" (V. Ostrom 1997, 271).

Vincent Ostrom took as a key task of his scholarship

... the development of a science of citizenship that might enable human beings to use the arts and sciences of association to diagnose their sources of trouble and to learn from their mistakes. My effort is to deepen the foundations implicit in Tocqueville's analysis so that we might recognize the theoretical merit of Tocqueville's achievements and begin to explore potentials for crafting democratic societies built on principles of self-governance. (V. Ostrom 1992, 30)

The exercise is almost a textbook illustration of what we have already seen Schumpeter (1954) call pre-analytical vision: a cognitive act teaching us to *see* things in a certain light. Indeed, once the role of citizens and their capabilities to self-govern are brought to salience, a new view of what governance is opens up. The architecture of formal institutions and the structures of power and authority (that otherwise are center stage in standard analysis, geared more toward the tutelage and steering end of the continuum) recede to the background, becoming an instrumental role for the citizen. Major differences of approach and insights, and different landscapes of factors, structures, and processes are illuminated. One now has an approach in which the citizen, not the ruler or expert takes the foreground. The structures of power and authority traditionally salient in the spotlight now operate from a background position.

Conceptualizing political reality along those lines doesn't mean that the role of power and control is neglected. It just means that power and control are placed in a different position in the analytical and interpretive framework. In the citizen-centered approach, the dichotomy of rulers–ruled is realistically acknowledged. So is the need for a certain expertise or specialization in governing. Yet, the entire system, while acknowledging all this, is predicated on an assumption that citizens will be able to set up and collectively monitor and enforce the parameters of the rulers' authority and the limits of the power and authority of experts.

Analytically, in such a paradigm, such competencies are identified as the key factor in the process of governance. Citizens have the knowledge, will, skill, and capacity to govern. They are seen as an independent causal variable, drivers and entrepreneurs of political order and change, but at the same time, they may also be seen as a dependent variable – a result of the functioning of an institutional environment and institutional apparatus of governance that further fuels and increases citizens' competence. The virtuous cycle of self-governance is thus defined: a feedback loop in a Tocquevillian model of democracy, pivoting on citizens' actions and attitudes, values, and repertoires of strategies and public entrepreneurship. Turning to the normative side, the citizen-centered approach takes the "seeing like a citizen" perspective, as opposed to "seeing like a state." The result is both an analytically and normatively distinctive take on governance theories: an ideal theory, a model of governance systems, and a benchmark for applied approaches.

To sum up: First, at stake is not just a theory of social action but a coherent governance model backed by a coherent and respectable philosophy and theory. Second, the problem is not that one could not conceptualize things from a civics, citizen-centered angle or that one could not prove the theoretical possibility of such a system. As the previous chapters have shown, one is fully epistemologically and methodologically justified in engaging in such an exercise. The problem is that this entire system, impressive as it may be in its architecture and aspirations, hinges on the problem of the citizens' competence. To get from theoretical possibility to feasibility (or at least to practical relevance), such competence is essential. It would be naive and utopian to build a model of governance and have applied-level expectations in the absence of concern with the basic facts that give realism and feasibility to the model's applications. The empirical fact of citizens' capabilities is at the core of the feasibility assumption of the democratic self-governance proposition. That fact is intrinsically related to the issue of values and strategies, as it is deeply permeated with axiological and praxeological elements. A challenge to this fact is a challenge to the entire self-governance paradigm.

THE CHALLENGE

As we have already discussed, a citizen-centered perspective presupposes a certain model of man and rationality. Its entire analytical and normative structure depends on what that model assumes regarding the human capacity to correctly assess facts and to rationally implement strategies oriented by values. To ask and answer questions about how facts, values, and strategies can be recombined by social actors operating as citizens to generate self-governance institutions invites a discussion about what we should expect (or not expect) such citizens to be able to do in this respect in normal life circumstances. And this is precisely where the impact of the latest generation developments in social and behavioral sciences has struck the hardest, raising public choice questions that seem to undermine the very foundation of the self-governance paradigm.

The first generation of theories and models of citizens and citizen-centered governance was based on simple and robust notions of human rationality, decision-making, and action. An important part of the literature was written having in mind, explicitly or implicitly, a model of praxeologically rational, normatively reasonable, rule-guided, and self-regulated behavior. The literature took more or less for granted the relative effectiveness of rational self-monitoring, self-control, learning, and adaptation, based on communicative practices. Yet, during the last couple of decades, the twin behavioral and institutional revolutions taking hold in social and political sciences have brought to the fore a different understanding of individual and collective rationality and decision-making. The thrust was that individuals may not always act in ways that are fully rational, as their perception of facts and their judgment on values and strategy are unfavorably affected by various cognitive biases, failures of will, and difficulties of information gathering and processing. The citizens' own definition of their interests, of means and ends, the very perception of facts, may be affected in ways that have serious policy implications.

The literature identifying and documenting biases and deviations from expected rationality has exploded. Lists of biases, sometimes reaching hundreds of items, organized in various categories and at various levels, abound. A simple search indicates numerous such lists compiled and arranged in different classes. A closer look at one example (with four such categories: biases in probability and belief, decision-making and behavioral biases, social biases, and biases due to memory errors) gives a vivid sense of the magnitude of the challenge (Pohl 2004).

Let us start with an incomplete list of decision-making and behavioral biases. The Bandwagon Effect, the tendency to do (or believe) things because many other people do (or believe) the same; the Blind Spot, the tendency not to compensate for one's own cognitive biases; the Choice-Supportive Bias, the tendency to remember one's choices as better than they actually were; the Contrast Effect, the enhancement or diminishment of a weight or other measurement when compared with a recently observed contrasting object; the Endowment Effect, to demand much more to give up an object than one would be willing to pay to acquire it.

And the list goes on: Framing, Focusing Effect, Hyperbolic Discounting, Information Bias, Illusion of Control, Impact Bias, Irrational Escalation, Loss Aversion, Neglect of Probability, Obsequiousness Bias, Omission Bias, Outcome Bias, Planning Fallacy, Post-Purchase Rationalization, Pseudocertainty Effect, Reactance, Selective Perception, Status Quo Bias, Zero-Risk Bias.

Then there is the list of biases in probability and belief: Anchoring, the tendency to rely too heavily, or "anchor," on a past reference or on one trait or piece of information when making decisions; the Anthropic Bias, the tendency for one's evidence to be biased by observation selection effects; Attentional Bias, the neglect of relevant data when making judgments of a correlation or association; Availability Heuristic, a biased prediction due to the tendency to focus on the most salient and emotionally charged outcome. And this list also goes on: Clustering Illusion, Conjunction Fallacy, Frequency Illusion, Hindsight Bias, Illusory Correlation, Ludic Fallacy, Observer-Expectancy Effect, Overconfidence Effect, Positive Outcome Bias, Primacy Effect, Subadditivity Effect, Telescoping Effect, etc.

There is also the list of social biases: Actor-Observer Bias, Dunning–Kruger Effect, Egocentric Bias, False Consensus Effect, Fundamental Attribution Error, Halo Effect, Illusion of Asymmetric Onsight, Illusion of Transparency, In-Group Bias, Just-World Phenomenon, Out-Group Homogeneity Bias, Projection Bias, Trait Ascription Bias, Ultimate Attribution Error, etc., etc.

Last, but not least, is the list focused on cognitive functions such as memory and its errors: Consistency Bias, incorrectly remembering one's past attitudes and behavior as resembling present attitudes and behavior; Hindsight Bias; Selective Memory, False Memory, and so on.

One can easily understand how each of these biases could affect the ways social actors deal with the facts, values, and strategies that enter their decision-making process. Starting with the very perception of facts and continuing through the evaluation process and then on to planning and strategy implementation, the entire line of civic action seems to be fraught with serious tensions and ambiguities. Confirmation bias leads one to search for or interpret information in ways that confirm one's preconceptions. The contrast effect leads to the misspecification of the dimensions of an object when compared with a recently observed contrasting object. The focusing effect leads to prediction biases. Framing effects show that people are led to get different conclusions from the same information, a function of the different ways the same information is presented. To give a generic example, the ambiguity effect leads to the avoidance of those options defined by comparatively larger degrees of uncertainty. Anchoring and the availability heuristic induce a tendency to focus on information or expectations of outcomes in ways that diverge from the entire range of available facts and information on the ground. The Ash experiment and the Ash dilemma may be seen as emblematic: A group of subjects in a lab experiment are shown three lines of obviously different lengths. Then they are asked which of the three is longest. Confederates undercover among the participants loudly misstate the lengths. Again and again, a significant number of the targeted participants are likely to align their own assessment to the dominant view despite the obvious perceptual evidence of the facts. If, in such obvious conditions, one has such striking results, one should consider what happens in more ambiguous cases dealing not with facts but with values or strategies.

It is easy to see how each such finding undermines, bit by bit, gradually eroding, the very idea of political and civic competence. Separately, each may seem trivial or have a potential solution in the realm of social feasibility. In conjunction, they tell a different, overwhelming story. With it, by extension, the very notion of self-governance gets to be questioned. An entire apparatus of expertise, control, and paternalism seems to lurk behind each new item on the list.

These are precisely the kinds of problems that behavioral economics has indicated as plaguing people acting in the market setting. There is no reason to think that normal people, acting as citizens, would be able to solve the collective action problems they encounter as citizens if they are unable to solve similar problems when they encounter them as producers and consumers. Questioning the capabilities for rationality in the relatively stronger setting of markets leads to justified questions about the same capabilities in the reactively weaker nonmarket setting. There is no reason to think that a nonmarket setting – which has even fewer calculation signals and devices than the market setting – will induce higher levels of rationality and effectiveness in coordination. Self-governing individuals, following their biases and self-interests, fail to adjust and correct. As long as the symmetry of behavioral assumptions is upheld, the implications are unavoidable. The average individual will have similar problems in both market and nonmarket environments. The nonmarket environment is even worse given the absence of the signals from market processes and the profit and loss calculus.

It should be stressed again that we are not confronting here mere speculations based on laboratory experiments and theoretical seminars. These observations have been reinforced by the growth of the literature that goes beyond cataloging biases to gathering and analyzing evidence of the problem of ignorance and irrationality in public life (Shapiro and Bloch-Elkon 2008). This literature shows in multiple ways that facts are neglected or misinterpreted, while values and principles that are supposed to shape public life or its evaluations are rarely understood in their implications (or even articulated) by the average citizen of a modern industrial democracy. There is ample evidence that the general public is ignorant regarding not only the details of politics but also the basic elements and parameters of the public life (Friedman 2006; Bennett 2006). Basic logical or causal connections are missed, circumvented, or misinterpreted. The line of research opened up by Philip Converse (1964, 1975) has been bringing increasingly solid empirical evidence in this respect. As Jeff Friedman notes, "the widespread ignorance of the general public about all but the most highly salient political events and actors is one of the best documented facts in all of the social sciences." Naming "even the most prominent members of the cabinet is a real challenge for half of the public" and "only a third can name their two senators or their representative in Congress." It is only bare majorities that manage to know "the simplest facts about how government works, and fewer still hold 'real' attitudes toward even the most important political issues of the day" (Friedman 2006).

To make things even more confusing and unsettling, solid arguments have been made suggesting that citizens' behavior may, in fact, be rational in this respect: the rational ignorance or rational irrationality thesis. There are strong incentives and reasons for them to be rationally ignorant about politics. Ideology and partisanship come in this context as second-best substitutes, as cost-efficient heuristics used to orient the citizen when necessary through the maze of facts and interpretations of public issues (Lau and Redlawsk 2001). Downs (1957) first introduced the theory of rational ignorance to explain voters' ignorance on important issues for their public and even private lives: The expected benefits of information are deemed by them to be small relative to the costs. Being informed costs. Authors such as Bryan Caplan (2001) go even further in this respect: The theory of rational ignorance, he argues, explains only the low level of information. Caplan builds a more general model of "rational irrationality," which explains not only the bias to get little information but also the systematic biases and the high certainty that those biases display. According to the theory of rational irrationality, being irrational (that is to say, deviating from rational expectations) is a good like any other; the lower the private cost, the more agents buy (Caplan 2001). Caplan argues that "a peculiar feature of beliefs about politics, religion, etc. is that the private repercussions of error are virtually nonexistent, setting the private cost of irrationality at zero; it is, therefore, in these areas that irrational views are most apparent" (Caplan 2011, 25).

From here, things could get even direr. In parallel, the institutionalist revolution (the other major development in social sciences in the last several decades) has brought to the fore a different set of challenges. People may act rationally at the individual level, they may do their best to assess facts, judge values, and develop instrumental strategies, and yet, in the aggregation process from individual to the collective, something may happen, and irrational or counterintuitive and unexpected/undesired aggregated results may emerge. Institutional theory offers an entire set of models and theories to capture and describe these situations. Social choice aggregation problems (Arrow 1963; Sen 1970) and the problem of the social welfare function (Buchanan 1964) are some of the best known ways in which these problems were presented in technical terms. On top of that is the public choice literature bringing to light the problems of rent-seeking, perverse incentives, and an entire range of administrative and bureaucratic pathologies intrinsic to modern government (Reksulak, Razzolini, and Shughart 2013). Very serious questions regarding the capacity for collective action and public governance and administrations are thus raised in multiple ways and at multiple levels.

Obviously, all these have huge implications for a citizen-centered system of governance. Both the capabilities of citizens and the very process of self-governance (including the "virtuous cycles" of

Tocquevillian–Millian reinforcement in the practices of self-governance as mediated by the institutional environment) are questioned. These findings have significant applied-level implications. One of their consequences is a visible move in the public debate advancing a new rhetoric and a new set of paternalist designs. The last decades have witnessed the growth of an entire line of suggestions regarding interventions, manipulations, engineering, designing, and nudging via multiple and creatively combined tools of the government: education, persuasion, taxes and subsidies, time, place, and manner restrictions. The reasons are evident. With a perspective that has in the foreground the structures of power, coercion, and control, these challenges of authority and epistemic asymmetries seem to fit in a more realistic way (and this viewpoint navigates those challenges much better).

It is important to note that out of all these challenges, the behavioral challenge brings forth the most profound and strongest contestation to the idea of citizen self-governance. The reason is this: Aggregation phenomena induced by institutional and decision rules may, indeed, be important factors in distorting individual preferences and rationality, prompting collective irrationality and undesirable outcomes. However, as long as we assume that citizens have the capability to correctly perceive facts and assess values and decide rationally (or at least learn to adjust and adapt and thus gradually improve, through social technologies, their capacity to do those things), one should not be too pessimistic about the long-term future of self-governance. People will learn to build new institutions; to do institutional analysis and development; to create, negotiate, and change rules; and in general, to set into motion a gradual process of coevolution between the individual cognitive and emotional capacities and the institutional technology and environment supporting those psychological and behavioral features. Institutionalism finds recourse to a remedial and constructive logic of a Tocquevillian "science and art of association" operating in conjunction with a Hayekian trial and error and Popperian tinkering. In brief, institutionalism (with its social choice and public choice dimensions) may highlight problems, but it may also be a source of hope and solutions. On the other hand, the behavioral or statistical analytics of biases, ignorance, and irrationality don't have much to offer in the way of remedies. After all, the solution – if any solution is possible – has to go through the logic of institutions. Citizen efficacy and self-governance are intrinsically related to institutions and their design, as Vincent Ostrom has explicitly recognized:

When Tocqueville wrote *Democracy in America*, he recognized that a new con-ceptual-computational logic was required for the constitution of democratic socie-ties if human beings under conditions of increasing equality were to achieve and maintain substantial freedom in their relationships with one another. He was persuaded that alternatives were available so long as human beings might have recourse to a science of association in the conceptualization and design of human institutions. (V. Ostrom 1979, 20)

That being said, there is no doubt that the citizen-centered perspective is debilitated and put on the defensive by the findings questioning its very foundational assumptions. When citizens' political capabilities are ques-tioned, the very idea of civics is questioned. Self-governance has to be redefined to diluted versions of the initial expectations and aspirations. The center of gravity moves sharply toward the "guardians" and "tutelage" extreme of the continuum. Even if that side of the continuum is perceived as less normatively appealing (see, for instance, the problem of authoritar-ianism as implied by Arrow's [1963] or Sen's [1970] social choice analyses) the guardianship solutions are also seen as more realistic, more attuned to reality and the challenges of real-life societies and politics. The role of science, one would say, is precisely this: to give us the facts of the matter. And the facts dictate the diagnosis and, hence, the parameters of the solution. Guardianship based on asymmetries of capabilities and expertise seems the natural normative implication. It looks like the literature is pointing to a second-best: Government by experts and guardians operating under an indirect, institutionally mediated system of checks and balances and in which citizens have a precisely circumscribed role to play.

To sum up, seen in the light of the behavioral economics and rational irrationality literature, moving citizens and their capabilities of self-governance to the foreground (as the citizen-centered approach requires) seems to be fraught with difficulties both as an analytical approach and as a normative ideal. Vulnerabilities and difficulties abound. The behavioral economics revolution and the theorizing on rational ignorance and irra-tionality have brought a new understanding of the magnitude of the problem. The big winner of these developments seems to be a refurbished, refined, and reasserted paternalist–guardianship approach.

TUTELAGE AND PATERNALISM: REVIVED, REVAMPED, AND REASSERTED

The growth of a new form of paternalism is already featuring concrete applied formulas: At the most basic level, the so-called nudge technology of public policy, the basic building block of policy intervention. Then there is libertarian paternalism, the normative theory that justifies the technique and the intervention. On top of it all is epistocracy, as a doctrine of governance combining different interventions on the architecture of choice (and normative justifications to generate a model or ideal of a defensible system of governance that diverges from traditional notions of democracy).

Richard Thaler and Cass Sunstein (2003) are the authors most responsible for creating at the interface between law and behavioral economics the nudge doctrine and policy intervention strategy: That is, the theory and practice of influencing and manipulating choices by changing the choice architecture. The objective is not to directly impose but to structure a meta-level intervention on the settings and parameters of choice so that people are disposed to make better choices. That, it is argued, is libertarian paternalism, and as such, it does not affect freedom of choice. It just prestructures it. Thaler and Sunstein do not see a contradiction in the association of these two terms. The approach, they say, should be considered different from a regulation that leaves no other alternative but to comply: "Libertarian paternalism is a relatively weak, soft, nonintrusive type of paternalism because choices are not blocked, fenced off, or significantly burdened" (Thaler and Sunstein 2008, 5–6).

The governance formula incorporating all of the above still requires from citizens some competence in monitoring and running institutions and solving coordination and cooperation problems. Yet, the burden is lowered. We are in a model that is pushing civics to the background. Paternalism presents itself as the second-best solution in the absence of an optimality grounded in full rationality. Libertarian paternalism seems, in this context, rather enticing. With it on the table as a viable alternative, does it even make sense to engage in civics? Does trying to imagine, design, and advocate for governance systems that tend to get closer and closer to the "seeing like a state," citizen-centered social order make sense anymore? Is civics something utopian?

As these implications emerge with increasing clarity, a sense of uneasiness is palpable even among those engaged in advancing the paternalist arguments. Solutions such as nudge and libertarian paternalism seem to be favored as less intrusive ways of alleviating the tensions and dilemmas created in the field of governance by the new awareness of citizens' inherent shortcomings. The less intrusive is advocated as a preferable option to the ominous more intrusive ways. Yet, the discomfort persists. One could detect the plausible contours of a newly refurbished monitoring

and enforcement apparatus bolstered by technology and increasingly legitimized by the latest findings in behavioral sciences. The danger of sliding
into a sophisticated form of totalitarianism – brought to new Orwellian
and Huxleyan levels – is obvious.

Indeed, from all of the above, the emergence of models such as that of
epistocracy, advocated as an alternative to democracy as we know it, is just
one step. At the end of it all, if knowledge and epistemic competence are
the key, then sooner or later, rethinking the very foundation of our
governance system by questioning the equal right to vote comes naturally.
Epistocracy looks like a logical and natural outcome of the line of arguments challenging the civics paradigm.

In an epistocracy, explains Jason Brennan – the author who had the
stamina to articulate explicitly what others left implicit – votes are
weighted according to knowledge. Institutions such as political parties,
regular elections, constitutional review, checks and balances, and a bill of
rights continue to operate, but the basic allocation of political power is
prestructured. Some have additional voting power, or in a more extreme
form of the system, some may have their right to vote restricted in the
absence of passing a test of political knowledge. An epistocracy could thus
be organized in many ways: Everyone votes, but the citizens who pass a test
of political knowledge get more votes or their votes are weighted.
Alternatively, only the citizens who pass such a test may vote. Or one
may use an "enfranchisement lottery": a number of citizens are selected at
random, and then those citizens vote, but only after going through com-
petence-building training. There are many possible ways for arranging the
pieces of such a system (Brennan 2016a).

Epistocracy should not be confused with technocracy, as epistocracy
takes to its ultimate political consequences the logic underlying both.
In a technocracy, the emphasis is on the expert bureaucrats and their
paternalistic social engineering. Technocracy is about public policy and
public administration. On the other hand, epistocracy is about the very
nature of government and of the political process generating and maintaining it. Epistocracy is a total system, a radical restructuring of the system
from the electoral element to the legislative, executive, and public administration branches. Jason Brennan admits that such a system may seem
prima facie objectionable:

Some would object that epistocracy is essentially inegalitarian. In an epistocracy,
not everyone has the same voting power. But what's so wrong with that? Only some
people have plumbing or hairdressing licenses because we accept that only some

people are qualified to fix pipes or cut hair. Perhaps only some people, rather than everyone 18 and over, are truly qualified to decide who will lead the most powerful country on earth. (Brennan 2016b)

The claim is far from trivial. In fact, at a closer look, the argument has a double leverage, anchored in two major traditions of political philosophy – rights theory and consequentialist comparative institutional analysis: (1) people have a right to be governed by people who are good at governing, and (2) the choice between alternative systems is not an issue of absolute preferences between a perfect system and an imperfect one, but of relative performance of alternative systems. As Brennan explains it,

Any such system will be subject to abuse and will suffer from significant government failures. But that's true of democracy too. The interesting question is whether epistocracy, warts and all, would perform better than democracy, warts and all. (Brennan 2016c)

And thus, both a rights-based argument and a consequentialist argument are put to work in favor of the new guardian theory of governance. All elements are put in place for building a plausible technical case for the justification and legitimization of the system. At a closer look, the argumentative structure on which the case for epistocracy is erected is far from easy to dismiss. Today, any realistic and constructive discussion of civics and self-governance has to take as a starting point and benchmark the reality of the cumulative challenges that culminate in the epistocratic proposition.

AN OSTROMIAN RESPONSE

It is uncontroversial that the idea of self-governance is seriously challenged by the theories and doctrines noted above. The very idea of the viability of the "seeing like a citizen" perspective is questioned. Could we articulate new arguments for the viability of the self-governance, citizen-centered approach given these changing intellectual landscapes?

The question of what the main directions of this response should be becomes salient. This is the juncture where we turn back to the Ostroms' work under the conjecture that the Ostromian approach could offer resources and insights in this respect that few authors working at the interface between foundational and applied theory could (Levine 2011). The rest of this chapter will address this question from a perspective shaped by their work. The special relevance of that work comes from the fact that their empirical and analytical contributions are deeply permeated by a normative dimension solidly bolstered by a social philosophy of civics and even an action plan in this respect. One may even say that the Ostroms programmatically oriented their Bloomington Workshop for Political Theory and Public Policy toward the creation of knowledge that may improve citizens' capacity to organize for self-governance. They explicitly noted that one of the main priorities at the Workshop was to make sure that their research "contributes to the education of future citizens, entre-preneurs in the public and private spheres, and officials at all levels of government." A failure to make that type of contribution meant that "all our investigations and theoretical efforts are useless" (E. Ostrom in Aligica and Boettke 2009, 159).

Let us now take a closer look at how the empirical and analytical intertwine with the normative in the Ostroms' perspective and how that may inspire responses to the challenges of epistocratic paternalism and the rebuilding of the self-governance perspective. We'll be listing, one by one, the most important elements that may be used as vehicles or building blocks in this respect:

(1) Empirical Analysis

The simplest and most direct response to the behavioral economics chal-lenge is to critically revisit the empirical facts and their analyses, meaning, for instance, to counter the nature and significance of particular observa-tions and their interpretation by the behaviorists. That requires taking a closer look at the empirical settings, findings, and broader environmental and contextual factors. Elinor Ostrom's approach, coming from an insti-tutionalist angle, does precisely that. It essentially redefines the research design of decision-making under the assumption of bounded and imper-fect rationality. It shifts focus to decision arenas and social settings, thus putting into a new light the limits of the analytical framing used by the behaviorist mainstream.

As an institutionalist studying empirical phenomena, I presume that individuals try to solve problems as effectively as they can. That assumption imposes a discipline on me. Instead of presuming that some individuals are incompetent, evil, or irrational, and others are omniscient, I presume that individuals have very similar limited capabilities to reason and figure out the structure of complex environments. It is my responsibility as a scientist to ascertain what problems individuals are trying to solve and what factors help or hinder them in these efforts. When the problems that I observe involve lack of predictability, information, and trust, as well as high levels of complexity and transactional difficulties, then my efforts to explain must take these problems overtly into account rather than assuming them away." (E. Ostrom 1990, 25–26)

Gerd Gigerenzer's (2000) nuanced and well-grounded empirical take on some of the tenets of behavioral economics is an outstanding illustration of a similar type of approach, this time from a psychological standpoint. It is true, explains Gigerenzer, that taking decision shortcuts using heuristics, biased by emotion, may lead to less optimal decisions. But this is not always the case. In many cases, decisions taken by heuristics and intuition are correct, while the alternative, rational, calculative approach fails. Many decisions have to do with complex situations that our cognitive apparatus cannot handle. The gut, intuition, and heuristics approach is more viable, although one may be unable to articulate how it is working.

In brief, the empirical research could place the observations regarding biases and rationality in a larger context, illuminating different standards of performance and the role of the ecology of rationality, choice, and decision. Both Gigerenzer and Ostrom show that there is much more to be said and analyzed about the cases and findings flaunted by behavioral economics.

(2) The Plausibility of Self-Governance in Light of Existing Evidence

One of the most important elements of the Ostroms' contribution is the evidence – empirical and historical – generated as support for the feasibility of the normative stance encouraging self-governance (E. Ostrom 1990; Ostrom and Ostrom 2004). They documented the fact that, in some circumstances, people manage to solve the collective governance problems and social dilemmas that emerge from uncertainty, ignorance, and conflict of preferences. They have shown how people are able to overcome collective action problems by themselves, without externalizing governance functions or using third-party, exogenous authority. The empirical evidence is out there. Tendencies, patterns, sometimes successes, and sometimes arrangements that come closer and closer to approximating the ideals of self-governance could be empirically identified. They are present in various forms and at different levels (as large as the US experiment in constitutionalism or as small as the community-level management of natural resources in as diverse places as the Middle East, Africa, Nepal, and Latin America). Thus, they have shown that creating and maintaining a structure of self-governance within frameworks in which voluntary agreements play a key role is not utopian. Therefore, one could justifiably speak of self-governance not just as an argument of theoretical possibility or a mere "ideal theory" desideratum. The civics normative stance is not devoid of plausibility.

It is true that we are, indeed, living in new circumstances, and circumstances matter. Technological, demographic, and cultural change are pushing society into uncharted territories. But precisely because of that, one should not rule out ex ante the feasibility of civics self-governance. Some things were possible in the past. There is a likelihood that some things in this respect may be possible again in some form or another. Learning from the past and deliberating about the future, one may even be able to imagine the extension in scale and scope of these experiments in self-governance. One may even imagine that the new circumstances, the changed environment, may not just amplify the problems and dilemmas but also, at the same time, create new possibilities for alleviating them.

(3) Possibilism

Looking at the work of the Ostroms as a whole (empirical, theoretical, and normative) one can identify an underlying social philosophical standpoint that, in the absence of a better term, we'll call possibilism (with a nod to Albert Hirschman, 1971). We have already noted how, in analyzing the governance and human coordination and cooperation problems, Elinor Ostrom concluded that we are confronted with "a world of possibility rather than of necessity." In thinking and practicing governance, "we are neither trapped in inexorable tragedies nor free of moral responsibility for creating and sustaining incentives that facilitate our own achievement of mutually productive outcomes" (E. Ostrom 1998, 15–16).

Institutional order is not predetermined. Time and circumstances matter, but even more decisive are human deliberation, responsibility, and ideas. Human decisions are the basic building blocks of social order. And while there is a lot of determinism in structuring the choice set, in most cases, there is also a lot of freedom. Humans are moral agents able to imagine alternative scenarios and create alternative rules. They bear the responsibility for alternative courses of action. Governance is an amphibian, operating in both a space of determinism and a space of possibilism.

The corollary of the possibilist argument advanced by the Ostroms is that whatever progress is made on the path toward self-governance, it will not happen automatically. As Vincent Ostrom put it in a quip that has been repeatedly evoked in this book, the future of human civilization "will not just happen"; it "will be constructed and will require attentive care."

Citizenship implies a world of pluralism and multiple possibilities. The computational and combinatorial logics of alternative decisions of multiple and heterogeneous individuals leads to numerous alternative institutional arrangements. In a social universe in which the future is constantly constructed, Vincent Ostrom reminds us that we have a choice in the measure of how much of social order is going to be constructed by accident and force and how much by reflection and choice. Self-governance based on reflection and choice is coextensive with the notion of political and civic competence and with the constructive participation of citizens in the production and reproduction of social order (V. Ostrom 1979).

(4) Against Panacea

The underlying logic leads to the next major point: a warning against facile solutions (pseudo-solutions and panaceas). The Ostroms are antithetical to the notion that when it comes to governance, solutions will come more or less automatically due to the spontaneous work of "progress" and "history," as mediated by technological or political forces. In this respect, the fashionable optimism and high expectations that the internet and new technologies will create a new, more direct, form of democracy is exemplary. Given the strong impression made in the circles of civics-minded authors by the prediction that the technological wave will bring with it new levels of self-governance, any serious reassertion of the civics approach in the wake of the compounded recent revolutions in technology and social sciences needs to address this conjecture.

It should not be a surprise that an Ostroms-inspired position advises a guarded stance. Indeed, when it comes to the internet and its impact on democracy, so far, the evidence is mixed. The "networked democracy" doesn't seem to be working the way people expected it to work. The concerns about social media and its role in elections are a reminder of the Janus face of technological progress. Technology may create technical and instrumental capabilities, but it is not clear that it could induce the incentives and values, strategies, attitudes, and behaviors expected by the optimists.

More directly, and to the point of the behaviorist challenge, is the theme that the new technology and the internet will "make us smarter." The theme comes in multiple venues and from diverse sources, but several recent books have synthesized the arguments and their support that is scattered in the relevant literature. In *Smarter Than You Think* (2013),

Clive Thompson rebukes the thesis that technology makes citizens lazy, computer dependent, and incapable of independent thinking, thereby incapacitating human ability to think through individual and collective problems. He argues that technology and the internet revolution have instead bolstered the cognitive abilities of citizens, boosting individual and collective intelligence. They are better learners, able to access and retain more information and for a longer time, able to communicate better in writing and to think flexibly, calibrating to audiences able to identify connections while opening multiple channels of communication. The new tools allow "us to perform at higher levels, accomplishing acts of reasoning that are impossible for us alone" (Thompson 2013, 128). In the end, Thompson believes, these features of digital tools will allow us to not only think more deeply but also become more deeply connected, both as individuals and as a society.

Steven Johnson, in *Everything Bad Is Good for You* (2006), challenges the notion that the new forms of popular entertainment bolstered by the new technology – from computer and video games to new types of TV and interactive shows – have negative impacts on the cognitive, political, and moral development of citizens. The citizens exposed to and participating in today's pop culture are, in fact, induced to do more and more "cognitive work." Even when it comes to the much-derided television shows, one needs to separate the content from the cognitive challenges they pose. Johnson argues that "the content is less interesting than the cognitive work the show elicits from your mind." The result is an increase in the ability to identify relevant facts, to diagnose social situations, assess values, build up strategies, and make decisions in real life. Garett Jones's *Hive Mind* (2015) concentrates on the collective dimensions of these phenomena, using as a channel the nations' IQ. National IQ, argues Jones, is a good predictor of a country's performance as well as of the inequalities between countries. He looks at the statistical data that support the thesis that intelligence and cognitive skill are significantly more important on a national level than on an individual one because they have "positive spillovers." There is evidence that "qualities necessary to thrive in the complexity of modern societies and economies" rise "in a society as national test scores rise." The reason is that "the worker bees in every nation create a 'hive mind' with a power all its own. Once the hive is established, each individual has only a tiny impact on his or her own life." In a move that is very relevant for the current discussion, he finds a way to connect to the Flynn effect (the sustained increase of intelligence test scores measured in many parts of the world in the last hundred years or so) with the technological developments and the aggregated abilities of citizens. In brief, we could conclude that the hive mind, in combination with the Flynn effect, may lead to the solution, or at least an alleviation, of the cognitive and epistemic shortcomings problem as identified by behavioral economists.

All in all, the arguments presented by these books seem to indicate a way toward a possible solution: The deficiencies identified by the recent generations of behavioral economics and relevant literature seem to be on the way to being addressed by the technological forces that are acting both at the individual and the collective levels. It is rather tempting to conclude that technology and popular culture – without much deliberation, organization, or effort – will do the work for us.

This is precisely the type of conclusion that the Ostroms warn us against. The Ostromian perspective suggests the reverse of the complacency of expecting things to turn out well by the more or less spontaneous work of technological determinism. It may be the case that those technological developments create favorable conditions for self-governance. Yet, as Vincent Ostrom argued repeatedly, a serious effort and investment has to be made to engage with the future:

Those concerned with the constitution of democratic societies are required to give critical attention to the development of a science of citizenship and civic enlightenment. The idea of self-governance draws attention to the notion of constructive participation of citizens in social order. That science should not be confined to the education of students in schools. It should be a science of association that is studied and applied by all as we assume responsibility for living our lives and learning how to work with others under variable and changing conditions that reach out to global proportions. (V. Ostrom 1997, 271)

The bottom line is that whatever happens, it is not predetermined. Human ideas, values, and strategies matter; context matters, the relationships between social actors taking responsibility and acting in accordance to will and imagination and values matter. These seem simple, almost commonsense points. And yet, too often, they are forgotten.

(5) Institutions, Learning, Knowledge Processes, and Error

The Ostromian perspective equips us with a worldview, an attitude, and a social philosophy, but even more, all of these have an institutional theory and design extension of an unequivocal applied-level relevance. To elaborate this point, we have to return to the problem underlying the behavioral and rational ignorance challenge: the epistemic problem.

Ultimately, the discussion leads to the issues of the role, the production, and the diffusion of knowledge in society. It starts with the problem of rationality and biases, but it ends with the issues of learning and social adjustment via accumulated knowledge, including knowledge of institutional structures and processes.

As we have seen, far from denying or neglecting the problem of bounded or imperfect rationality, the Ostroms' approach takes it to a different level – a more complex stage operating above and beyond the behaviorist register. An Ostroms-inspired stance on the role and limits of paternalism and epistocracy is based on a sophisticated understanding of institutional order as a knowledge- and incentives-fueled process. First of all, if the behaviorists are right about the limits of individual rationality, then that should have some implications for experts and epistocrats as well. If institutionalists are right about the problems and puzzles of knowledge and preferences aggregation, then the knowledge base and rationality of social engineering and nudging should operate under similar conditions of indeterminacy and paradox. There are very serious reasons to think that many claims of knowledge (especially when it comes to the complexity of institutional arrangements) are limited. There are serious reasons to think that even when dealing with expert knowledge, one cannot escape the standard dilemmas and problems. Hence, experts and epistocratically enhanced rulers need in their turn the support of an institutional apparatus to correct their errors and enhance their own imperfect capacities.

But the point goes even deeper than that: Social order and institutions are emergent phenomena, aggregations of diverse decisions and actions of individual human actors with diverse values, perceptions of facts, preferences, and strategies who, by their very nature, could act nondeterministically. Human action, the basic building block of social order and change, has a reflexive nature. Humans have the ability to react, adapt and adjust to changes in rules, the environment, or the ideas inspiring or orienting them. Institutional design, social engineering, and nudging are not simple acts of imposing order on inert matter. Each change is confronted with reactions, feedback, adaptation, etc. Social systems, and especially governance systems, are domains where ideas and expectations are always challenged by other ideas, undergoing endless transformations when applied to practice. Taking ideas and epistemic processes seriously leads to more understanding, which is precisely what defines the core of civics.

An emphasis on the intellectual, epistemic element ensures continuity with older traditions ... Thomas Hobbes, David Hume, Adam Smith, and others give us foundations for dealing with language, learning, knowledge, communication, artisanship, and moral judgment in the exercise of choice ... the contingencies of language and their relationships to knowledge, choice, and action are at the focus of attention. (V. Ostrom 1997, 91)

If that is the case, it is clear that institutional theory (and implicitly, institutional design) cannot guarantee error-free operation and full control over a governance system. Uncertainty looms large because of the reflexivity of the system. Error is unavoidable. To try to eliminate error is impossible and counterproductive. In fact, the actual objective should be to make a virtue out of necessity and use the errors and learn from them. Thus, we come to understand why Vincent Ostrom emphasizes so much the notion of fallibility as a key element of thinking about civics and self-governance.

If a society accepts the potential fallibility of all decision-makers, then it recognizes that the key goal is not to try to create a perfect social mechanism engineered to be operated under the assumption of quasi-total control of main factors and circumstances. The goal should instead be to try to reduce error proneness by building "error-correcting procedures in the organization of decision-making processes" (V. Ostrom 1982a, 32; 1990; V. Ostrom and Parks 1973). The very nature of the system's performance is shaped by these error-correcting procedures. Their essence is learning and adaptation as they are basically organizational and institutional processes aimed at facilitating and speeding up the rate of learning. In doing so, they are shaping the social change process. Learning is the essence of reflexivity, and at the same time, it is the quintessence of error-fighting mechanisms. Reflexivity and error correction are major domains of social change. If that is the case, systems of organization, including large-scale systems of governance, could be viewed as arrangements that either facilitate or stifle opportunities for learning to occur. The question is what kind of institutional and decision-making arrangements facilitate error correction? What kind of arrangements are to be preferred – those that involve a dispersion of authority or those that require a centralization of authority? In what measure and how is it that the institutional system creates "opportunities for critical scrutiny and review and facilitates the pursuit of error-correcting strategies"? In what measure and how do the institutional and political arrangements "facilitate concurrent deliberation and action in response to diverse environmental conditions and to diverse communities of 'interest'?" (V. Ostrom 1982a, 31–32; 1973).

Thus, the Ostroms-inspired approach takes us beyond behaviorism. It emphasizes more complex socially embedded and situated forms of rationality, decision-making, and epistemic processes. Many of the issues of interest identified and studied by behaviorists come to be seen in a new and different light. A vision of governance systems setting in motion knowledge, learning, and adaptation processes suggests solutions operating in the realm of institutional processes: Dispersed knowledge and competences, integrated and combined in a structure that collectively engenders a learning, error correction driven social change. It is a vision that resonates with a more sophisticated view of knowledge as advanced by the sociological and political economy of knowledge processes. The developments in social epistemology and political epistemology rooted in ecological rationality take center stage, redefining the terms of the debate. We are now starting to gauge the contours of a response to the contemporary behavioral literature and theories using equally up-to-date literature and theories. A complex theoretical structure grounded in psychology and ending in political theory, via sociology and social theory, could now be mobilized by the defenders of self-governance and civics.

As Todd and Gigerenzer (2003) put it, ecologically rational means "making good decisions with mental mechanisms whose internal structure can exploit the external information structures available in the environment" (Todd and Gigerenzer 2003, 144). The ecological rationality model sees human rationality as part of an adaptive fit between the human mind and the environment; it emphasizes both the bounded rational decision mechanisms and the epistemic structure/properties of the environment. As such, it brings to the table social epistemology, the study of knowledge as a collective phenomenon, or more precisely, the study of the social dimensions of knowledge or information, with an emphasis on the epistemic effects of social interactions and social systems (Goldman 1999; Goldman and Whitcomb 2011). The focus on how knowledge is shaped by social relationships and institutions helps explain many of the epistemic problems and properties of the phenomena of interest in governance studies (Landemore 2013). That, in turn, creates the possibility to further engage and integrate the political epistemology perspective, the new subfield, exploring the mechanisms of collective intelligence in governance and politics. With that, one has all the instruments to analyze how the collective and distributed intelligence of the many, via democratic mechanisms such as deliberation and majority rule with universal suffrage, "combine their epistemic properties to maximize the chances that the group picks the better political answer within a given context and a set of values" (Landemore 2012b, 251).

The case of self-governance is thus renewed and reformulated in a rather profound and refined manner. Assuming sufficient cognitive diversity and appropriate mechanisms of deliberation and collective decision, solid arguments could be made that the rule of the many has "an epistemic edge over any variant of the rule of the few. In the end, and rather counterintuitively, the logic of good governance and democracy may be not so much a function of the separated individual ability of the citizen but rather of the cognitive diversity of the citizens and of the rules, procedures, and institutions that they put in place for making their collective decisions" (Landemore 2013, 21–22).

In brief, an Ostroms-inspired approach shifts the weight from individuals onto institutional processes and their social and political epistemological features, creating the possibility of building a framework that incorporates cutting-edge insights and arguments from contemporary psychology, sociology, and political theory. Thus, it could respond to the challenges of behavioral economics and epistocratic paternalism, advancing counterarguments at a new level of complexity and sophistication.

(6) A Conceptual Apparatus

Last but not least, in addition to all of the above, the Ostroms have created a conceptual apparatus precisely fitted to analyzing and designing institutional arrangements relevant for the processes and issues identified above. Two already discussed concepts are of special significance – polycentricity and coproduction – and could be used as illustrations.

The Ostroms' work on polycentricity offers both (i) a conceptual apparatus that helps identify and explain the epistemic and incentive structures of governance systems and (ii) a normative ideal that could alleviate the epistemic challenges pointed out by behaviorists. We have seen how a polycentric system functions as a dynamic order based on multiple overlapping layers of governance arenas, structuring at different levels the collective action problems and solutions in a countervailing system of cooperation and competition. Polycentricity is, hence, a structural feature of the governance arrangements creating not only the conditions for public entrepreneurship to emerge but also the conditions for the institutional processes associated with the political epistemological arguments noted above. It is a system of diversity and pluralism that aggregates, sorts, clusters, and calibrates preferences and strategies, in the function of levels and areas of decision. Freedom of association in institutional pluralist environments generates the conditions for experiments, error, learning, and error correction. Polycentricity, with its intrinsic diversity and freedom of choice, is a naturally supportive environment for self-governance.

The other concept, coproduction, illuminates a crucial but usually ignored facet of governance. The Ostroms' studies revealed an entire series of cases in which the collaboration between those who produced and/or supplied a public good or service and those who consumed it was the factor determining the effective delivery of the service. Without the efforts of consumers, the service may not even exist or could "deteriorate into an indifferent product with insignificant value." In coproduction, the consumer is a necessary part of the production process. Users of services also function as coproducers. Examples from education and health care to police and fire protection show how the inputs of beneficiaries are decisive. The key point is that good governance is one of the services or goods of this type. The framework of standard consumer theory that assumes a radical separation between producer and consumer is deficient in capturing that. Good governance is a coproduction process. To have good governance, the consumer – that is to say, the citizen – is a necessary part of the production process. Self-governance and good governance are, thus, intrinsically related. The entire self-governance perspective could be simply rebuilt around this model in which the citizen – both as a producer and a consumer of governance – again takes center stage.

We have seen so far how public entrepreneurship and citizenship and the conceptual and theoretical apparatus they bring with them help us understand the nature and future of self-governance systems. It is now time to move one step further and address these systems in the context of current political doctrines and theories to identify and illuminate the distinctiveness of self-governance among the diversity of alternative governance systems.

PART III

SELF-GOVERNANCE

The argument so far has identified several fundamental aspects of a form of governance in which individuals' initiative and responsibility as citizens and public entrepreneurs is essential to the organization, operation, and performance of the system. Crucial links between public entrepreneurship, citizenship, and the very idea of self-governance have been illuminated and elucidated. The question is what kind of system is more precisely the governance system whose contours have been encountered and outlined in the previous chapters? Where should one place it, given the existing array of political doctrines? What is its nature if seen through the lenses offered by the principles and criteria that define the familiar range of ideological positions?

This question is very important. Sooner or later, both the public and the scholarly discourse use the shortcuts and heuristics of ideological benchmarks to frame and understand a topic like the one discussed in this book. A set of publicly shared frameworks provide the background against which every doctrinal or ideological proposition is projected, interpreted, and assessed. One may respond that making an appeal to notions, themes, and dichotomies that are at the foundation of familiar ideological landscapes may seem to be a questionable strategy. Shouldn't we keep things away from the muddy waters of ideology? Yet, as Michael Freeden (2015), one of the preeminent scholars of ideology, has repeatedly noted, ideological taxonomies are, in fact, vital cognitive maps, instruments that people use to order and orient their perspectives and actions in the complex political reality. Freeden reminds us that ideology is a sui generis social phenomenon, an indispensable feature of the political and that "no academic course of political studies and no political activist can expect to attain professional and practical competence in their endeavors, unless the role of ideologies – as action oriented ideas concerning human communities seeking to achieve public influence and control – is appreciated" (Freeden 2015, 1). Irrespective of how sophisticated the answers to a political question may be, the starting point is almost always the reference to the existing range of emblematic ideologies and political doctrines.

If that is the case, then it should be no surprise that the ideologically related questions get to the forefront sooner or later when articulating a specific theoretical position on governance; in our case, on self-governance. This section of the book engages the problem of self-governance as developed in the previous chapters in an attempt to answer precisely this type of question. The section will use as a frame the main dichotomies and themes that are at the core of the ways we commonly think about political doctrines. In doing that, a clearer and more nuanced perspective on the problem of self-governance and the nature of self-governance systems will emerge.

First, in Chapter 7, the classical, traditional anarchy versus Leviathan, state versus libertarianism, seeing like a state versus seeing like an individual citizen set of dichotomies will be mobilized. They are all touching on the problem of system and structure in governance and the role of centralized (and monopolized) force in social order. The chapter will show why the self-governance position is neither statist nor anarchist nor, for that matter, libertarian. The intellectual tradition of classical liberalism is, thus, brought to light as the closest equivalent in the range of familiar political doctrines. Textual evidence will be used in an attempt to establish the grounding of the conceptual reconstruction and interpretation developed by this chapter and by the volume in general.

Chapter 8 will continue this effort of profiling. This time, the defining framework will not be given by the political system perspective, based on the place of the state in governance systems, but by the different alternative stances toward social change implemented by and via the state through social intervention. Recent developments in social sciences – institutionalism, public choice, behavioral economics, and social and political philosophy – have converged in raising important questions regarding these problems. Given these developments and the insights they bring, how are we to interpret and translate the basic dichotomy between the interventionist and the conservative status quo orientations? Where should we place the self-governance approach, given this dichotomy? Is self-governance a progressive or a conservative project? Responding to these challenges, a nuanced stance will be articulated, navigating through the conservative resistance to change and the progressive interventionist enthusiasm while moving toward a special position that revives and reconstructs an older tradition anchoring participatory democracy elements into a classical liberal framework.

7

Anarchy, Statism, and Liberalism

The Self-Governance Alternative

How can one describe self-governance in the context of the various alternative political doctrines and ideologies that shape contemporary public debates? This chapter will try to contribute to answering this question by placing self-governance in a dialogue and comparing it with other, more familiar positions. More precisely, in this chapter, we'll use some customary dichotomies at the core of modern political theory and ideology – anarchy versus Leviathan, statism versus anti-statism, seeing like a state versus seeing like a citizen – as part of a strategy of delineating the relevant distinctions that circumscribe the particular character of self-governance.

The starting point is a simple observation: In the practice of construing institutions and governance arrangements, one may take one of these two stances, based on two distinct views: On the one hand, implicitly or explicitly, consciously or not, one may imagine and assess situations from a privileged imaginary commanding height. One may take the perspective of the benevolent and omniscient ruler, of a being (a consciousness) operating at the center of power and decision-making. This abstract mind is the bearer of an objective, unique, and well-defined public interest, of a well-defined and objectively identifiable public domain. The view also assumes, for practical purposes, a considerable degree of command and control and assumes that control is vested in a centralized institutional structure. That is to say, to adopt this approach means to approach issues from the stance of "viewing like a state."

On the other hand, one may take the perspective of the individuals in their various capacities as producers, consumers, citizens, and self-governing beings. That is to say, normal human beings, without an overarching knowledge, who live and operate in local conditions, in domains that are more often than not in the fuzzy area between the public and the private, in conditions of relative uncertainty, having a mixture of public and private interests. The latter perspective is closer to viewing like an individual or a social actor or a citizen. That is the pre-analytic act of the citizen-centered approach to governance: the instinct to escape the temptation of "viewing like a state" and to take the "viewing like a citizen" stance.

Obviously, the two positions are to be thought of as ideal types. In practice, it is very difficult, if not impossible, to maintain full consistency of perspectives either way. Yet usually, various views on governance gravitate toward one of the two poles or can be understood in relation to them. The direction toward which one inclines, even if ideal purity is not achieved, matters a lot. These ideal types and the space between them are an excellent foil for assessing the nature of various other ideological or policy positions. Let us take a closer look at the two, trying to determine how the self-governance perspective is faring given the conceptual space they create.

STATISM: SEEING LIKE A STATE AND SELF-GOVERNANCE

Statist discourse is obviously organized around the state as a premier instrument. Analytically and normatively, the state is the focal point, the main vehicle, and the assumption and implication of the analytical or normative exercise. There is a strong social engineering presumption: economic and technological efficiency, social justice, and equality could and should be achieved through top-down interventions and constraints based on superior motives and expert, privileged knowledge, all mobilized and rendered practical by the state. By assumption, irrespective of the way the state is organized (democratic or authoritarian), the statist rhetoric and knowledge production are meant for a special audience or social group: those who are in charge of running the state. As Abram Bergson (1954, 237–238) put it in his discussion of the theoretical articulation of a democratic version of statism, according to this view, the problem is to counsel not citizens generally but public officials. Furthermore, the values to be taken as data are not those that would guide the official if he were a private citizen. The official is envisaged instead as more or less neutral, ethically. His one aim in life is to implement the values of other citizens as given by some rule of collectivist decision-making (Bergson 1954, 237–238).

Let us emphasize at this juncture that the goal of our current discussion is not to criticize the views in point. It is simply to spotlight the differences between perspectives and to note that (be these differences of nature or only of degree) they are real and significant for our major theme: governance, and more precisely, self-governance. The statist instinct, with its pre-analytical bias, means to think in terms of the state; to define the problems and their solutions using as a mental device the "eye" of the state and assuming a very special and idealized set of capabilities on behalf of the state.

It is a separate discussion if that propensity is merely the result of a romantic view of politics very popular in modernity (Buchanan 1984) or if it is something based in the deep structure of mythical thought; the function of myth is man's social life (Cassirer 1961). For our discussion, the important point is the mere observation that, empirically and historically, as a matter of intellectual and psychological basic observations, there is a discernable centripetal pattern in the statist thought and attitude. That pattern allows us to contrast it to the self-governance view tentatively sketched in the first part of the book, which tries to evade this centralizing tendency, opposing it as a centrifugal force. The fact that such an effort may be seen in this context as part and parcel of the long struggle against myth in the history of political thought or as an attempt to replace the myth of the state with alternative, more benign, myths is the substance of a discussion we are, obviously, not going to pursue here.

Irrespective of interpretation, as James Scott has noted, "seeing like a state" is linked to a strong social engineering mentality that, at its roots, aims to "arrange the population in ways that simplified the classic state functions of taxation, conscription, and prevention of rebellion" (Scott 1998, 2). For that, one needs a detailed map of the social territory to be restructured, rebuilt, rationalized, and systematized. The social engineer – expert or decision-maker – requires "a measure, a metric, which would allow it to 'translate' what it knew into a common standard necessary for a synoptic view." The result is a systematic attempt toward a simplified and hands-on perspective of social order with a view to controlling it:

These state simplifications, the basic givens of modern statecraft, were . . . rather like abridged maps. They did not successfully represent the actual activity of the society they depicted, nor were they intended to; they represented only that slice of it that interested the official observer. They were, moreover, not just maps. Rather, they were maps that, when allied with state power, would enable much of the reality they depicted to be remade. Thus, a state cadastral map created to designate taxable property holders does not merely describe a system of land tenure; it creates such a system through its ability to give its categories the force of law. (Scott 1998, 3)

And thus, we have seen evolving along with the growth of the modern state (in fact supporting its growth) an entire intellectual domain that rationalizes, legitimizes, and refines in multiple ways along social engineering lines the tools of modern statecraft. It is an intellectual history phenomenon but also an economic and political history one. Although taken for granted today, one can hardly overestimate its peculiarity and influence on modern and contemporary history. The domain and practice of public administration preexisted this particular development. To be sure, governance could always be imagined operating along lines that are either divergent or at least are not fully consistent with the commanding heights, monocentric, centripetal stance. Yet the monocentric social control view had a huge impact on the way the problems of governance and public administration were defined in the twentieth century and continues to have an impact to this day.

In this historical context, the intellectual tradition inspiring the self-governance approach, and of which the Ostroms' perspective was a family member, may be interpreted as initially articulating a skeptical position and then as advancing a counterreaction to this commonly held monocentrism and its increasing institutionalization. It was an effort taking place in the midst of and against what has been called the high-modernist enthusiastic, self-confident, strong faith in "the mastery of nature (including human nature), and above all, the rational design of social order commensurate with the scientific understanding of natural laws" (Scott 1998, 7). The citizen-centered approach brings a correction and is an attempt to build an alternative based on a tempered and restrained attitude toward the power and limits of science and progress. It does so in a climate of public opinion and scholarly environment otherwise suffused with an ideological faith "that borrowed, as it were, the legitimacy of science and technology," and converted that into an "uncritical, unskeptical, and thus unscientific optimism about the possibilities for the comprehensive planning of human settlement and production." Again, as Scott put it,

The carriers of high modernism tended to see rational order in remarkably visual aesthetic terms. For them, an efficient, rationally organized city, village, or farm was a city that looked regimented and orderly in a geometrical sense ... Not surprisingly, its most fertile social soil was to be found among planners, engineers, architects, scientists, and technicians whose skills and status it celebrated as the designers of the new order. High-modernist faith was no respecter of traditional political boundaries; it could be found across the political spectrum from left to right but particularly among those who wanted to use state power to bring about huge, utopian changes in people's work habits, living patterns, moral conduct, and worldview. (Scott 1998, 7)

Obviously, the tension between the two approaches has massive implications for the ways one sees the problems of governance. These are ultimately two attitudes toward the relationship between human knowledge (scientific and know-how) and their application to social institutions and human society in general. The problem of the role of knowledge in society in its many forms (from local/personal knowledge to highly abstract and formalized scientific generalizations) is thus deeply intertwined with the problem of governance. While both approaches claim to build on modern understanding of science and on modern sensibilities regarding human nature and its condition, their concrete, applied-level strategies have to be different. The science, the art, and the practice of governance are unavoidably shaped by the way the practitioners understand, internalize, and assume these alternative interpretations and positions.

In brief, buried in the common scientific and philosophical language, and underlying the debates about modes of governance, rests a conflict of visions. Following Scott, we have already identified and depicted the perspective that "implies a viewer whose place is central and whose vision is synoptic" (Scott 1998, 78). We have also noted how "state simplifications" work to "provide authorities with a schematic view of their society, a view not afforded to those without authority." We are now fully aware that in this perspective, "the authorities enjoy a quasi-monopolistic picture of selected aspects of the whole society." It is a "privileged vantage point" which is "typical of all institutional settings where command and control of complex human activities is paramount" (Scott 1998, 79).

First, before moving ahead, Scott's observation allows us to note similar points made by many critics not necessarily sharing the citizen-centered self-governance ethos (Foucault 1977). But second, and even more important, it allows us to see that the problem is not only one of power and authority. It is also one of epistemic content, epistemic reach, of the type and quality of knowledge mobilized and used in governance. Self-governance is, in part, necessary because it is a way to circumvent what Hayek calls "the synoptic delusion," i.e., "the fiction that all the relevant facts are known to some one mind, and that it is possible to construct from this knowledge of the particulars a desirable social order" (Hayek [1973] 1998, 14). The relevance of that observation for governance systems is hard to overestimate, and it is worthwhile to delve into it for a moment.

Hayek notes that people may imagine an art of simultaneous thinking, "the ability to deal with a multitude of related phenomena at the same time, and of composing in a single picture both the qualitative and the quantitative attributes of these phenomena" (Hayek [1973] 1998, 14). Yet those who try to think about governance under that assumption "seem completely unaware that this dream simply assumes away the central problem which any effort toward the understanding or shaping of the order of society raises: our incapacity to assemble as a surveyable whole all the data which enter into the social order" (Hayek [1973] 1998, 14–15). The "synoptic delusion" draws attention to the limits of our knowledge in designing and running governance systems and to the necessity to engage local, dispersed, tacit, personal knowledge. Thinking, designing, and managing governance systems needs to acknowledge

the fact that knowledge of the circumstances of which we must make use never exists in concentrated or integrated form, but solely as the dispersed bits of incomplete and frequently contradictory knowledge which all the separate individuals possess ... It is rather a problem of how to secure the best use of resources known to any of the members of society, for ends whose relative importance only these individuals know. Or, to put it briefly, it is a problem of the utilization of knowledge. (Hayek 1945, 519–520)

The assumption that there is a mind somewhere (the state) for which every fact required for control is known (and the implicit assumption that this mind has the capabilities to control the facts and the intended and unintended consequences of the controlling intervention, being able to foresee and anticipate them) becomes, thus, the way in which the vision of seeing like a state is converted into institutional design (and even analytical principles) by the statist, high-modernist social scientists and economists. Knowledge – full knowledge from a privileged perspective – is wedded to power.

Confronted with the high-modernist social engineering and their top-down plans and designs, the self-governance approach draws attention to the intrinsic operational problems of these designs. Such designs make heroic assumptions about knowledge and its use in social systems. Also, they assume incentive structures that do not fit with what we know about typical human behavior. Creating and operating the monocentric hierarchies required by the statist vision generates huge incentive problems and social dilemmas irrespective of the specific form of institutional arrangements the statist vision may take at one point or another.

Last but not least, the self-governance approach also asks the basic question what is the ultimate legitimacy and justification of these schemes, based on what one could justify as the top-down intervention into the lives of individuals and communities? Based on what normative principles could one justify the social engineering and centralized control of basic individual decisions regarding occupation, location, associations, lifestyle, production, and consumption? Or, alternatively, what is the justification for governance regimes that allow the individuals to have a choice of occupation, associations, lifestyle, location, production, and consumption? What is the nature of the normative principles imposing as a prima facie standard the respect for individuals' preferences and not the collectivist or authoritarian approaches? In brief, should these forms of organization, governance systems, or regimes be considered preferable or superior to the alternative regimes that limit, restrict, or interdict individual choice or subsume them to collective choices?

All of the above illuminate the gap between the two positions. Out of the two ideal types, the self-governance approach is much closer to the seeing like a citizen end of the spectrum than the seeing like a state end. By all accounts, it is an approach that tries to set up an alternative to the dominant high-modernist mainstream, and it tries to do that while still mindful of the profound epistemic problems that can plague the foundations of any governance system.

Once we have established this basic point, a new question naturally arises: In what measure does distancing from the seeing like a state approach (and from the modern doctrines that are in large degree based on that vision) mean that the self-governance approach has to be, by default, associated with the best known anti-statist doctrines of the libertarian and anarchist traditions? It becomes evident that defining the self-governance position and delineating its conceptual perimeter requires a double effort. On the one hand, one needs to assert its distinctiveness from those positions that are organized around the statist viewpoint. Yet, on the other hand, one has to clarify its relationship to and family resemblances with the anarchist side. We have thus come to identify the uneasy predicament at the core of the self-governance perspective.

VARIETIES OF ANARCHISM AND SELF-GOVERNANCE

Given the fact that, more often than not, in the public discourse and the scholarly literature, self-governance may be easily conflated and considered identical to the anarchist anti-statism, the effort to conceptually and theoretically de-homogenize them is crucial. However, as soon as the nontrivial differences existing between an anarchist position and self-governance positions are identified and elucidated, the self-governance position has to respond again to nontrivial charges. The main challenge is that once it distances itself from the anarchist anti-statist principles, it becomes too easy to conflate again with the mainstream (high) liberal positions that have evolved and gained ground during the last century or so. This predicament of carving a space under the pressure of these two powerful ideological blocks is one of the most important features of the self-governance stance articulated by the Ostroms in the wake of the public choice revolution. The constant struggle to articulate an alternative to both anarchy and Leviathan, as Buchanan put it, without simply succumbing to the mean of the average middle of the road is one of the most interesting and challenging features of the intellectual tradition the Ostroms were part of and that they tried to advance.

At this juncture of the argument, the task to identify the defining elements of the self-governance position shifts to the ambiguities inherent in the non-statist spectrum of views that includes libertarianism and classical anarchism but is not limited to them. (For a discussion of the modern state and the alternative forms of political organization, including the problem of their legitimacy, see Morris 2002, 2008). Elinor Ostrom's work was, from time to time, associated with classical anarchism, "landing somewhere between Hayek and Kropotkin" (Walker 2012). Indeed, there are some salient affinities between the classical anarchist and self-governance positions. Vincent and Elinor Ostrom have been very clear in their rejection of the doctrines and theories that make the state the alpha and omega of governance, being critical of "the amorphous, fictitious and omnicompetent entity called 'the government'" (E. Ostrom 1990, 216). In this respect, it is hard to see them objecting to Bakunin's credo: "We think that people can be free and happy only when organized from the bottom up in completely free and independent associations, without governmental paternalism, though not without the influence of a variety of free individuals and parties" (Bakunin 1990).

Indeed, at a deeper level, in both the self-governance and the classical anarchist stance, there is an evident focus on individuals, each employing methodological individualism with an evolutionary twist. As Kropotkin put it, the anarchist follows "the course traced by the modern philosophy of evolution." The anarchist studies human society without "endowing humanity as a whole, or separate individuals, with superior qualities which they do not possess." Moreover, the anarchist "merely considers society as an aggregation of organisms trying to find out the best ways of combining the wants of the individual with those of cooperation for the welfare of the species" (Kropotkin 1987, 5). The Ostroms' use of methodological individualism both in its public choice form and its behavioral form is well documented (Ostrom and Ostrom 1977). And it is safe to conjecture that they would not find anything objectionable with stances like those quoted above.

The interest in the diversity and evolutionary aspects of cooperation and cooperative institutions is another element that has facilitated and instigated the analogies and links between the Ostroms' work on self-governance and classical anarchism. Kropotkin defined his intellectual strategy as based on documenting "the number and importance of mutual-aid institutions" developed by the "creative genius" of humankind "from the savage and half-savage masses" down to the present times, while trying to indicate "the immense importance which the mutual-support instincts, inherited by mankind from its extremely long evolution, play even now in our modern society" (Kropotkin 2012). Again, in this case, the similarities with the Ostroms' work is evident, and the convergence is easy to establish.

Yet, despite these and other related similarities and even commonalities of perspective, the self-governance approach is not and could not be subsumed to the classical anarchist stance. When all is said and done, it simply does not fit the standard definition (as featured in the *Merriam-Webster* dictionary) of classical anarchism, i.e., "a political theory holding all forms of governmental authority to be unnecessary and undesirable and advocating a society based on voluntary cooperation and free association of individuals and groups." The self-governance approach has a more nuanced understanding of institutional diversity, of the mix of markets and hierarchies and networks. Most importantly, it has a nuanced understanding of the inescapable presence of social dilemmas and tragedies in social order. After all, self-governance not only recognizes the Faustian bargain at the core of any governance system but also considers it a tragic, ineluctable feature of the social condition of humankind.

Vincent Ostrom notes that there is, indeed, an inescapable division of labor principle at work when it comes to governance, too. It means that there are certain social roles, functions, and positions of authority, and it means the existence of asymmetries of power and decision rights. Vincent Ostrom writes that the most fundamental source of inequalities in human societies derives from the inevitable use of rules to order social relationships. The problem of rules is amplified by the fact that social order has to ultimately depend on the use of sanctions. That means that social order "not only requires an assigning of authority to those who govern but also requires giving them the right to use coercion" (V. Ostrom 1982, 22–23). As social beings, humans are forced to "accept coercion as a use of instruments of evil to permit orderly social relationships." The ubiquity of coercion means that order and predictability in human societies "depend upon a Faustian bargain where the use of instruments of evil, i.e., sanctions, including those of organized force, become necessary conditions for deriving the advantages of social organization" (V. Ostrom 1982, 210). This is the condition of human societies.

No one can escape from the burden of using such instruments of evil to do good . . . We are all intricately bound in a Faustian bargain which we as human beings cannot avoid. At most, we can attempt to understand the fundamental tensions that are inherent in such a bargain and conduct ourselves accordingly. We are all potential tyrants unless we learn to act justly. (V. Ostrom 1982, 35)

Force and political constraint can be used both as "instruments of tyranny as well as instruments to support productive and mutually advantageous relationships." In other words, "political relationships are sensitive relationships; and, like fire, need to be treated with care in devising solutions to the structuring of decision-making arrangements among people." If that is the case, the question "whether people can develop appropriate precautions in the use of such instruments of evil and constrain them from dominating organized activities" becomes the central problem of political thinking and governance (V. Ostrom 1982, 24).

Despite this recognition of the significant presence of force and evil in social order, the self-governance perspective could not be reducible to Emma Goldman's reading of the problem, a reading which leads her to announce a "philosophy of a new social order based on liberty unrestricted by man-made law" under "the theory that all forms of government rest on violence and are therefore wrong and harmful, as well as unnecessary" (E. Goldman 2012, 56). Neither does the self-governance perspective follow the militant implications of this philosophy as described by Michael Bakunin (1990):

Anarchism has declared war on the pernicious influences which have so far prevented the harmonious blending of individual and social instincts, the individual and society. Religion, the dominion of the human mind; Property, the dominion of human needs; and Government, the dominion of human conduct, represent the stronghold of man's enslavement and all the horrors it entails. (Bakunin 1990)

It goes without saying that a citizen-centered approach to governance in which public entrepreneurship is crucial could not be explained, understood, and advanced as a declaration of war like those endemic to classical anarchism: "We declare ourselves the enemies of every government and every state power, and of governmental organization in general" (Bakunin 1990). Neither does the self-governance approach embrace any of the naive undertones about social cooperation and organization so present in the classical anarchist vision.

In brief, there are, indeed, some converging and intersecting aspects of the two perspectives. Yet, such convergence points exist between all governance doctrines and political ideologies. Doctrines are combinations of distinctive features and building blocks. In many cases, some building blocks are shared by different doctrines. It is not the separated elements but the specific configuration of features (how these building blocks are put together and the logic connecting them) that give meaning and identity to a governance doctrine. And in this respect, the configuration and semantic space of self-governance are substantially different from that of classical anarchism.

One could restate these conclusions from an additional angle, which moves things from intellectual history toward more philosophical and foundational viewpoints. Following David Miller's taxonomy of anarchism, we could use three forms or models of anarchism as benchmarks: philosophical anarchism, communist (or collectivist) anarchism, and individualist anarchism (Miller 1984, 1).

Philosophical anarchism is basically a methodical critique of the idea of authority itself. At its core is the notion that "no man can ever rightfully exercise political authority over another"; that is to say "to have a right to issue directions which the other has an obligation to obey" (Miller 1984, 15). It is a radical principle, indeed, and it is rich in philosophical and speculative implications and assumptions. Yet this principle could hardly be part of the core set of ideas defining the self-governance position. In general, authority is a key ingredient of governance systems. The problem – assuming a realistic discussion focusing on the feasibility space – is not of the presence or absence of authority in a system, but the forms it may take and whether those forms are legitimate or not. And when it comes to the Ostroms, they have never been shy about repeatedly assuming explicit positions (especially Vincent Ostrom) on foundational normative issues. However, as far as one could tell, this specific a stance on authority was never embraced or asserted in their writings.

Next in Miller's nomenclature comes communist anarchism. Anarcho-communists, he explains, "maintain that the natural and proper relationship between people is one of sympathy and affection, expressed in acts of mutual aid and cooperation." The doctrine involves a criticism of the status quo, noting that despite the natural order, in existing societies, "solidarity is displaced (though not extinguished) by antagonism and competition." Competition entails a distorted view of the world. A climate of opinion is induced in which "people see themselves as isolated and self-sufficient" while other people are seen as rivals and enemies. The status quo has to be challenged. The goal should be a return to the natural harmony: "Everyone would be better off, in both material and human terms if social harmony could be established instead of the present system" (Miller 1984, 45).

Again, the dissimilarity between these views and those defining the self-governance stance is transparent. As we have already seen, the assumptions about human nature and social order at the foundation of the self-governance perspective are of a much more realistic nature. Conflict, opportunism, competition, and disharmony are part and parcel of the phenomena that self-governance efforts have to deal with. They are not contextual or accidental features. The Faustian bargain is an unescapable reality. The self-governance perspective could not be associated with this "natural harmonies" doctrine.

The fact that solving social dilemmas that involve commons or collective action/public goods may be possible in certain situations outside the mechanism of the state or the market (an important contribution of the Ostroms' work) has almost nothing to do with (or is only marginally related to) the belief in natural communistic affective properties of the kind that play such a preeminent role in the doctrine of communistic anarchism. To claim that the complex multidimensional and contextually calibrated analyses advanced by the Ostroms are an endorsement of such "natural harmonies" communistic doctrines – although tempting – is missing exactly the essence of the Bloomington School research program.

The third and last type of anarchism in Miller's classification is indi-vidualist anarchism. He associates it with the liberal tradition of Locke, the founding fathers, and nineteenth-century classical liberalism. At its core is the notion that each person has "an inviolable sphere of action within which he reigns supreme, encompassing both the body and the property rightfully acquired" (Miller 1984, 30). Within this sphere, one can act just as one pleases, and moreover, one is "entitled to give away and exchange anything that fell within it." The legitimate relationships between persons are those of exchange, contract, and gift. This type of individualism is intrinsically connected to the defense of the sphere of freedom: "Invasion in the private sphere may be resisted, by force if necessary," while "a sharp moral distinction is drawn between the use of force by an aggressor and the use of force by a victim of aggression" (Miller 1984, 30).

At a closer look, out of the varieties of anarchism, what is dubbed (in Miller's classification's terms) individualist anarchism seems closer to the self-governance perspective. Indeed, even as a matter of intellectual history or genealogy, the contributions to the self-governance perspective come mostly from the classical liberal tradition and its twentieth-century revival – such as the contributions of the public choice revolution in social sciences. The problem is that there are several inheritors of that tradition. This basic observation allows us to take a step further in our attempt to delineate the contours and nature of the self-governance perspective.

LIBERTARIANISM, SELF-GOVERNANCE, AND CLASSICAL LIBERALISM

Separating what is called left-wing non-statism from right-wing non-statism is relatively easy. In addition to the anarchist tenets outlined above, there are always things like private property rights and the role of markets and corporate industrial organizations, which come in handy as demarcation criteria. The real difficulty is not on the left – although the tradition associated with workers' self-management and democratic firms poses some serious problems to simple taxonomies (Ellerman 1999, 1986) – but on the right side of the spectrum. As already mentioned, there are more than a couple of non-statist positions on that side. Most of them adhere to or have roots precisely in the classical liberal tradition identified by Miller as a main source of individualist anarchism. The problem is that in most cases, they appear to both supporters and critics as conflated into one single entity of vague contours and confusing texture. Couldn't we simply say that the self-governance position is just a form of modern libertarian anarchism?

The short answer is no. The de-homogenization strategy has several steps and starts by being clear what are the real features of libertarian anarcho-capitalism at its theoretical core. Then, based on that, we go on to establish how and why self-governance is related to, but different from, the radical anti-statism specific to anarcho-capitalism. A quick take in this respect is to say that the former does not allow for a legitimate domain of the public in a meaningful way; the latter acknowledges it. The former denies the need for public governance; the latter accepts its inevitability.

A huge source of ambiguities and misunderstandings is eliminated if this distinction is elucidated. Yet, given the stakes of this clarification effort, it is worthwhile to delve into the issue a little bit more. Let us take a closer look at the distinguishing features of anarcho-capitalist libertarianism.

Anarcho-capitalism is inherently and radically anti-state, but it goes beyond that by questioning broader notions of publicness and collectivity. Even if it recognizes the existence of something resembling a collective social space or a public arena, it does not seem interested in it other than as a target of criticism and of theoretical speculations regarding its aberrant nature in comparison with the normative ideal residing in the private.

Murray Rothbard's work is emblematic of this school of thought, and we'll use it as a reference and as a vehicle. His argument is more sophisticated than simply asserting the primacy of the private by invoking natural rights and a priori reasoning. Rothbardian anarcho-capitalism questions in a rather subtle way the notion of public goods and, by implication, the justification for collective action. But it does so by claiming that these concepts have too large a sphere to be useful as tools in an argument for compulsory provision. For instance, the arguments building on the need to preempt free riding in collective action via coercive provision entail too much (Rothbard and Salerno 2011). There are precious few services that do not have externalities or spillover effects. The notion that the public/private distinction could be pinpointed through models of collective action, externalities, and public goods is leading to absurd implications.

At a deeper level, the case is based on a set of rather astute theoretical insights, and briefly noting them illustrates why the anarcho-capitalist position has interesting things to say about self-governance and why it is not so easy to dismiss. Also, it illustrates why its family relationship with classical liberalism (and, for that matter, with the self-governance perspective articulated in this volume) is so tense.

First is a radical adherence to a specific interpretation of the subjectivist conception of value (which defines a service as something someone wishes to consume, and hence, it has a value only in light of the subjective preference of that individual). There is no objective public value, just private subjective values. Hence, any theory of value worth its name cannot be mobilized in support of a theory of public or collective goods. Second, only the preferences revealed in actual voluntary exchanges are meaningful as criteria for social production and provision. If people do not express a preference in a voluntary exchange, then there is no room to speculate about what they truly prefer. Individuals may actually enjoy an already provided, unpurchased good or service offered free by the state. But if there is no way one may identify a concrete and measurable manner of determining how much they are prizing something, if it is impossible to know whether they are prepared or not to trade off other resources to get it, then one has no idea how much and at what cost that good or service should be publicly produced. If, for various reasons, individual preferences fail to translate into market demand, they fail to create prices and, thus, fail to provide rational standards of overinvestment or underinvestment. State-like collective action, by definition involving compulsory provision and taxation, is all the more arbitrary when it claims to serve preferences explicitly contested by subjects.

One has to keep in mind that a public goods argument justifying compulsory provision via collective/state mechanisms is compelling only in conjunction with an acknowledgment that the good in question is important or essential. The anarcho-capitalists appeal to the theory of marginal utility to argue that a public goods argument for state-scale collective action proves too much. Incongruous implications ensue. If we consider services in terms of large classes, then not only defense, but food and clothing, too, seem essential preconditions of anything (Rothbard and Salerno 2011). But all services and actions are marginal, says Rothbard. Not even security is a "single, indivisible lump" (Osterfeld 1989, 2). Thus, in addition to invoking marginalism, it is suggested that security and other public goods may practically come in increments small enough and affordable enough to be produced, provided, and bought on the market by private agents. Legislation, for instance, a service seemingly provided for all if intentionally provided for any, can be replaced by a rule of law that spontaneously emerges with many judge-found solutions.

Anarcho-capitalists' suggestion of sweeping substitutability looks less outlandish if we consider that the public good characteristics of some services are not intrinsic, but are, instead, relational properties depending on the surrounding structure of action arenas and the existing institutional arrangements and technologies. For instance, the costs of excludability are modified not only with the literal replacement of goods but also with the evolution of institutions and technologies that govern their provision and consumption.

The bottom line is simple: anarcho-capitalism denies with rather robust and sophisticated arguments the reality and legitimacy of the collective public domain by attacking the very core of collective action and collective goods theories. The applied-level governance implication is straightforward: One can always find ways to convert the public into private.

Dedicating time and effort to something called public administration seems to be a diversion, a detour from the correct approach.

The objective of this discussion is not to debate the merits of the anti-statist anarcho-capitalist stance on collective goods and public action arenas. The goal is merely to make clear that there is a foundational difference between, on the one hand, the position on self-governance, citizenship, and public entrepreneurship advanced in this book and, on the other hand, the anarcho-capitalist positions. However, before moving forward in further describing the far from trivial grounds of that difference, let us briefly make one observation about the anarcho-capitalist stance.

One of its major underlying themes seems to be that the undeniable blurriness at the edge between the public and the private is generating, at the applied level, a slippery slope leading inevitably to abuse. This invocation of the slippery slope argument in multiple reiterations is tantamount to denying the relevance of any second-best, real-life arrangements in the slippery slope area. If "jointness of consumption" is a myth, if "externalities" are a misunderstanding leading inevitably to gross coercion and abuse, etc., all one has left to do is to preach the first best scenario, the pure private – a space free of collective action or spillover ambiguities. There are no institutional designs and criteria relevant for the worlds of second-best, hybridity, and comparison and assessment of competing alternatives in real historical time. To administrate something that is public or collective and to try to find the intellectual and conceptual means of organizing that effort is a meaningless, if not downright evil, task.

That being said, note that the idea that the public or private nature of goods and actions is determined by relational properties, depending on the surrounding structure of institutions, technologies, and arenas, cuts both ways. Hence, it may well be a way to acknowledge the existence and legitimacy of a public domain. However, anarcho-capitalists simply eliminate this possibility by ethical and methodological assumption: A normative injunction, reinforced by a conceptual one, precludes exploring that avenue.

Anarcho-capitalism claims the mantle of classical liberalism, but this is definitely not a classical liberal position. As already noted, it is a historical fact that classical liberals have acknowledged the existence and necessity of a public collective realm. They went beyond criticism and deconstruction and took seriously the institutional and operational challenge that required them to think in applied terms about the complex real-life circumstances that preclude the mirage of easy, ideal theory solutions. Accepting this challenge while acknowledging the validity of the criticism brought against collectivism and power systems centralized and legitimized by collective choice is what gives classical liberalism its specific distinctiveness.

If that is the case, then by all accounts, the self-governance perspective is closer to the classical liberal perspective than to any other alternative. As opposed to the anarcho-capitalist stance, defining figures of the twentieth-century classical liberal tradition such as F. A. Hayek and James Buchanan did recognize the reality of common concerns, collective purposes, and collective action. Even in Hayek's thought, one can always detect a tension between, on the one side, skepticism regarding the state and its role and capabilities and, on the other side, arguments according to which "there is little reason why the government should not also play some role, or even take the initiative in such areas as social insurance and education or temporarily subsidizing certain experimental developments" (Hayek [1960] 1978, 258). Hayek admits to compulsory provision of standards of cooperation with strangers applying uniformly over an open or great society (Hayek [1973] 1998). In addition to that, the free rider problem – a typical collective action challenge – may require compulsory provision of certain infrastructure, standards, and services, including protection against violence, epidemics, and natural disasters (Hayek [1973] 1998).

James Buchanan was explicit in distancing his views from the anarcho-capitalist libertarianism:

We can, I think, dismiss the anarchist positions readily, whether this be the romantic or libertarian variety. Public choice theory deals with persons as utility maximizing beings not with disembodied spirits full of love or even as mindful of each other's "natural boundaries." (Buchanan 1979, 273)

Buchanan's work explicitly engages in the study of the public realm and his public choice theory develops a contractarian mode of determining when the government should produce public goods (Buchanan [1968] 1999). He insisted that the question "under what circumstances will collective-governmental supply be more efficient than private or non-collective supply?" requires case-by-case evaluations of the goods in point together with case-by-case comparisons of how various non-collective and collective organized supply arrangements can perform the functions of financing, allocating, and distributing the goods (Buchanan [1968] 1999, 162). Once framed in the classical liberal tradition, they are to be seen as part of a large social system created by division of labor, specialization, and cooperation based on exchange and voluntary action.

All of the above reveal not only the distinctiveness of the self-governance approach, with its classical liberal roots, but also the fact that it operates in a space riddled with an uneasy tension. On the one hand is the issue of the desirability of a voluntary action and an association-based society. On the other hand is the problem of the feasibility of such an ideal.

Once we accept the ideal of a purely voluntary and contractual society, it follows that a contractual society of voluntary association and cooperation, without central government, has to be a desirable ideal end state of affairs (Crowder 1992). Because what we called government action involves forced inclusion and forced participation and it is ultimately backed by the threat of force in case of noncompliance, government, as we know it, is difficult to fit with the ideal of a voluntary society. As Buchanan noted, "the ideal society is anarchy, in which no one man or group of men coerces another" (Buchanan 1975, 117). This ideal is, to some extent, embedded in human nature given that "[m]an's universal thirst for freedom is a fact of history, and his ubiquitous reluctance to 'be governed' insures that his putative masters, who are also men, face never-ending threats of rebellion against and disobedience to any rules that attempt to direct and to order individual behavior" (Buchanan 1975, 117). But if this is so, why wait and put up with injustice? Why not just embrace radicalism and attempt a complete reboot of society on just grounds?

Anarcho-capitalism may ultimately be seen as a particular vision of anarchism according to which, in order to achieve this utopia, one simply needs to privatize everything (Friedman 1973; Rothbard 1973; Murphy 2002; Huemer 2012). Given the liberal emphasis on the primacy of the individual and normative individualism, anarcho-capitalism seems the logical conclusion. Why not a full embrace by classical liberals of this stance?

If all men are viewed as moral equals, why not institute the anarchist utopia in the here and now? Must the utopia remain unattained because some men cannot qualify as brothers? Is the problem centrally one of broadening the anarchist elite until all men become capable of the challenge? This line of thought may character-ize the anarchist-cum-elitist, but it offers neither the direct nor the detour route to the construction of a free social order. (Buchanan 1975, 118)

This is the point where the feasibility issue reenters the stage. The classical liberal response is, thus, simply that the anarcho-capitalist position may be valid as an ideal theory. As a general normative ideal, it captures a strong and coherent dimension of desirability. Yet, like all ideal theories, it under-estimates the actual complexity of human nature and of social problems.

Hence, it has rather limited range as an applied theory of governance. Governance theories need to be operational; they need to pass basic tests of feasibility and need to be flexible enough to fit the contextual conditions in place in various social settings. Governance theory has to be, in the end, applied theory. The applied theory level is precisely the domain of the self-governance perspective advanced in this volume.

Moreover, there is an additional substantive aspect that needs to be taken into account. Any system based on voluntary exchange and voluntary association has to stay true to its normative individualist foundations. That is to say, it has to remain open to any possible outcome resulting from the freedom of choice and association of the individuals operating in the diverse and complex circumstances of life. Self-governance starts from the thesis that individuals are the ultimate authority – the sovereigns – in matters of governance: the governance systems under which individuals live are to be decided, adjusted, and replaced by following the preferences of the individuals who have to live their lives in those systems (Buchanan 1991). In operational terms, the normative individualism principle means that the ultimate legitimacy of institutions and social order has to be based on various forms and systems of voluntary arrangements or that use the notion of agreement and voluntary action as a benchmark. Delegation, indirect and mediated binding, responsibility in collective action, and the associated constraining and control mechanisms are recognized as inescapable, but all come, in the end, to the idea that the individual is the sovereign. This is the difference between self-governance and other theories of governance: a systematic and consistent attachment to the principle of normative individualism. It is the insistence that the individual social actor, the citizen, is the principal in a system of governance in which the trade-offs of agent–principal representation and the constraints of collective coordination and action are unavoidable and create many dilemmas and paradoxes.

The classical liberalism of authors like Friedrich Hayek, James Buchanan, and Vincent Ostrom seriously took into account the radical ideal of a purely voluntary and contractual society and its corollary, i.e., the advice to stay open to the variety of possible outcomes resulting from the freedom of choice and association of the individuals operating in the diverse circumstances of life. Therefore, they were led by logical necessity to be skeptical that one could rationally construct the details of what that end state of affairs would actually look like, including an anarcho-capitalist libertarian one.

As Buchanan noted, "we made no attempt to generate specific predictions as to what might emerge from the prospective agreement among contractors who choose behind the veil of ignorance" because reality is too complex to allow for a single general solution to all problems, and thus, "no single decision rule was likely to be chosen for general applicability over the whole range of political action" (Buchanan 1987, 74).

This is the core of the self-governance perspective. Self-governance is precisely about the constitution of a system in which citizens and public entrepreneurs operate in an open society with the goal of maintaining and expanding an open society, a society whose arrangements could not be predetermined ex ante.

The position that I advance is neutral with respect to ideological or normative content. I am simply proposing, in various ways, that economists concentrate attention on the institutions, the relationships, among individuals as they participate in voluntarily organized activity, in trade or exchange, broadly considered. People may . . . decide to do things collectively. Or they may not. The analysis, as such, is neutral in respect to the proper private sector–public sector mix. I am stating that economists should be "market economists," but only because I think they should concentrate on market or exchange institutions, again recalling that these are to be conceived in the widest possible sense. This need not bias or prejudice them for or against any particular form of social order. (Buchanan [1964] 1999, 41–42)

At the same time, self-governance is more than merely a doctrine of institutional design based on normative individualist principles. In the measure to which it is associated with classical liberalism, it is not limited to just a coherent set of principles. It is also about the minds and hearts of the individuals:

While customs, norms, and rules can be presumed to exist as features or attributes of a community, they also exist in each individual's mind and become habituated in the ways that people relate to one another. Whatever you and I do is always intermediate between what has been and what might be. We take habituated routines for granted without a thought, but habits of the heart and mind are always grounded in the moral and intellectual traditions of people unless those are forgotten. (V. Ostrom 1997, 286)

As James Buchanan (2000) has insisted, there is also "a vision of an ideal, over and beyond science and self-interest, a soul of classical liberal tradition," an "animating or vital principle" with "attributes that would seem equally applicable to persons and to philosophical perspectives" (112).

The work of Adam Smith, along with that of his philosophical predecessors and successors, created a comprehensive and coherent vision of an order of human interaction that seemed to be potentially approachable in reality, at least sufficiently so to offer the animating principle or moving spirit for constructive institutional change. At the same time, and precisely because it is and remains potentially rather than actually attainable, this vision satisfies a generalized human yearning for a supraexistent ideal. Classical liberalism shares this quality with its archrival, socialism, which also offers a comprehensive vision that transcends both the science and self-interest that its sometime advocates claimed as characteristic features. That is to say, both classical liberalism and socialism have souls, even if those motivating spirits are categorically and dramatically different. (Buchanan 2000, 113)

The self-governance perspective outlined in this volume is, thus, way closer to the classical liberal paradigm than to the anarchist or statist alternatives. It advances the open-ended aspect of the classical liberal vision. It is based on an acute awareness of the heterogeneity of preferences, beliefs, endowments, and capabilities of social actors. It acknowledges the complexity and the challenges of collective action, public choices, and collective goods under assumptions of normative individualism and circumstances of deep heterogeneity. It follows through the overall implications of all of the above for governance arrangements. Its operational objective is to create a structure able to manage continuity and change at the dynamic interface between the private and the public spheres with the view to what is *potentially* rather than *actually* attainable, as inspired by a soul and a vision channeling a generalized human yearning for a supraexistent ideal.

With that, and with the pivotal theme of continuity and change in social order, we have reached a crucial point that allows us to take one final step forward in identifying the distinctiveness of the self-governance perspective. The problem of continuity and change brings to the fore another basic framework and set of themes shaping the landscape of modern political doctrines and ideologies: a propensity for intervention versus a propensity for status quo, for conservatism versus dynamism, evolutionary change versus socially engineered change. Chapter 8 will further illuminate the self-governance perspective by projecting it on the background of these basic tensions.

8

Conservatism, Interventionism, and Social Evolution

The Self-Governance Alternative

Chapter 7 delineated the contours of the self-governance approach using as a foil one of the most basic frameworks of thinking about political doctrines and systems: the problem of the state and its centralized authority and monopoly of power and violence. By looking at this in light of the tension between the statist and anarchist standpoints, the ways self-governance is different from both was illustrated. This chapter will continue this effort of identification and specification by opening an additional dimension. This time, it will use as a defining framework not the political system based on the place of the state in governance, but a policy framework based on stances toward social change and, more specifically, intentional, state-generated change via policies and social interventions.

The starting point is the simple observation that the problem of social change is at the core of our understanding of political and governance positions. The nature, scale, scope, rhythm, and instruments of social change, the legitimacy and responsibility for the implications, processes, and outcomes associated with it, converge to put forward one of the most important sets of parameters when it comes to governance doctrines and political ideologies. Hence, one of the best ways of understanding a position is to look at it using as a background the theme of social change and that stance's most common ways of framing it: status quo versus drastic change, social evolution versus social engineering, spontaneous order versus managed interventionism. Where should we place the self-governance approach, given these dichotomies in dealing with social continuity and change? Given the developments in institutional theory and collective action research that we have discussed due to their relevance for governance, how are we to interpret and translate the basic dichotomy between the interventionist and conservative status quo orientations?

Again, the initial vehicle to be used in approaching the theme will consist of some of the implications of the institutionalist and collective action research already discussed in previous chapters: one of the most powerful research programs in contemporary policy and social sciences and one of the main intellectual sources for the self-governance perspective discussed in this book. As we have seen, it also happens that the Ostroms were important contributors there. As extensively discussed in Chapter 5, that line of research brings to the table some fresh challenges and insights regarding the problem of social change and, more specifically, on the ways the feasibility issue in policy and institutional design is understood. What is feasible and what is not in our attempts to design, induce, and control social change? Of special bearing has been the new emphasis put on (a) the problem of the contextual and combinatorial nature of the conditions of feasibility and (b) the complex aspects of the diverse forms and uses of knowledge in society (especially social knowledge). That, in turn, has led to a much more nuanced view on the task of institutional design and policy intervention, both issues at the core of any governance theory.

THE FEASIBILITY ISSUE

As argued in the previous chapters, the insights brought by collective action and institutionalism studies have put a special emphasis on the notion that context matters and that the range of possibilities where the relevant variables may combine is so vast, it precludes any analytical or normative fixed formula of feasibility. Not only is the standard logic of policy intervention challenged in its external validity assumptions, but also, the very notion of feasibility gains additional and complex facets, emerging to salience in a new light. The ways of thinking about governance and governance systems have to be amended. A renewed and updated effort is required to precisely capture the combination of empirical, counterfactual, contextual, normative, and philosophical elements involved in the variety of facets of socially managed social change. Huge epistemic problems, including problems involving expert knowledge and its applications, are revealed.

An entire array of feasibility criteria emerges. Disentangling them contextually seems to be critical. Different dimensions of a philosophical, applied-level, and social science nature intertwine with local and tacit knowledge. The tensions between the long run and the short, between evolutionary and revolutionary change, between tinkering and radical change, gain a renewed significance. In brief, when it comes to the feasibility of interventions, the message is a reminder that one needs to think beyond deceptive epistemic certainties and not take the notion for granted, not assume its reducibility to a formula or model or consider that it is just a matter of a simple, technical, practical task. It is naive to think that big data, better methods or technologies, or hypothetical agreements on values under the pressure of "reality" will solve the foundational feasibility problems identified in the collective action and institutionalist research.

Things are further complicated if one introduces into the picture the issue of desirability. What is desirable and what is not in our attempts to design, induce, and control social change? As opposed to the feasibility issue, where the basics of the discussion continue to be framed and constrained in some measure by causality and malleability concerns, when it comes to desirability, the issue is far from having an intrinsic disciplining element. Introducing desirability increases even more the complexity of indeterminacy of governance and its associated policies and intervention. In many cases, the dimensions and criteria overlap in confounding ways due to the difficulty of determining where considerations of feasibility stop and where considerations of desirability start. Possibilism – including the standards of social responsibility brought by it – raises the challenge to a new level.

The message of the institutionalist and collective action research that we are taking as a starting point for our discussion has been thus pretty consistent in tempering the enthusiasm of social engineering schemes aimed at social change via interventions on social institutions or ambitious quantitative policy targeting. When it comes to social interventionism driven social change, facts, data, and generalizations are necessary, but in the end, not only desirability but even feasibility may mean many things. Unintended consequences, social reflexivity, and external validity loom large. The very effort of pinpointing what feasibility necessitates in specific circumstances entails an engagement that involves substantial heuristic, philosophical, and normative elements. It is a discussion in itself how the various factors, forces, and criteria shaping an individual's or group's assessment of feasibility and desirability are determining the range of political and policy positions. For our purposes, the focus will be on how these insights and considerations about the feasibility and desirability of policy intervention help us to locate and specify the distinctiveness of the self-governance perspective.

Confronted with these challenges, the easiest and most tempting reaction seems to be to retreat to a more guarded position. A certain skepticism toward social engineering is, obviously, underlying the insights coming from research on the institutional and collective action aspects of govern- ance. We have seen that context matters. It is not hard to note that when public policy and institutional design are seen in important ways as matters of context and circumstances, a certain skepticism toward the potentialities of social engineering is not far away. When the informal, the role of the social norms in complex combinatorial systems, is seen as pivotal for policy, a rather agnostic, skeptical demeanor seems hard to avoid. From there, the traditional conservative stance seems the natural rallying point. Indeed, whether one likes it or not, the language of context, limits, and unintended consequences in complex path-dependent systems, the caution against hubris and centralized control, is a conservative language.

Hence the question: Do these insights truly support a conservative stance in public policy? What does that mean for governance theories in general and for the self-governance perspective in particular? We are now confronting what seems to be one of the most intriguing aspects of the intellectual developments related to the public choice institutionalist revo- lution discussed in this book. How are those insights and findings reflect- ing on the self-governance approach that seems to rely so much on that line of research for building its case? A case could obviously be made for a conservative reading. Yet, at the same time, a substantially different reading could be advanced. Let us take them one by one.

BETWEEN CONSERVATISM AND INTERVENTIONISM

The aforementioned evolutions of the institutionalist program are, in a sense, all ironic. It looks like an entire research cycle started decades ago in search of a grand theory of collective action and institutional design, with a view to creating a scientific basis for designing social change schemes, has apparently come to speak of conservative themes and in something that resembles a conservative idiom. The institutional theorists scrupulously avoid the ideological or public philosophy tangent, but then all that is left to debate is a matter of semantics: How should one label this renewed understanding of the limits of policy interventions and centra- lized social control? What is the best way to characterize its insights on social continuity and change? It is intriguing and significant that looking at major figures of the neo-institutionalist movement, such as D. C. North and Elinor Ostrom, one could hardly find any enthusiasm for this or that policy blueprint (or the very idea of such blueprints), but finds instead abundant caveats regarding the dangers of hubris or the limits of prediction and control when confronted with the complexity, variety, and multiple dimensions of institutional order.

This could be seen in an even clearer light if contrasted with the optimist interventionist ethos currently fueled by behavioral economics through its influence in law and economics as described in the previous chapters. It is very intriguing that, in many cases, this literature simply glosses over the difficulties and problems identified by the institutionalist research. Richard Thaler and Cass Sunstein are the leading examples in this respect as the authors of the nudge approach, a consistent doctrine of intervention at the interface between law and behavioral economics (Thaler and Sunstein 2008). One could look long and hard for an equivalent similar stance in the institutionalist literature. How one might label those two contrasting stances – one fueled by institutionalism, the other by behaviorism – is, in the end, secondary. The point is the stark differences.

In any case, the law and economics literature seems to inspire the most policy intervention relevant work building on the interface between social sciences and law and picking up elements that help articulate the normative or conceptual case for various types and strategies of intervention. Several examples will give a sense of the spirit of the enterprise that took off a couple of decades ago: Cooter (1998) sponsored a theory of expressive law aimed at creating a focal point when norms generate multiple equilibria. The recommended policy intervention is, obviously, the design and creation of the focal point. Lessig (1995) introduced the distinction between behavioral and semiotic techniques of norm change. On the semiotic side are techniques of tying and ambiguation, and on the behavioral side are techniques of inhibiting and inducing a certain behavior. Richard A. Posner (1998) discussed legal interventions using ideas such as signaling games and talked about mechanisms of norm violation and norm transformation through the introduction of new signals. One could induce norm transformations via changes in the costs of signaling and changes in the senders' and receivers' gains from cooperation as well as via changes in beliefs about the distribution of types. We have seen how Thaler and Sunstein, of the nudge doctrine and policy intervention strategy, have inspired an entire body of literature suggesting interventions, manipulation, engineering, designing, and nudging using multiple creatively combined tools of the government to change norms: education, persuasion, taxes and subsidies, time, place, and manner restrictions.

The literature has also generated a set of heuristics for intervention. The "norm failure theory" is illustrative in this respect. Just as regulations ideally correct failures in markets, laws ideally correct failures in social norms. The theory of normative failures is a diagnostic tool for explaining if, when, and how the state should intervene by imposing law (Cooter 1997, 1998). That doesn't mean that law and economics is a domain of unhinged interventionism. Obviously, there are nuances and differences of emphasis as well. But the bottom line is this: There is a visible difference in tone and approach between the institutionalist and collective action research program, with its more guarded approach to intervention, and its more acute sense of the limits and problems of designing and engineering social change through collective action governmental instruments. The way the feasibility issue has emerged to salience in that line of research has led to a substantially different perspective.

In brief, we have so far seen, again and again, how the very research program that has offered so many insights to the public choice and institutionalist conceptual apparatus that we associate with the self-governance perspective seems to bring with it a revamping of older arguments regarding the limits of social engineering, arguments that may be qualified as noninterventionist, even conservative. This is an intriguing observation, and it requires a closer look at the spectrum of such conservative interpretations and positions in order to see in what measure the self-governance position qualifies. Clarifying this issue has important implications for the argument advanced by this book.

The point is that it is easy to see how the feasibility complications revealed by the collective action, critical mass, social norms centered institutional analysis of causality, malleability, and validity in policy designs may lend support to a conservatist interpretation. For instance, in many cases, the emerging skepticism of policy interventions based on the analysis of informal institutions and social norms sounds somewhat familiar because it resonates as a microlevel version of the already familiar macro-sociological theme of neoconservative tones articulated by, among others, authors such as Robert Nisbet (1953). The gist is that in order to function, the institutions of modernity (capitalism and democracy) need the existence of functional premodern institutions and social norms that generate a certain social environment, a certain set of social relations and attitudes. The complexity of the systems that are created by their combinations is daunting. Yet one could still remark that there is a social and cultural dimension that makes the more preeminent and visible capitalist and democratic arrangements work tolerably well. Modern economic and governance performance depend on that underlying and neglected social dimension that acts as a necessary condition of their functioning. Hence, there is a concern of having this constitutive resource undermined, shattered, and consumed without replacement by the formal, main institutions, in their operations and expansion, under the drive of a too-powerful modern state.

With or without any analogy to that literature, it is tempting to see in the institutionalist results a more technical up-to-date version of what Albert Hirschman dubbed the "rhetoric of reaction" – i.e., better empirically grounded versions of the "perversity thesis," the "futility thesis," and the "jeopardy thesis" (Hirschman 1991). Indeed, the most vivid rendering of conservatism is the almost cartoonish version of this stance as presented in the "rhetoric of reaction" model. Hirschman's rhetoric of reaction argument described it through three theses: the perversity thesis – any deliberate social intervention will only exacerbate the condition the intervention aims to remedy; the futility thesis – any such intervention will simply fail to make a difference; and the jeopardy thesis – the intervention will endanger some social equilibrium or some valuable social state. It is easy to see how the difficulties of centrally designed and controlled social change revealed by collective action, critical mass, social norms, and institutional logics brought to the fore by the institutional analysis perspective may lend support to such an interpretation (Hirschman 1991).

Yet, when all is said and done, that is obviously not the self-governance position as described and reconstructed in the argument of this book. At a closer look, the thrust of a self-governance system is not on inertia but on dynamics, not on status quo but on change, as shaped by public entrepreneurship and the judgment, preferences, and capabilities of citizens. The emphasis on the difficulties, dangers, and uncertainties of interventions is meant to give a realistic sense of the true challenges and accomplishments with acting and changing such an environment. Some things are possible, and some are not. Self-governance is not a naive and utopian ideal theory. So, from the very beginning, the extreme version of Hirschman's rhetoric of reaction has to be rejected as alien to the very spirit of citizenship and public entrepreneurship view of governance.

Next, moving on the spectrum of possible interpretations of the stances that are skeptical of intervention and a social change dirigisme is a popular interpretation of Hayekian agnosticism and spontaneous order that makes spontaneous selection of institutions and norms the ultimate principle of social order and change. Hence, any policy intervention or correction of the results of spontaneous forces selecting a certain social norm or set of social norms are, by definition, dubious and undesirable. It is an extreme interpretation of Hayek's own take, but it is a legitimate position in itself – with or without the reference to Hayek. Moreover, it is a position invoked by many in public and even academic debates. Change is accepted, but only if it results from something more or less arbitrarily labeled as spontaneous or natural.

A version of that position introduces criteria of efficiency into the picture. A good example is Donald Wittman's take on democracy. It is not a universal argument but one dealing with a specific aspect of the social system – the democratic political system. Yet it vividly illustrates the Panglossian logic that could be applied to other areas and generalized to the entire system. Wittman argues that under conditions of democracy, voters seek wealth maximization and that politicians have, thus, the incentive to operate toward wealth-maximizing policies along the lines sought by voters. Hence, the democratic political system is moving in a natural way on the efficiency frontier. Because such a political economic system allocates to private markets the tasks at which they are most efficient and to political markets those tasks for which they are best suited, there is not much one can say or do about such arrangements other than to note that they are efficient in that way. Hence, given market-efficient allocation by market and political-efficient allocation by democracy, the need for intervention is taken out of the picture. There is a great variety of nonintervention positions of this type, but the point is to illustrate the nature of this type of position for analytical and taxonomical purposes. The bottom line is that none of them allow much discussion of the applied level as the ideal social order of natural harmony or that evolutionary selection is rarely, if ever, improved by interventions or deliberate social change.

Again, this is not the position that we have described under the label of self-governance. First, Hayek's work itself could be interpreted (and, as was shown earlier in this volume, has in fact been interpreted) in a different light, closer to what we have dubbed the self-governance position. But even more important (and setting aside the many arguments outlined so far pointing to the contrary) is the resounding argument from authority coming precisely from the scholars who were most involved in the tradition we associate with self-governance. They have openly and explicitly, with great accuracy and without acrimony, distanced themselves and their work from the conservative standpoint. There is no need to speculate about that; the textual evidence is unambiguous. Two major examples, one of them being Hayek himself, will illustrate this point.

Both Buchanan and Hayek define conservatism as a form of status quo bias. Buchanan (2006) imputes this bias to the conservative's distinctive valuation of the status quo. For Hayek, it is more the expression of a mere instinctive resistance to rapid or radical change. As Hayek explains, there are some affinities between conservatism and his own stance claiming the mantle of classical liberalism, but in the end, the differences are decisive:

[T]hough the position I have tried to define is also often described as "conservative," it is very different from that to which this name has been traditionally attached. There is danger in the confused condition which brings the defenders of liberty and the true conservatives together in common opposition to developments which threaten their ideals equally. It is therefore important to distinguish clearly the position taken here from that which has long been known – perhaps more appropriately – as conservatism. (Hayek [1960] 1978, 397)

Ultimately, both Hayek and Buchanan not only distance themselves from conservatism but they are also not shy about explicitly assuming an alternative position, which they use as a point of comparison. That position is – as already discussed in Chapter 7 – shaped by the tradition of classical liberalism:

The conservative assigns a value privilege to the status quo, as such. The classical liberal may recognize that the status quo is privileged by the fact of its existence, but there is no independent positive value assigned. The liberal is willing to examine alternatives without surmounting the threshold that the conservative places between what is and what might be. (Buchanan 2006, 2)

At the same time, Hayek goes further in comparing and contrasting the two stances. He notes that there is one respect in which there is justification for considering that liberalism has a position midway between the socialist and the conservative. It is "as far from the crude rationalism of the socialist, who wants to reconstruct all social institutions according to a pattern prescribed by his individual reason," as it is "from the mysticism to which the conservative so frequently has to resort." That standard of comparison is crucial, indeed, as the rational reconstruction of institutional order is at the core of what is at stake:

What I have described as the liberal position shares with conservatism a distrust of reason to the extent that the liberal is very much aware that we do not know all the answers and that he is not sure that the answers he has are certainly the rights ones or even that we can find all the answers. He also does not disdain to seek assistance from whatever nonrational institutions or habits have proved their worth. The liberal differs from the conservative in his willingness to face this ignorance and to admit how little we know, without claiming the authority of supernatural forces of knowledge where his reason fails him. It has to be admitted that in some respects the liberal is fundamentally a skeptic – but it seems to require a certain degree of diffidence to let others seek their happiness in their own fashion and to adhere consistently to that tolerance which is an essential characteristic of liberalism. (Hayek [1960] 1978, 406–407)

Reviewing and further explaining the misunderstandings generated by the conflation of these two distinct positions, Hayek wraps up his argument: "What I have said should suffice to explain why I do not regard myself as a conservative." A similar statement has been made by James Buchanan, published under the suggestive title of *Why I, Too, Am Not a Conservative: The Normative Vision of Classical Liberalism* (2006).

Such statements are replete in the intellectual tradition that inspires the self-governance perspective, a tradition in which the Ostroms themselves were anchored in multiple ways via public choice Tocquevillian and Federalist roots. As the arguments advanced in especially this part of the book make increasingly clear, this tradition and the type of governance formula it advocates are distinctive in ways that transcend the standard formulas used to frame the political and ideological arenas for public understanding. Such frameworks are very useful in helping us illuminate, in preliminary ways, that distinctiveness. Yet, they need to be cast off if one wants to take further steps in exploring and articulating the self-governance perspective. Let us turn to this task, describing this perspective as it is now reshaped in the aftermath and light of the most recent developments in social sciences and political philosophy, where the line of arguments explored in this book – with their focus on entrepreneurship and citizenship – have contributed so much.

SELF-GOVERNANCE: A DISTINCTIVE APPROACH TO GOVERNANCE

The argument advanced in this book is that at a closer look, an equally plausible and tempting interpretation brings itself to our attention: It is actually a case not for conservatism but for a certain form of institutionalized, dynamic pluralism. In this view, policy problems are seen as part of a larger, complex, and evolving system. It is a case for institutional diversity, for polycentric systems of overlapping and competing jurisdictions, of pluralist ongoing experimentation and tinkering, probing and adjusting the justice and feasibility frontiers. Indeed, this has to be a case not for conservatism but for dynamism. At its core is, first, the idea of a meta-level institutional framework of "the rules of the game" constituting social arenas through systems of overarching rules. Second is the notion that social actors interact via voluntary exchanges and voluntary associations within those general rules. Thus, they generate the trends in institutional and social change (including change of social norms, as well as of the meta-level constitutive rules) in accordance with the dynamics of

the aggregation of individual preferences and the collective action parameters in place. A large space is created for such bottom-up solutions
driven by public entrepreneurship, while the space of top-down targeted
interventions becomes more circumscribed. The desirable and feasible
are constantly defined, redefined, calibrated, probed, and experimented
with as part of this multifaceted evolutionary process.

In this alternative view, public policy is seen less as a targeted intervention using instrumental variables to change dependent malleable variables
and more as an indirect approach. The policy (both in diagnosis and
solutions) is projected as part of a broader process taking place in an
evolutionary system of nested institutional arrangements and decision
arenas. We are now probably getting closer to Hayek's position, the one
he described using the metaphor of gardening. The activities "in which we
are guided by a knowledge merely of the principle of the thing," he
suggested,

should perhaps better be described by the term "cultivation" than by the familiar
term "control" – cultivation in the sense in which the farmer or gardener cultivates
his plants, where he knows and can control only some of the determining circumstances, and in which the wise legislature or statesman will probably attempt to
cultivate rather than control the forces of the social process. (Hayek 1967, 66–81)

If that is the case, the feasibility of various interventions has to look
different in a gardening mode than in an engineering mode.
The distinctiveness of the gardening approach is the combination between
an organically evolving process and a process in which reflection, choice,
and design may nonetheless play a definite role.

And thus, the issues of collective action, critical mass, circularity, contextual validity, etc. as brought to the fore by modern institutional analysis,
with its theoretical and empirical revelations, could offer support to
a governance approach in which the public choice process is mainly
defined as endogenized, socialized, and institutionalized as opposed to
formalized, intellectualized, and externalized. In this respect, its status of
the feasibility issue is not much different from the status of the desirable
ideals of justice as discussed in the social philosophy dealing with the
tension between ideal and nonideal theory (Gaus 2016).

In fact, it is even more evident than in the case of ideals of justice that the
matter cannot be dealt with without bringing into the picture the more
complex social–epistemological processes and the institutional arrangements that frame them. In the absence of clear-cut epistemic criteria and
scientific formulas, a context-based iterative procedure of trial and error is

deemed to be the second-best. As already mentioned, it is a case for institutional diversity, for polycentric systems of overlapping and competing jurisdictions and of ongoing experimentation, tinkering, probing, and adjusting the justice and feasibility frontiers. All the inhibiting challenges of complexity, malleability, validity, contextualism, and indeterminacy revealed by the institutionalist analysis of social norms and social change, are acknowledged. Yet, it circumvents the tempting case for conservatism and instead puts forward a case for dynamism and polycentric social experimentation.

With a close look, we recognize that this is a *process perspective* that shifts the focus from an ideal, final state or goal to decentralized activity and the interaction between social actors (Barry 1988). The objective of governance is not so much to achieve a predetermined configuration or a particular state. Instead, the focus shifts on the rules and the general principles that those rules reflect and the process they shape. That doesn't mean a lack of concern with the end results. It means that when evaluating for policy and design purposes a situation or a system, the various states emerging are always judged in parallel with the rules and procedures generating them. Instead of being absorbed with a particular fixed configuration of arrangements and outcomes – an end state – the change process and its parameters become preeminent. The ultimate governance ideal is making the system flexible and adaptable, resonating closely with the changes of the environment and responding to the dynamics of the preferences of social actors on the ground, with public entrepreneurship and citizenship pivotal to the ongoing system and its processes. The materialization of such a governance objective necessarily has to take the form of a polycentric system of institutional diversity and experimentation. The conceptual framework used to generate "policy theory" for such an objective has to go beyond a mere model of localized intervention. Thinking about institutional change, institutional design, and feasibility requires conceptualizing these multiple level, multiple speed, and multiple intensity nested processes.

An example of thinking along these lines is Knight and Johnson (2011), who introduced the distinction between the first-order functions and the second-order functions of institutions. The first-order task of institutions is a role a specific institution has in solving a particular economic, social, or political problem. The first-order function of democracy, for instance, is the facilitation of collective action regarding substantive policy issues to generate consensus, or at least commonalities, and legitimize the decisions made. The second-order tasks are a meta-level phenomenon. Their function is to monitor and manage the entire institutional set of a society. This involves an "ongoing process of selecting, implementing and maintaining effective institutional arrangements," i.e., feedback function, monitoring the functioning and performance of the institutional mix, identifying failures, dysfunctions, externalities, and coordination problems, as well as remedies for them (Knight and Johnson 2011, 19). The effectiveness of first-order mechanisms is enhanced by an effective second-order mechanism. Even the process approach seems to need such a mechanism. It is a necessary feedback function to have a recourse to such a social instrument able "(1) to coordinate effective institutional experimentation, (2) to monitor and assess effective institutional performance for the range of institutions available in any society, and most importantly, (3) to monitor and assess its own ongoing performance." In brief, to assume mechanisms through which the members of a society "can collectively assess the interrelationship of conditions and consequences over time" (Knight and Johnson 2011, 169). One may agree or not with Knight and Johnson's specific interpretation of democracy as a second-order mechanism. The point is that the notion offers an excellent example of thinking about governance in complex, polycentric, multi-layered, dynamic systems while trying to stay as close as possible to normative individualist principles.

At a closer look, this is, in fact, the essence of what James Buchanan and his collaborators called the constitutional political economy approach (Vanberg 2005). Constitutional political economy sets a meta-level pre-analytical vision that "looks at market and state as different kinds of social arenas in which people may realize mutual gains from voluntary exchange and cooperation." The nature of those arenas and their functioning are shaped by "the rules of the game that define the constraints under which individuals are allowed, in either arena, to pursue their interests." In this respect, a policy to improve markets means mainly "to adopt and to maintain an economic constitution that enhances consumer sovereignty." Similarly, a policy to improve the political arena "means to adopt and to maintain an economic constitution that enhances citizen sovereignty" (Vanberg 2005, 1). This is also reflecting Richard Wagner's (2016) theory of entangled political economy or Easterly's stance on the bottom-up view of institutions, a view that is "more open to the possibility that societies evolve different institutions, even in the long run" and that, more often than not, considers that the top-down approach is responsible for development policy fiascoes (Easterly 2008, 95). This, as already noted, is probably closer to Hayek's gardening metaphor (1967). This is, indeed, the Ostroms' polycentric democratic public administration idea that has to be analyzed as an interplay of three institutional levels (constitutional, public choice, and operational) and that has been extensively investigated both theoretically and empirically by them and their associates. And this is also convergent with the efforts to revamp and rearticulate the Popperian notion of open society, "a framework in which different perspectives can search, share, debate, and dismiss each other's insights while engaging in cooperative social relationships" (Gaus 2016, 243). This is the tradition defined by Kukathas as

A political outlook which responds to human diversity by advocating institutions that permit different beliefs and ways of life to coexist; it accepts the fact of the plurality of ways of life – of the multiplicity of religious and moral values in the modern world – and favors toleration ... [I]t rejects the idea of an organic and spiritually unified social order in which the interests of the individual are brought into perfect harmony with the interests of the community. Individuals have different ends; there is no single, common goal that all must share; and, necessarily, these ends come into conflict. The problem, from a liberal point of view, is to regulate rather than eradicate these conflicts. (Kukathas 2003, 2)

This is – as we'll see – the tradition that is being revamped by Gaus (2016) and his collaborators through updating its political and social philosophy foundations, starting from the very criteria of analysis and assessment of the justice and desirability of alternative governance systems.

Obviously, if that is the case, then the question to ask is what are the criteria, the operating principles that the process defining these diverse polycentric systems will be geared toward? Multiple such criteria are possible. And given a complex and diverse society, multiple interpretations of each criteria should not be a surprise. The challenge of diversity looms large. It may be that the constitutional meta-level is structured to increase individual liberty and citizen sovereignty, as Vanberg and Buchanan argue, but other criteria are possible. Some may suggest economic efficiency; others, social justice; others, resilience; and yet others, stability. Rawls and Nozick are just some better-known examples of authors approaching the problems from this angle and tightening up the constitutive meta-level framework with the view of channeling the process in certain directions. But the idea is the same: a meta-structure that disperses the decision-making across various levels alleviates the pressure to centrally intervene. All these are implying a robust structure of governance in which multiple checks and balances interplay with social forces at multiple levels, but at the same time, they imply specific policy interventions (Pennington 2011). In the end, it all comes down to the issues of polycentricity and feasibility.

The critical point to be made at this juncture is that these and related themes are not a matter of mere intellectual history. This is a vibrant research domain at the interface between political philosophy and social science, as illustrated by Gerald Gaus's work – the contemporary theorist who has probably done the most to elucidate the logic and tensions of diversity in reference to such criteria of institutional performance out of which justice is preeminent. Gaus has pushed the debate "to a second phase, in which the problem of diversity became deeper, involving reasonable disagreements about justice" (Gaus 2017, 27). He has challenged the simplistic solutions to the intellectual and governance puzzles created by social diversity and the diversity of views, preferences, and options of real-life social actors that define real-life situations. His main target was the contractarian strategy of "normalization of interests attributed to the parties," usually done under the assumption that if we normalize the choosers by designating a shared evaluative point of view, then a social contract (a meta-level institutional structure) will arise smoothly. From the 1960s through the 1980s, Gaus explains, "philosophical inquiry into justice was largely dominated by the pursuit of an Archimedean point: a description of an impartial, normalized chooser such that his choice would identify the correct principles of justice" (Gaus 2017, 29). But what happens if that is not the case and, while living in a much more heterogeneous world, we are unable to reach that normalization?

Gaus (2016) emphasizes the dynamic, multifaceted process nature of the search for the common good and for justice in conditions of diversity. Echoing the results of Scott Page's (2008) investigations, he argues that one should not see diversity and difference only as problems to be coped with but also as resources to be employed in justifying and changing our institutions, laws, and social rules. Once we make that step, our understanding of the institutional structure needed for such a process changes at the same time as the entire paradigm of governance:

Once we understand the role of diversity in reasoning about the common good, we shall see that the general will in a diverse society is a matter of both discovery ("Just what norms and laws promote the common good?") and a matter of social choice ("Given that we have different views of this question, how can all free and equal persons come to endorse common norms and laws?"). Such a contract of "bounded diversity" gives us genuine insight into how a diverse society can come to share a general will, and so a common moral life. (Gaus 2011, 71)

Gaus's student, Brian Kogelmann, has further anchored the institutionalist governance theory of polycentricity to the public reason and political philosophy discussion. Rendering the problem of polycentric governance in political theory terms, he has shown that there is a polycentric model of the well-ordered society distinct from both the unifying model and the deliberative model:

Like the deliberative model, there is no overarching conception of justice governing society as a whole. But like the unifying model, there is some form of unification in that there are pockets of governance jurisdictions that are unified around one and only one political conception of justice from the family of liberal conceptions. We can thus think of the polycentric model as a hybrid of the two. (Kogelmann 2017, 682)

Using the same criteria advanced by mainstream political philosophy as defined in the Rawlsian literature, he has shown that the polycentric model thus realizes all those ideals, all those normatively attractive features that Rawls enumerates when introducing the idea of the well-ordered society and has to be the preferred model for a society defined by heterogeneity and value pluralism (Kogelmann 2017).

In brief, the institutionalist approach and its implications for the key problems of feasibility and desirability of governance arrangements suggests a social–epistemic approach combining incentives, knowledge elicitation, and mobilization, in which the ideal and the feasible are constantly explored and tested via a diversity of collective and interactive polycentric arrangements and processes. It is a process in which the diversity of social actors matter. The frontiers of ideals of justice or of the practically implementable are continuously probed, configured, and reconfigured while tinkering "in the neighborhood."

What is important on this view is the way in which morality, social rules and institutions arise out of real social processes: it not a social contract in the form of an imaginary agreement, but a dynamic process of social discovery and choice that creates an actual social and moral fact – a social world that all will. Note that this selection process is an actual collective social choice. It is a collective choice that arises out of the social nature of individual choices: each person choosing to do what his perspective recommends given what others are doing. (Gaus 2011, 92)

To sum up, it is a remarkable convergence of views, social, scientific, and philosophical, in dealing with the challenges of articulating a consistent view along these lines, lending support to various facets of self-governance. In what measure we are justified to consider it an intellectual tradition, from Hayek and Buchanan to Ostrom and Gaus, may be a separate discussion. By all accounts, it looks like it is offering not only a nuanced understanding of institutional design but also an alternative to the standard public philosophy and ideology taxonomy: It is distinctive enough from both the conservative reluctance to intervene and the progressive interventionism that currently defines the ideological spectrum, and it is backed up by an impressive theoretical and empirical body of literature.

Seen in this light, the institutionalism program (and the developments fueled by its insights) may be considered a direct contribution to this alternative tradition. If that is the case, we are confronted perhaps with the most important and intriguing contribution of the institutional revolution. Unfortunately, it is also its less-often discussed, noted, and used aspect. And yet, if one goes beyond the agnostic, cautious lessons of the institutional analysis literature overviewed in our discussion, one can discover the elements of a fresh view of governance, a distinct analytical and theoretical universe irreducible to the currently dominating political doctrines or social scientific orthodoxies. And thus, the message of institutionalism seems to be more coherent and far-reaching in its foundational philosophical and applied directions than either its supporters or critics have been prepared to admit. If we add to that the themes of public entrepreneurship and citizenship as key elements in understanding and coping with the challenges of polycentric governance, the significance of the Ostromian contribution to this distinctive tradition of political philosophy and governance theory gains new dimensions.

KNOWLEDGE, EVOLUTION, INSTITUTIONAL DIVERSITY, AND SEEING LIKE A CITIZEN

We have now reached a point in which the broader context and relevance of the Ostroms' work on public entrepreneurship and citizenship has become unmistakably evident. Following the logic of public entrepreneurship and citizenship, we have reconstructed the basic elements of a distinctive way of thinking about governance and governance systems. At the same time, we have illuminated how that is part and parcel of a tradition and a larger debate about political order and social change, and we have linked it to that tradition and the ongoing developments in social science and philosophy that support or challenge it.

Any overview and reconstruction of the Ostromian contribution – and especially once it has been placed in the context of the aforementioned tradition – has to sooner or later touch upon one of the major underlying themes of their work: the role of scholarship and scholars in dealing with institutional diversity, polycentricity, and the evolutionary processes taking place in systems driven by public entrepreneurship and citizenship aiming toward the ideals of self-governance. We have already noted that, consistent with their Tocquevillian and civil society orientation, the Ostroms were vocal in advancing a seeing like a citizen perspective in a deliberate attempt to challenge the dominant seeing like a state predisposition of twentieth-century economics and political science. Their intellectual endeavor was based on the conviction that the knowledge they produced was meant to be useful to citizens. Social scientists have to create and disseminate knowledge not for social engineering purposes but for citizens and their self-governance. The Ostroms – as conveyed by a quote that we have already encountered but which deserves to be reiterated – have insisted that one of their greatest priorities

has been to ensure that our research contributes to the education of future citizens, entrepreneurs in the public and private spheres, and officials at all levels of government. We have a distinct obligation to participate in this educational process as well as to engage in the research enterprise so that we build a cumulative knowledge base that may be used to sustain democratic life. Self-governing, democratic systems are always fragile enterprises. Future citizens need to understand that they participate in the constitution and reconstitution of rule-governed polities. And they need to learn the "art and science of association". If we fail in this, all our investigations and theoretical efforts are useless. (E. Ostrom in Aligica and Boettke 2009, 159)

The multiple tracks of knowledge production and uses in society (the personal and local knowledge of citizens, the codified and general knowledge of specialized researchers of social order, the epistemic processes produced by knowledge aggregation processes, the wisdom of the many, etc.) converge in a process that combines the theory of participatory democracy with an institutional political economy framework. The emerging construct is a model that puts at the center the ideal of a rational, active, and informed democratic individual. Knowledge production and dissemination is central – epistemic choice, as Vincent Ostrom (1997) put it, is at the core of public choice. The emerging governance model is built on the traditional participatory democracy awareness that the continuing interrelationship between the working of institutions and the epistemic and psychological features of social actors is the basis of both continuity and change of the system, of its dynamics and its stability:

Social training for democracy must take place through the process of participation itself. The major function of participation in the theory of participatory democracy is therefore an educative one, educative in the widest sense, including both the psychological aspect and the gaining of practice in democratic skills and procedures. Thus there is no special problem about the stability of a participatory system; it is self-sustaining through the educative impact of the participatory process. Participation develops and fosters the very qualities necessary for it; the more individuals participate the better able they become to do so. Subsidiary hypotheses about participation are that it has an integrative effect and that it aids the acceptance of collective decisions. (Pateman 1970, 42–43)

This synthesis of the institutionalist and participatory traditions is paralleled and reinforced by a rather sophisticated theory of evolutionary institutional change that integrates a strong epistemic factor. The elements of this theory could be identified both in Vincent's papers on social order and change as a function of the tension of "artisanship and knowledge versus uncertainty and ignorance" and in Elinor's work touching on evolutionary theory themes. It is worthwhile dwelling on both. In doing that, we'll also be touching on a tension between assuming the role of specialized producer of knowledge in the larger social division of labor and assuming the role of a challenger of those who claim expert knowledge relevant to interventions and social engineering. One cannot complete the overview of the self-governance perspective without self-reflectively revisiting the place of the scholarly producers of knowledge relevant for our understanding of institutions, institutional design, and governance systems.

We have seen how Vincent Ostrom drew attention to the fact that the increase of knowledge is, by its nature, not stabilizing but destabilizing to a governance system. An increase of knowledge generates increased social uncertainty, a paradox and a challenge: "Since new knowledge opens new possibilities that could not have been imagined in the absence of that knowledge, the most capable learners face the highest level of uncertainty in anticipating the future course of development" (V. Ostrom 1982a, 27). A society that is rapidly expanding its stock of knowledge has, thus, a predictability problem where any long-term, comprehensive planning is impossible, and also has a knowledge management problem, broadly defined. While new knowledge may reduce uncertainty in some areas, it may increase it in many others. One needs to not only reduce uncertainty in specific domains but also to manage it in the aggregate. The impossibility of planning as a result of humans' capabilities to generate new knowledge is an observation that takes us to the core of governance theory and its paradoxes.

In the end, we need to be reminded that institutional design – irrespective of how sophisticated – cannot guarantee control over the governance system. Uncertainty remains an issue because of the very dynamic and reflexivity of the system. This is precisely why Vincent Ostrom put at the center of self-governance the notion of *fallibility* as an implicit element of the conceptual set we need to develop when thinking about institutional design and governance. If a society accepts that all decision-makers are fallible and reflexivity increases exponentially the chances of error and unintended consequences to occur, then it recognizes that the most important thing is "to create institutional bulwarks against error" and to encourage citizens to partake in the self-enforcing process of democratic participation, which increases the error-correcting epistemic capabilities of the system.

That effort requires the development of a special body of knowledge. Institutional theory, broadly defined as systematic knowledge about institutions, is a significant contribution to that effort. Based on all of the above, one can see why a theory of social order as a knowledge process is central to the entire enterprise. At the same time, we can see the pivotal relevance of the social scientist as both a producer of social knowledge and as a citizen. The Ostroms' notions of public entrepreneurship and citizenship are profoundly related to this knowledge process that is at the core of self-governance systems.

In her turn, Elinor Ostrom advances a comparable argument. Sketching a cultural–institutional evolutionary model, Elinor Ostrom makes an analogy between biological evolution and institutional evolution: rules and norms are the equivalents of genes, while the resulting social system, with its incentives structures, is the equivalent of the phenotype (E. Ostrom 2008, 57). That leads to the notion that cultural evolution is a competition between different systems of rules and norms rather than a competition between people themselves (who are subjected to those rules and norms). Rules and norms are instruments used at individual and community levels to achieve various goals, some of them having to do, indeed, with interindividual or intercommunity competition. Yet, communities are not necessarily seen as being in conflict, and while some norms and rules might be used as weapons in conflicts, they mostly are not. On the other hand, systems of rules and norms are in competition with one another even in the absence of any conflict between the communities organized on their basis. That is to say, the competition between systems of rules and norms has a broader dimension than the competition between social actors or communities and may be used as an analytical device to understand patterns of social order and change.

That brings to the fore the issue of the cultural mechanisms conducive to new arrangements and that induce and spread a particular institutional variation. With that, the role of scholars generating and transmitting knowledge about institutional diversity moves to center stage as well. Elinor Ostrom's cultural evolution perspective assumes that the evolution of institutional rules is not shaped solely by biologically determined social intuitions, but also by social choice and by rational institutional design (E. Ostrom 2000). The variation of rules and norms is often the result of reason, based on learning, social knowledge processes, and foresight. Rather than taking the path of mere randomness and accident, people experiment and learn from different institutional arrangements. In time, they have learned to do all that in a rather sophisticated way, operating within purposefully fashioned meta-rules (such as constitutions) that frame at multiple levels the processes by which the rules are to be created and changed.

Instead of relying entirely on blind variation . . . human agents frequently try to use reason and persuasion in their efforts to devise better rules (for themselves and their supporters or for a broader community). The process of choice, however, always involves experimentation. Self-organized . . . governance systems use many types of decision rules to make collective choices ranging from deferring to the judgment of one person or elders, to using majority voting, to relying on unanimity. (E. Ostrom 2008, 58)

The end result of such endeavors to evade the evolutionary path of mere randomness is that in polycentric systems, with their rich institutional diversity, the speed of institutional development can be much faster, while deleterious path dependencies and dead ends have better chances of being avoided. Failure and error, intrinsic parts of the human condition, are easier to correct in such a system. By dispersing the risks and opportunities, they increase the overall resilience. In parallel, they permit the use of errors as a learning source for their adaptive strategies. Evolution by blind variation and natural selection tinkers slowly and quasi-mechanically with existing designs. However, rational variation can involve substantial redesigns based on deliberation and choice, grounded in knowledge processes. In a broader system of division of labor, a niche is created for specialization in this respect: Systematizing, producing, and transmitting information and knowledge regarding institutions, institutional performance, and institutional design.

One may now see more clearly the role of scholars in studying institutions and institutional diversity and, even more precisely, of those exploring the complex territory of natural experiments in governance. The danger of institutional mono-cropping is evident: "Relying on any single institutional model ... produces far less information about alternatives and consequences than allowing multiple institutions to exist side by side" (E. Ostrom and Davis 1993, 49). The area of interface between the private and the public is a reservoir or hotbed of institutional experimentation and public entrepreneurship. By cataloging, analyzing, and assessing it, scholars focusing on the analysis of the diverse institutional formulas and their performance provide an important service to citizens. They, themselves, are citizens serving their fellow citizens in the larger division of labor of their society. They make possible much better informed institutional design decisions based on deliberation and choice – a necessary (although not a sufficient) condition for citizens' self-governance, the Ostromian ideal.

That being said, the Ostroms consider that these scholars have the responsibility to constantly remind their fellow citizens and their political leaders of the limits of human knowledge as well as the limits of their institutional design capabilities. When it comes to social order and human governance, it is always tempting to think that we know or can do more than is the case. The Bloomington scholars are weary that people may imagine they have social engineering capabilities that are simply unattainable, epistemologically, logically, and ontologically. They repeatedly warn that "given the logic of combinatorics, it is impossible for public officials or for direct beneficiaries to conduct a complete analysis of the expected personal benefits or broader performance of all of the potential rule changes that could be made by the individuals served by ... a governance system trying to improve its performance" (E. Ostrom 2008, 57). Too many times in the twentieth century, scholars operating in the monocentric paradigm have assumed that they have such capabilities. The sensible thing is to be wary of the pretenses of knowledge of both experts and political leaders and skeptical about top-down, formulaic, and general solutions. Even more, one has to always keep in mind the fact that when it comes to governance, there is no correct, universal solution, one method, one formula, one recipe, and that kind of healthy skepticism should be applied to even our most cherished governance ideals and institutional designs.

Conclusion

"If you and I are to be self-governing, how are we to understand and take part in human affairs?"

(V. Ostrom 1998, 117)

The notions of public entrepreneurship and citizenship offer two distinct but related ways of articulating, in a theoretically informed manner, a set of answers to that question. They identify two central elements of any system of governance in which the members function as sovereign representatives in a network of reciprocal accountability and associated arrangements based on self-responsibility, voluntarism, dispersal of authority, contestability, and balance (V. Ostrom 1998, 223). Bridging political economy and political theory via Public Choice and Institutionalist models, the twin concepts substantiate, for analytical and normative purposes, the social mechanisms at the core of that type of governance system. Focusing on the concepts, we get a more profound sense of both the potential and the limits of self-governance, while the normative ideal of a citizen-centered society could be better articulated and defended. This volume has tried to engage all these themes and contribute in a tentative and modest way to their elucidation, interpretation, and elaboration.

Probably the most important insight emerging from this effort is that despite the recent setbacks – intellectual and political – the ideal of self-governance is both intellectually viable and worth pursuing as a governance system formula. The growth of new forms of social control, authoritarianism and illiberalism bolstered by new arguments questioning the feasibility and even the desirability of democratic self-governance could be met and countered. We have the intellectual resources to respond to those challenges in a spirit combining both intellectual ambition and intellectual humility while building on the remarkable scholarly tradition that inspired the arguments of this book.

The arguments advanced have, indeed, strived to stay as close as possible to the lines defined by the influential scholars who have revived and redefined in the second half of the twentieth century the great tradition of thinking about governance in ways that resist the "seeing like a state" and synoptic vision of social order. They embrace normative individualism as an axiomatic principle together with its twin corollaries – freedom of choice and freedom of association – while operating under the assumptions that both humans and their institutions are imperfect and prone to failure. In this tradition, one starts by acknowledging the diversity of individuals' preferences and their freedom of choice and association. With that, the focus goes to the process and the variety of governance arrangements that emerge at the interface between the public and the private as a result of the private and public choices of the social actors operating in specific, real-life circumstances. In this view, the function of governance is the collective management of an ongoing process driven by individuals' preferences and values and in which different institutional environments induce different decision-making costs; technology affects rivalry and excludability and culture matters in determining the range of acceptability of diverse solutions.

This is the territory of public entrepreneurship and citizenship. Because of the heterogeneity of human beliefs and preferences and of the limits and imperfection of the institutions emerging at the private–public interface, the most prudent approach to governance under normative individualistic assumptions is to encourage dynamic adaptability and flexibility. Individuals – acting as citizens engaged in public entrepreneurship – are thus encouraged to organize at different levels, in the ways they see as most effective for realizing their individual or collective objectives. That approach aligns the normative desideratum of individual freedom with the desiderata of efficacy and resilience through flexibility and adaptability. In the end, the label "classical liberal" – suggested at one point in this volume – may or may not be used to denote that specific take. What matters for the argument is to establish and acknowledge the unique distinctiveness of this position.

This position comes always with a caveat regarding the limits of our institutional design capabilities and the limits of prediction and control when it comes to social arrangements and their governance. When it comes to social order and human governance, we need to resist the temptation to think that we know or can do more than is the case. It is both an intellectual and civic virtue to be wary of the pretenses of knowledge of both experts and political leaders, including our own knowledge.

There is no correct universal solution, no one method, one formula, or one recipe. This simple statement goes hand in hand with two other related observations. On the one hand, we should avoid the radical stance that claims that we are unable to understand our institutional environment and, hence, we need to let rules and norms vary at random. On the other hand, we need not fall to the opposite, social engineering extreme that claims in various forms omniscience and control. That is to say, the task is, indeed, a profoundly challenging one and cannot be circumvented by any intellectual and technological shortcut. We simply have to be clever and alert and make judicious use of our capabilities of deliberation and choice in conditions of relative ignorance, while assuming that error and failure are unavoidable and, hence, that learning and flexibility are mandatory. Whether we like it or not, understand it or not, institutional diversity and institutional evolution are part and parcel of our condition and social destiny. As modern social beings, we are the result of an institutional process of evolution in the same measure that we are the result of a biological evolutionary process. We need to accept this predicament as part of the human condition. We are fallible but capable social beings striving for self-governance by crafting institutions and tinkering with them in a universe we only partially understand and, even less, control.

Bibliography

Alchian, A. A., and Demsetz, H. (1972). Production, Information Costs, and Economic Organization. *The American Economic Review,* **62**(5), 777–795.

Aligica, P. D. (2003). *Rethinking Institutional Analysis: Interviews with Vincent and Elinor Ostrom.* (Interview), Mercatus Center at George Mason University.

Aligica, P. D. (2014). *Institutional Diversity and Political Economy,* New York: Oxford University Press.

Aligica, P. D. (2016). Neither Market nor State Domain: Nonprofits from the Ostroms' Theoretical Perspective. *Nonprofit and Voluntary Sector Quarterly,* **45**(4_suppl), 43S–60S.

Aligica, P. D., and Boettke, P. J. (2009). *Challenging Institutional Analysis and Development: The Bloomington School,* New York: Routledge.

Aligica, P. D., & Tarko, V. (2013). Co-Production, Polycentricity, and Value Heterogeneity: The Ostroms' Public Choice Institutionalism Revisited. *American Political Science Review,* **107**(4), 726-741.

Anheier, H. K. (2005). *Nonprofit Organizations: Theory, Management, Policy,* New York: Routledge.

Anheier, H. K., and Ben-Ner, A. (Eds.). (2003). *The Study of the Nonprofit Enterprise: Theories and Approaches,* New York: Springer.

Arrow, K. J. (1963). Social Choice and Individual Values. *Cowles Foundation for Research in Economics at Yale University Monograph 12,* New Haven, CT: Yale University Press.

Audretsch, D. B., Grilo, I., and Thurik, A. R. (Eds.). (2007). Explaining Entrepreneurship and the Role of Policy: A Framework. In *Handbook of Research on Entrepreneurship Policy,* Cheltenham, UK: Edward Elgar Publishing, pp. 1–17.

Bakunin, M. A. (1990). *Bakunin: Statism and Anarchy,* edited by M. Shatz. Cambridge: Cambridge University Press.

Barnett, R. E. (1998). *The Structure of Liberty: Justice & the Rule of Law,* Oxford University Press.

Barry, N. P. (1988). *The Invisible Hand in Economics and Politics: A Study in the Two Conflicting Explanations of Society: End-States and Processes,* London: Institute of Economic Affairs.

Baumol, W. J. (1990). Entrepreneurship: Productive, Unproductive, and Destructive. *Journal of Political Economy*, **98**(5), 893–921.

Ben-Ner, A. (1986). Nonprofit Organizations: Why Do They Exist in Market Economies? In S. Rose-Ackerman, ed., *The Economics of Nonprofit Institutions: Studies in Structure and Policy*, New York: Oxford University Press, pp. 94–113.

Ben-Ner, A., and Gui, B. (2003). The Theory of Nonprofit Organizations Revisited. In H. K. Anheier and A. Ben-Ner, eds., *The Study of the Nonprofit Enterprise: Theories and Approaches*, Boston: Springer, pp. 3–26.

Bennett, S. E. (2006). Democratic Competence, Before Converse and After. *Critical Review*, **18**(1–3), 105–141.

Bergson, A. (1954). On the Concept of Social Welfare. *The Quarterly Journal of Economics*, **68**(2), 233–252.

Boettke, P. (2010). *Handbook on Contemporary Austrian Economics*. Cheltenham, UK: Edward Elgar Publishing.

Boettke, P. J., and Coyne, C. J. (2008). The Political Economy of the Philanthropic Enterprise. In G. E. Shockley, P. M. Frank, and R. Stough, eds., *Non-Market Entrepreneurship: Interdisciplinary Approaches*, Cheltenham, UK: Edward Elgar Publishing, p. 71–88.

Boettke, P., and Prychitko, D. (2004). Is an Independent Nonprofit Sector Prone to Failure? Toward an Austrian School Interpretation of Nonprofit and Voluntary Action. *Conversations on Philanthropy*, **1**(1), 1–63.

Boulding, K. E. (1981). *A Preface to Grants Economics: The Economy of Love and Fear*, New York: Praeger.

Boyte, Harry. (2011). Public Work and the Politics of the Commons. *The Good Society*, **20**(1), 84–102.

Brennan, G., Eriksson, L., Goodin, R. E., and Southwood, N. (2013). *Explaining Norms*, Oxford University Press.

Brennan, J. (2016a). *Against Democracy*, Princeton University Press.

Brennan, J. (2016b, June 24). Ethicist Jason Brennan: Brexit, Democracy, and Epistocracy. *Princeton University Press Blog*. Retrieved from http://blog.press.princeton.edu/2016/06/24/ethicist-jason-brennan-brexit-democracy-and-epistocracy/

Brennan, J. (2016c, August 28). Can Epistocracy, or Knowledge-Based Voting, Fix Democracy? *Los Angeles Times*. Retrieved from http://www.latimes.com/opinion/op-ed/la-oe-brennan-epistocracy-20160828-snap-story.html

Brennan, J. (2017). *Against Democracy*, new preface edition, Princeton University Press.

Breton, A. (1996). *Competitive Governments*, Cambridge University Press.

Buchanan, J. M. (1964). What Should Economists Do? *Southern Economic Journal*, **30**(3), 213–222.

Buchanan, J. M. (1965). An Economic Theory of Clubs. *Economica*, **32**(125), 1–14.

Buchanan, J. M. ([1968] 1999). *The Collected Works of James M. Buchanan Vol. 5: The Demand and Supply of Public Goods*, Indianapolis: Liberty Fund.

Buchanan, J. M. (1975). *The Limits of Liberty: Between Anarchy and Leviathan*, University of Chicago Press.

Buchanan, J. M. (1979). *What Should Economists Do?* Indianapolis: Liberty Fund, Inc.

Buchanan, J. M. (1984). Politics Without Romance: A Sketch of Positive Public Choice Theory and Its Normative Implications. In J. M. Buchanan and R. D. Tollison, eds., *The Theory of Public Choice II*, Ann Arbor: University of Michigan Press, pp. 11–22.

Buchanan, J. M. (1987). Justification of the Compound Republic: The Calculus in Retrospect. *Cato Journal*, 7(2), 305–315.

Buchanan, J. M. (1990). The Domain of Constitutional Economics. *Constitutional Political Economy*, 1(1), 1–18.

Buchanan, J. M. (1991). The Foundations of Normative Individualism. In J. M. Buchanan, ed., *The Economics and the Ethics of Constitutional Order*, Ann Arbor: University of Michigan Press., pp. 221–229.

Buchanan, J. M. (1999). *The Collected Works of James M. Buchanan Vol. 1: The Logical Foundations of Constitutional Liberty*, Indianapolis: Liberty Fund.

Buchanan, J. M. (2000). The Soul of Classical Liberalism. *The Independent Review*, 5(1), 111–119.

Buchanan, J. M. (2006). *Why I, Too, Am Not a Conservative: The Normative Vision of Classical Liberalism*, Cheltenham, UK: Edward Elgar Publishing.

Caplan, B. (2001). Rational Irrationality and the Microfoundations of Political Failure. *Public Choice*, 107(3), 311–331.

Caplan, B. (2008). *The Myth of the Rational Voter: Why Democracies Choose Bad Policies*, new edition with a new preface by the author, Princeton University Press.

Carson, K. (2013). Governance, Agency and Autonomy: Anarchist Themes in the Work of Elinor Ostrom. The Center for a Stateless Society Paper No. 16 (Second Half 2013).

Cartwright, N., and Hardie, J. (2012). *Evidence-Based Policy: A Practical Guide to Doing It Better*, Oxford University Press.

Cassirer, E. (1961). *The Myth of the State*, New Haven: Yale University Press.

Chamlee-Wright, E. (2010). *The Cultural and Political Economy of Recovery: Social Learning in a Post-Disaster Environment*, New York: Routledge.

Clark, J. P. (2013). *The Impossible Community: Realizing Communitarian Anarchism*, New York: Bloomsbury Publishing USA.

Clemens, E. S. (2006). The Constitution of Citizens: Political Theories of Nonprofit Organizations. In W. W. Powell and R. Steinberg, eds., *The Nonprofit Sector: A Research Handbook*, New Haven: Yale University Press, pp. 207–220.

Converse, P. E. (1964). The Nature of Belief Systems in Mass Publics. *Critical Review*, 18 (1–3), 1–74.

Converse, P. E. (1975). Public Opinion and Voting Behavior. In F. I. Greenstein and N. W. Polsby, eds., *Handbook of Political Science*, Vol. 4, Boston: Addison-Wesley, pp. 75–169.

Cooter, R. (1997). Normative Failure Theory of Law. *Cornell Law Review*, 82(5), 947–979.

Cooter, R. (1998). Expressive Law and Economics. *The Journal of Legal Studies*, 27(S2), 585–607.

Coyne, C. (2013). *Doing Bad by Doing Good: Why Humanitarian Action Fails*, Stanford University Press.

Crowder, G. (1992). *Classical Anarchism : The Political Thought of Godwin, Proudhon, Bakunin, and Kropotkin*, 1st edition, Oxford University Press.

Dahl, R. A. (1989). *Democracy and Its Critics*, New Haven, CT: Yale University Press.

Dollery, B. E., and Wallis, J. (2003). *The Political Economy of the Voluntary Sector: A Reappraisal of the Comparative Institutional Advantage of Voluntary Organisations*, Cheltenham, UK: Edward Elgar Publishing.

Downs, A. (1957). *An Economic Theory of Democracy*, New York: Harper.

Durieux, H. (2011). Subsidiarity, Anarchism, and the Governance of Complexity. Koninklijke Vlaamse Academie van België voor Wetenschappen en Kunsten, Contactforum.

Easterly, W. (2008). Design and Reform of Institutions in LDCs and Transition Economies Institutions: Top Down or Bottom Up? *American Economic Review*, **98** (2), 95–99.

Elkin, S. and Soltan, K. (Eds.). (1999). *Citizen Competence and Democratic Institutions*, University Park: Pennsylvania State University Press.

Ellerman, D. P. (1986). The Employment Contract and Liberal Thought. *Review of Social Economy*, **44**(1), 13–39.

Ellerman, D. (1999). The Democratic Firm: An Argument Based on Ordinary Jurisprudence. *Journal of Business Ethics*, **21**(2), 111–124.

Elster, J. (1989). *The Cement of Society: A Survey of Social Order*, Cambridge University Press.

Epstein, R. A. (2003). *Skepticism and Freedom: A Modern Case for Classical Liberalism*, University of Chicago Press.

Epstein, R. A. (2009). *Simple Rules for a Complex World*, Cambridge, MA: Harvard University Press.

Ferguson, W. D. (2013). *Collective Action and Exchange: A Game-Theoretic Approach to Contemporary Political Economy*. Stanford University Press.

Foss, N. (1994). The Theory of the Firm: The Austrians as Precursors and Critics of Contemporary Theory. *Review of Austrian Economics*, **7**(1), 31–65.

Foucault, M. (1977). *Discipline and Punish: The Birth of the Prison*, New York: Vintage Books.

Freeden, M. (2015). In M. Freeden, L. T. Sargent, and M. Stears, eds., *The Oxford Handbook of Political Ideologies*, Reprint edition, Oxford University Press.

Friedman, D. (1973). *The Machinery of Freedom*, Chicago: Open Court Publishing Company.

Friedman, J. (2006). Democratic Competence in Normative and Positive Theory: Neglected Implications of "The Nature of Belief Systems in Mass Publics." *Critical Review*, **18**(1–3), 1–43.

Galston, W. A. (1991). *Liberal Purposes: Goods, Virtues, and Diversity in the Liberal State*, Cambridge University Press.

Gaus, G. (2010). *The Order of Public Reason: A Theory of Freedom and Morality in a Diverse and Bounded World*, Cambridge University Press.

Gaus, G. (2011). Between Discovery and Choice: The General Will in a Diverse Society. *Contemporary Readings in Law and Social Justice*, **3**(2), 70–95.

Gaus, G. (2013). The Evolution, Evaluation, and Reform of Social Morality: A Hayekian Analysis. In S. J. Peart and D. M. Levy, eds., *F. A. Hayek and the Modern Economy: Economic Organization and Activity*, New York: Palgrave Macmillan, pp. 59–88.

Gaus, G. (2016). *The Tyranny of the Ideal: Justice in a Diverse Society*, Princeton University Press.

Gaus, G. (2017). Is Public Reason a Normalization Project? Deep Diversity and the Open Society. *Social Philosophy Today*, **33**, 27–52.

Gigerenzer, G. (2000). *Adaptive Thinking: Rationality in the Real World*, Oxford University Press.

Goldman, A. I. (1999). Social Epistemology. *Crítica: Revista Hispanoamericana de Filosofía*, **31**(93), 3–19.

Goldman, A. I., and Whitcomb, D. (Eds.). (2011). *Social Epistemology: Essential Readings*, 1st edition, Oxford University Press.

Goldman, E. (2012). *Anarchism and Other Essays*, Mineola, NY: Courier Corporation.

Goodin, R. E. and Tilly, C. (Eds.). (2008). *The Oxford Handbook of Contextual Political Analysis*, 1st edition, Oxford University Press.

Granovetter, M. (1978). Threshold Models of Collective Behavior. *American Journal of Sociology* **83**(6), 1420–1443.

Green, D., and Shapiro, I. (1996). *Pathologies of Rational Choice Theory: A Critique of Applications in Political Science*, New Haven, CT: Yale University Press.

Groenewegen, J. (2011). The Bloomington School and American Institutionalism. *The Good Society*, **20**(1): 15–36.

Grube, L., and Storr, V. H. (2013). The Capacity for Self-Governance and Post-Disaster Resiliency. *Review of Austrian Economics*, **27**(3), 301–324.

Gutmann, A. (1980). *Liberal Equality*, Cambridge University Press.

Hammack, D. C., and Young, D. R. (1993). *Nonprofit Organizations in a Market Economy: Understanding New Roles, Issues, and Trends*, San Francisco, CA: Jossey-Bass Publishers.

Hansmann, H. (2003). The Role of Trust in Nonprofit Enterprise. In H. Anheier and A. Ben-Ner, eds., *The Study of the Nonprofit Enterprise: Theories and Approaches*, Boston: Springer, pp. 115–122.

Hansmann, H., and Powell, W. W. (1987). Economic Theories of Nonprofit Organization. In W. W. Powell and R. Steinberg, eds., *The Nonprofit Sector: A Research Handbook*, New Haven, CT: Yale University Press, pp. 117–139.

Harper, D. A., and Lewis, P. (2012). New Perspectives on Emergence in Economics. *Journal of Economic Behavior & Organization*. **82**(2–3), 329–37.

Hayek, F. A. (1945). The Use of Knowledge in Society. *American Economic Review*, **35** (4), 519–30.

Hayek, F. A. (1948). Economics and Knowledge. Reprinted in *Individualism and Economic Order*, Chicago: University of Chicago Press, pp. 33–56.

Hayek, F. A. ([1960] 1978). *The Constitution of Liberty*, University of Chicago Press.

Hayek, F. A. (1967). Notes on the Evolution of Systems of Rules of Conduct. In *Studies in Philosophy, Politics and Economics*, Chicago: University of Chicago Press, pp. 66–81.

Hayek, F. A. (]1973] 1998). *Law, Legislation and Liberty, Volume 1: Rules and Order*, unknown edition, Chicago: University of Chicago Press.

Hayek, F. A. ([1976] 1998). *Law, Legislation and Liberty, Volume 2: The Mirage of Social Justice*, Chicago: University of Chicago Press.

Hayek, F. A. ([1979] 1998). *Law, Legislation and Liberty, Volume 3: The Political Order of a Free People*, Volume 3 in series; softcover edition, Chicago: University of Chicago Press.

Hayek, F. A. (1992). Why I Am Not a Conservative. *The Centre for Independent Studies*, **41**, 1–28.

Heckathorn, D. (1996). The Dynamics and Dilemmas of Collective Action. *American Sociological Review*, **61**(2), 250–277.

Helmke, G., and Levitsky, S. (2004). Informal Institutions and Comparative Politics: A Research Agenda. *Perspectives on Politics*, **2**(4), 725–740.

Hirschman, A. O. (1971). Introduction: Political Economics and Possibilism. In *Bias for Hope: Essays on Development and Latin America*, 1st edition, New Haven, CT: Yale University Press, pp. 26–37.

Hirschman, A. O. (1991). *The Rhetoric of Reaction: Perversity, Futility, Jeopardy*, 1st edition, Cambridge, MA: Belknap Press.

Huemer, M. (2012). *The Problem of Political Authority: An Examination of the Right to Coerce and the Duty to Obey*, Basingstoke, UK: Palgrave Macmillan.

Iannaccone, L. (1998). Introduction to the Economics of Religion. *Journal of Economic Literature*. **36** (3), 1465–1495.

James, E., (Ed.). (1989). *The Nonprofit Sector in International Perspective: Studies in Comparative Culture & Policy*. New York: Oxford University Press.

James, E. (1990). Economic Theories of the Nonprofit Sector: A Comparative Perspective. In H. K. Anheier and W. Seibel, eds., *The Third Sector: Comparative Studies of Nonprofit Organizations*, Berlin: Walter de Gruyter, pp. 21–30.

Johnson, J., and Orr, S. (2017). Institutions, Capabilities, Citizens, paper presented at Fact/Values/Strategies, Tisch College of Civic Studies, Tufts University.

Johnson, S. (2006). *Everything Bad is Good for You: How Today's Popular Culture is Actually Making Us Smarter*, 1st reprint edition, New York: Riverhead Books.

Jones, G. (2015). *Hive Mind: How Your Nation's IQ Matters So Much More Than Your Own*, 1st edition, Stanford, CA: Stanford Economics and Finance.

Keefer, P., and Knack, S. (2008). Social Capital, Social Norms and the New Institutional Economics. In C. Ménard and M. M. Shirley, eds., *Handbook of New Institutional Economics*, Dordreccht, The Netherlands: Springer, pp. 701–725.

Kirzner, I. (1973). *Competition and Entrepreneurship*, University of Chicago Press.

Kirzner, I. (1992). *The Meaning of the Market Process: Essays in the Development of Modern Austrian Economics*, London: Routledge.

Kirzner, I. M. (1960). *The Economic Point of View: An Essay in the History of Economic Thought*, Auburn, AL: Ludwig von Mises Institute.

Kirzner, I. M. (1997). Entrepreneurial Discovery and the Competitive Market Process: An Austrian Approach. *Journal of Economic Literature*, **35**(1), 60–85.

Klein, P., Mahoney, J., McGahan, A., and Pitelis, C. (2010). Toward a Theory of Public Entrepreneurship. *European Management Review*, **7**(1), 1–15.

Kliemt, H. (2011). Tayloring Game Theory the Ostrom Way. *The Good Society*, **20**(1), 37–50.

Knight, F. H. (1921). *Risk, Uncertainty and Profit*, Boston: Houghton Mifflin.

Knight, J., and Johnson, J. (2011). *The Priority of Democracy: Political Consequences of Pragmatism*, Princeton University Press.

Kogelmann, B. (2017). Justice, Diversity, and the Well-Ordered Society. *The Philosophical Quarterly*, **67**(269), 663–684.

Kropotkin, P. (1987). *Anarchism and Anarchist Communism: Its Basis and Principles*, (edited by N. Walter), London: Freedom Press.

Kropotkin, P. (2012). *Mutual Aid: A Factor of Evolution*, Courier Corporation.

Kuhnert, S. (2001). An Evolutionary Theory of Collective Action: Schumpeterian Entrepreneurship for the Common Good. *Constitutional Political Economy*, **12**(1), 13–29.

Kukathas, C. (2003). *The Liberal Archipelago*, Oxford University Press.

Kuran, T. (1997). *Private Truths, Public Lies: The Social Consequences of Preference Falsification*. Cambridge, MA: Harvard University Press.

Kuran, T., and Sunstein, C. R. (1999). Availability Cascades and Risk Regulation. *Stanford Law Review*, **51**(4), 683–768.

Lachmann, L. M. (1966). Sir John Hicks on Capital and Growth. *South African Journal of Economics*, **34**(2), 113–123.

Lachmann, L. M. (1971). *The Legacy of Max Weber: Three Essays*, Berkeley: The Glaendessary Press.

Lachmann, L. M. (1986). *The Market as an Economic Process*, Oxford: Blackwell.

Landemore, H. (2012a). Democratic Reason: The Mechanisms of Collective Intelligence in Politics. In H. Landemore and J. Elster, eds., *Collective Wisdom: Principles and Mechanisms*, Cambridge University Press, pp. 251–289.

Landemore, H. (2012b). Why the Many are Smarter Than the Few and Why it Matters. *Journal of Public Deliberation*, **8**(1).

Landemore, H. (2013). *Democratic Reason: Politics, Collective Intelligence, and the Rule of the Many*, reprint edition, Princeton University Press.

Lau, R. R., and Redlawsk, D. P. (2001). Advantages and Disadvantages of Cognitive Heuristics in Political Decision Making. *American Journal of Political Science*, **45**(4), 951–971.

Lessig, L. (1995). The Regulation of Social Meaning. *University of Chicago Law Review*, **62**(3), 943–1045.

Levine, P. (2011). Seeing Like a Citizen: The Contributions of Elinor Ostrom to "Civic Studies." *The Good Society*, **20**(1), 3–15.

Levine, P. (2014). The Case for Civic Studies. In P. Levine and K. Soltan, eds., *Civic Studies: Approaches to the Emerging Field*, American Association of Colleges & Universities, pp. 3–8.

Levine, P., and Soltan, K., (Eds.). (2014). *Civic Studies: Approaches to the Emerging Field*, American Association of Colleges & Universities.

Levy, J. T. (2015). *Rationalism, Pluralism, and Freedom*, Oxford University Press.

Lewis, P. A. (2011). Varieties of Emergence: Minds, Markets and Novelty. *Studies in Emergent Order*. **4**, 170–92.

Link, A. (2007). Public Policy and Entrepreneurship. In D. Audretsch, I. Grilo, and A. R. Thurik, eds., *Handbook of Research on Entrepreneurship Policy*, Cheltenham, UK: Edward Elgar, pp. 130–139.

Macedo, S. (1990). *Liberal Virtues: Citizenship, Virtue, and Community in Liberal Constitutionalism*, Oxford University Press.

Marwell, G., and Oliver, P. (1993). *The Critical Mass in Collective Action*, Cambridge University Press.

Marwell, G., Oliver, P., and Prahl, R. (1988). Social Networks and Collective Action: A Theory of the Critical Mass. *The American Journal of Sociology*, **94**(3), 502–534.

McGinnis, M. D. (1999). *Polycentricity and Local Public Economies: Readings from the Workshop in Political Theory and Policy Analysis*. Ann Arbor, MI: University of Michigan Press.

McGinnis, M. D. (2005). Self-Governance, Polycentrism, and Federalism: Recurring Themes in Vincent Ostrom's Scholarly Oeuvre. *Journal of Economic Behavior and Organization* 57(2): 173–188.

McGinnis, M. D., and Walker, J. M. (2010). Foundations of the Ostrom Workshop: Institutional Analysis, Polycentricity, and Self-Governance of the Commons. *Public Choice*, 143(3): 293–301.

Merton, R. K. (1948). The Self-Fulfilling Prophecy. *Antioch Review*, 8, 193–210.

Mill, J. S. (1859). *On Liberty*, Ontario: Batoche Books Limited.

Miller, D. (1984). *Anarchism*, London: JM Dent.

Mises, L. (1920). Economic Calculation in the Socialist Commonwealth. In F. A. Hayek, ed., *Collective Economic Planning*, London: George Routledge & Sons, pp. 87–130.

Mises, L. (1922). *Socialism: An Economic and Sociological Analysis*, New York: Mcmillan Co.

Mises, L. (1998). *Human Action*, Auburn, AL: The Ludwig von Mises Institute.

Morris, C. (2002). *An Essay on the Modern State*, Cambridge University Press.

Morris, C. (2008). State Legitimacy and Social Order. In J. Kühnelt, ed., *Political Legitimization Without Morality?* Springer Netherlands, pp. 15–32.

Munger, M. (2010). Endless Forms Most Beautiful and Most Wonderful: Elinor Ostrom and the Diversity of Institutions. *Public Choice*, 143(3): 263–268.

Murphy, R. P. (2002). *Chaos Theory*, Auburn, AL: The Ludwig Von Mises Institute.

Nisbet, R. A. (1953). *The Quest for Community: A Study in the Ethics of Order and Freedom*, Oxford University Press.

North, D. C. (1993). Institutions and Credible Commitment. *Journal of Institutional and Theoretical Economics (JITE)/Zeitschrift für die gesamte Staatswissenschaft*, 149 (1), 11–23.

North, D. C. (1997). Some Fundamental Puzzles in Economic History/Development. In *Santa Fe Institute Studies in the Sciences of Complexity-Proceedings*, Vol. 27, Addison-Wesley Publishing, pp. 223–238.

O'Driscoll, G. P., and Rizzo, M. J. (1985). *The Economics of Time and Ignorance*, London: Routledge.

Oliver, P. (1993). Formal Models of Collective Action. *Annual Review of Sociology*, 19, 271–300.

Oliver, P., and Marwell, G. (1988). The Paradox of Group Size in Collective Action: A Theory of the Critical Mass. II. *American Sociological Review*, 53 (1), 1–8.

Oliver, P., and Marwell, G. (2001). Whatever Happened to Critical Mass Theory? A Retrospective and Assessment. *Sociological Theory*, 19(3), 292–311.

Oliver, P., Marwell, G., and Teixeira, R. (1985). A Theory of the Critical Mass. I. Interdependence, Group Heterogeneity, and the Production of Collective Action. *American Journal of Sociology*, 91(3), 522–556.

Olson, M. (1971). *The Logic of Collective Action: Public Goods and the Theory of Groups*, Cambridge, MA: Harvard University Press.

Ortmann, A. (1996). Modem Economic Theory and the Study of Nonprofit Organizations: Why the Twain Shall Meet. *Nonprofit and Voluntary Sector Quarterly*, 25(4), 470–484.

Osterfeld, D. (1989). Anarchism and the Public Goods Issue: Law, Courts, and the Police. *The Journal of Libertarian Studies*, 9(1), 47–68.

Ostrom, E. (1965). *Public Entrepreneurship: A Case Study in Ground Water Basin Management*, Los Angeles, University of California. Retrieved from https://dlc.dlib .indiana.edu/dlc/handle/10535/3581

Ostrom, E. (1972). Metropolitan Reform: Propositions Derived from Two Traditions. *Social Science Quarterly*, 53(3), 474–493.

Ostrom, E. (Ed). (1982). *Strategies of Political Inquiry*, Beverly Hills: Sage Publications.

Ostrom, E. (1986). An Agenda for the Study of Institutions. *Public Choice* 48(1): 3–25.

Ostrom, E. (1990). *Governing the Commons. The Evolution of Institutions for Collective Action*, Cambridge University Press.

Ostrom, E. (1991). Rational Choice Theory and Institutional Analysis: Towards Complementarity. *American Political Science Review*, 85(1), 237–250.

Ostrom, E. (1994). *Neither Market Nor State: Governance of Common-Pool Resources in the Twenty-First Century*, Washington, DC: International Food Policy Research Institute.

Ostrom, E. (1996). Crossing the Great Divide: Coproduction, Synergy, and Development. *World Development*, 24(6), 1073–1087.

Ostrom, E. (1998). A Behavioural Approach to the Rational Choice Theory of Collective Action. *American Political Science Review*, 92(1), 1–22.

Ostrom, E. (2000). Collective Action and the Evolution of Social Norms. *Journal of Economic Perspectives*, 14(3), 137–158.

Ostrom, E. (2005a). *Understanding Institutional Diversity*, Princeton University Press.

Ostrom, E. (2005b). Unlocking Public Entrepreneurship and Public Economies. Discussion Paper No. 2005/1, EGDI-WIDER Conference on Unlocking Human Potential – Linking the Informal and Formal Sectors, Helsinki, 17–18 Sept. Retrieved from https://www.wider.unu.edu/sites/default/files/dp2005-01.pdf

Ostrom, E. (2008). Developing a Method for Analyzing Institutional Change. In S. S. Batie and N. Mercuro, eds., *Alternative Institutional Structures: Evolution and Impact*, New York: Routledge, pp. 48–76.

Ostrom, E. (2011). Background on the Institutional Analysis and Development Framework. *Policy Studies Journal*, 39(1), 7–27.

Ostrom, E. (2014). Collective Action and the Evolution of Social Norms. *Journal of Natural Resources Policy Research*, 6(4), 235–252.

Ostrom, E. (2016). The Comparative Study of Public Economies. *American Economist*, 61(1), 91–107.

Ostrom, E., and Ahn, T. K. (2007). The Meaning of Social Capital and its Link to Collective Action. Available at SSRN: https://ssrn.com/abstract=1304823 or http://dx.doi.org/10.2139/ssrn.1304823

Ostrom, E., and Davis, G. (1993). Nonprofit Organizations as Alternatives and Complements in a Mixed Economy. In D. C. Hammack and D. R. Young, eds., *Nonprofit Organization in a Market Economy: Understanding New Roles, Issues, and Trends*, San Francisco, CA: Jossey-Bass Publishers, pp. 23–56.

Ostrom, E., and Ostrom, V. (2004). The Quest for Meaning in Public Choice. *American Journal of Economics and Sociology*, 63(1), 105–147.

Ostrom, E., and Parks, R. B. (1973). Neither Gargantua nor the Land of Lilliputs: Conjectures on Mixed Systems of Metropolitan Organization. In M. D. McGinnis, ed., *Polycentricity and Local Public Economies: Readings from the Workshop in Political Theory and Policy Analysis*, Ann Arbor: University of Michigan Press, pp. 284–305.

Ostrom, E., and Walker, J. (Eds.). (2003). *Trust and Reciprocity: Interdisciplinary Lessons from Experimental Research*, New York: Russell Sage Foundation.

Ostrom, V. (1972). Polycentricity. Workshop Working Paper Series, Workshop in Political Theory and Policy Analysis, Presented at Annual Meeting of the American Political Science Association, Washington, DC, Sept. 5–9.

Ostrom, V. (1979). A Conceptual-Computational Logic for Federal Systems of Governance. In D. J. Daniel, ed., *Constitutional Design and Power-Sharing in the Post-Modern Epoch*, Lanham, MD: University Press of America, pp. 2–22.

Ostrom, V. (1982). The Human Condition. In *Indiana University Archives*, Vol. 82, pp. 3–29.

Ostrom, V. (1984). The Meaning of Value Terms. *American Behavioral Scientist*, **28**(2), 249–262.

Ostrom, V. (1986). The Constitutional Level of Analysis: A Challenge. Bloomington: Workshop Working Paper Series, Workshop in Political Theory and Policy Analysis, Indiana University.

Ostrom, V. (1987). *The Political Theory of a Compound Republic: Designing the American Experiment*, Lincoln, NE: University of Nebraska Press.

Ostrom, V. (1990). Problems of Cognition as a Challenge to Policy Analysts and Democratic Societies. *Journal of Theoretical Politics* 2(3): 243–262.

Ostrom, V. (1993). Opportunity, Diversity, and Complexity. In V. Ostrom, D. Feeny, and H. Picht, eds., *Rethinking Institutional Analysis and Development: Issues, Alternatives, and Choices*, San Francisco: ICS Press, Institute for Contemporary Studies, pp. 389–407.

Ostrom, V. (1994). *The Meaning of American Federalism: Constituting a Self-Governing Society*, San Francisco, Calif: ICS Press.

Ostrom, V. (1997). *The Meaning of Democracy and the Vulnerability of Democracies: A Response to Tocqueville's Challenge*, Ann Arbor: University of Michigan Press.

Ostrom, V. (2006). Citizen-Sovereigns: The Source of Contestability, the Rule of Law, and the Conduct of Public Entrepreneurship. *PS: Political Science & Politics*, **39**(1), 13–17.

Ostrom, V. (2008 [1973]). *The Intellectual Crisis in American Public Administration*, 3rd edition [1st ed. 1973; rev. ed. 1974; 2nd ed. 1989], Tuscaloosa, AL: University of Alabama Press.

Ostrom, V., and Allen, B. (2008). *The Political Theory of a Compound Republic: Designing the American Experiment*, 3rd revised edition, Lanham, MD: Lexington Books.

Ostrom, V., and Ostrom, E. (1965). A Behavioral Approach to the Study of Intergovernmental Relations. *Readings from the Workshop in Political Theory and Policy Analysis*, **359**(1), 135–146.

Ostrom, V., and Ostrom, E. (1977). Public Goods and Public Choices. In M. McGinnis, translator, *Readings from the Workshop in Political Theory and Policy Analysis*, Boulder, CO: Westview Press, pp. 75–105.

Ostrom, V., Bish, R., and Ostrom, E. (1988). *Local Government in the United States*, San Francisco: ICS Press.

Ostrom, V., Tiebout, C. M., and Warren, R. (1961). The Organization of Government in Metropolitan Areas: A Theoretical Inquiry. *American Political Science Review*, **55**, 831–842.

Ott, J. S. (Ed.). (2001). *The Nature of the Nonprofit Sector*, Boulder, CO: Westview Press.

Page, S. E. (2008) *The Difference: How the Power of Diversity Creates Better Groups, Firms, Schools, and Societies*, Princeton University Press.

Parks, R. B., Baker, P. C., Kiser, L., . . . Wilson, R. (1981). Consumers as Coproducers of Public Services: Some Economic and Institutional Considerations. *Policy Studies Journal*, **9**(7), 1001–1011.

Pateman, C. (1970). *Participation and Democratic Theory*, Cambridge University Press.

Pennington, M. (2011). *Robust Political Economy: Classical Liberalism and the Future of Public Policy*, Cheltenham: Edward Elgar Publishing.

Platteau, J.-P. (1996). Traditional Sharing Norms as an Obstacle to Economic Growth in Tribal Societies. (Working Paper), Notre-Dame de la Paix, Sciences Economiques et Sociales. Retrieved from https://econpapers.repec.org/paper/fthnodapa/173.htm

Platteau, J.-P. (2000). *Institutions, Social Norms and Economic Development*, 1st edition, Amsterdam, The Netherlands: Routledge.

Platteau, J.-P. (2006). Solidarity Norms and Institutions in Village Societies: Static and Dynamic Considerations. In S.-C. Kolm and J. M. Ythier, eds., *Handbook of the Economics of Giving, Altruism and Reciprocity*, Vol. 1, Oxford: Elsevier, pp. 819–886.

Pocock, J. G. A. (2016). *The Machiavellian Moment: Florentine Political Thought and the Atlantic Republican Tradition*, Princeton University Press.

Pohl, R., (Ed.). (2004). *Cognitive Illusions: A Handbook on Fallacies and Biases in Thinking, Judgement, and Memory*, New York: Psychology Press.

Polanyi, M. (1951). *The Logic of Liberty*, University of Chicago Press.

Posner, E. A. (Ed.). (2007). *Social Norms, Nonlegal Sanctions, and the Law*, Cheltenham, UK: Edward Elgar Publishing.

Posner, R. A. (1998). Rational Choice, Behavioral Economics, and the Law. *Stanford Law Review*, 1551–1575.

Powell, W., and Steinberg, R. (2006). *The Nonprofit Sector: A Research Handbook*, New Haven, CT: Yale University Press.

Pressman, J. L., and Wildavsky, A. B. (1973). *Implementation: How Great Expectations in Washington Are Dashed in Oakland; Or, Why It's Amazing that Federal Programs Work at All*, Berkeley, CA: University of California Press.

Pryor, F. L. (2005). *Economic Systems of Foraging, Agricultural, and Industrial Societies*, Cambridge University Press.

Putnam, R. D., Leonardi, R., and Nanetti, R. Y. (1994). *Making Democracy Work: Civic Traditions in Modern Italy*, Princeton University Press.

Radnitzky, G. (Ed.). (1992). *Universal Economics: Assessing the Achievements of the Economic Approach*, New York: Paragon House.

Radnitzky, G., and Bernholz, P. (1987). *Economic Imperialism: The Economic Approach Applied Outside the Field of Economics*, New York: Paragon House.

Raiser, M. (1997). Informal Institutions, Social Capital and Economic Transition: Reflections on a Neglected Dimension. European Bank for Reconstruction and Development. http://citeseerx.ist.psu.edu/viewdoc/download?doi=10.1.1.194.8230&rep=rep1&type=pdf

Raiser, M. (2001). Informal Institutions, Social Capital, and Economic Transition: Reflections on a Neglected Dimension. In G. A. Cornia and V. Popov, eds., *Transition and Institutions: The Experience of Gradual and Late Reformers*, Oxford University Press, pp. 218–239.

Reksulak, M., Razzolini, L., and Shughart, W. F. (Eds.). (2013). *The Elgar Companion to Public Choice*, Cheltenham, UK: Edward Elgar Publishing.

Rose-Ackerman, S. (Ed.). (1986). *The Economics of Nonprofit Institutions: Studies in Structure and Policy*, Oxford University Press.

Rose-Ackerman, S. (1997). Altruism, Ideological Entrepreneurs and the Non-Profit Firm. *VOLUNTAS: International Journal of Voluntary and Nonprofit Organizations*, 8(2), 120–134.

Rossi, P. H., Lipsey, M. W., & Freeman, H. E. (2004). *Evaluation: A Systematic Approach*. Thousand Oaks, CA: SAGE Publication.

Rothbard, M. N. (1973). *For a New Liberty: The Libertarian Manifesto*, New York: Collier Books.

Rothbard, M. N., and Salerno, J. T. (2011). *Man, Economy, and State with Power and Market, Scholar's Edition*, 2nd edition, Auburn, Alabama: Ludwig von Mises Institute.

Sabetti, F. (2011). Constitutional Artisanship and Institutional Diversity: Elinor Ostrom, Vincent Ostrom, and the Workshop. *The Good Society*, 20(1), 73–83.

Sabetti, F. (2014). Artisans of the Common Life: Building a Public Science of Civics. In P. Levine and K. Soltan, eds., *Civic Studies: Approaches to the Emerging Field*, Vol. 3, Washington, DC: Bringing Theory to Practice, pp. 23–32.

Sabetti, F., Allen, B., and Sproule-Jones, M. (Eds.). (2009). *The Practice of Constitutional Development: Vincent Ostrom's Quest to Understand Human Affairs*, New York: Lexington Books.

Salamon, L. M. (1987). Of Market Failure, Voluntary Failure, and Third-Party Government: Toward a Theory of Government–Nonprofit Relations in the Modern Welfare State. *Nonprofit and Voluntary Sector Quarterly*, 16(1–2), 29–49.

Salamon, L. M. (1995). *Partners in Public Service: Government–Nonprofit Relations in the Modern Welfare State*, Baltimore, MD: Johns Hopkins University Press.

Salamon, L. M., and Anheier, H. K. (1998). Social Origins of Civil Society: Explaining the Nonprofit Sector Cross-Nationally. *VOLUNTAS: International Journal of Voluntary and Nonprofit Organizations*, 9(3), 213–248.

Salamon, L. M., Sokołowski, C. W., and Anheier, H. K. (2000). *Social Origins of Civil Society: An Overview*, Baltimore, MD: Johns Hopkins Center for Civil Society Studies.

Schmidtz, D. (1995). *Rational Choice and Moral Agency*, Princeton University Press.

Schmidtz, D. (2006). *The Elements of Justice*, Cambridge University Press.

Schmidtz, D., and Brennan, J. (2011). *A Brief History of Liberty*, Hoboken, NJ: John Wiley & Sons.

Schumpeter, J. (1954). *History of Economic Analysis*, New York: Oxford University Press.

Schumpeter, J. A. (1976). *Capitalism, Socialism, and Democracy*, London: Allen & Unwin.

Scott, J. C. (1998). *Seeing Like a State: How Certain Schemes to Improve the Human Condition Have Failed*, New Haven, CT: Yale University Press.

Selgin, G. (1988). *Praxeology and Understanding: An Analysis of the Controversy in Austrian Economics*. Auburn, AL: Ludwig von Mises Institute.

Sen, A. (1970). The Impossibility of a Paretian Liberal. *Journal of Political Economy*, 78 (1), 152–157.

Shackle, G. L. S. (1973). *Epistemics and Economics: A Critique of Economic Doctrines*, Cambridge University Press.

Shapiro, R. Y., and Bloch-Elkon, Y. (2008). Do the Facts Speak for Themselves? Partisan Disagreement as a Challenge to Democratic Competence. *Critical Review: A Journal of Politics and Society*, **20**(1–2), 115–139.

Shockley, G. E. (Ed.). (2009). *Non-Market Entrepreneurship*, Cheltenham, UK: Edward Elgar Publishing.

Skinner, Q. (1998). *Liberty Before Liberalism*, Cambridge University Press.

Smith, S. R., and Grønbjerg, K. A. (2006). Scope and Theory of Government–Nonprofit Relations. In W. W. Powell and R. Steinberg, eds., *The Nonprofit Sector: A Research Handbook*, 2nd edition, pp. 221–242.

Smith, V. L. (2003). Constructivist and Ecological Rationality in Economics. *The American Economic Review*, **93**(3), 465–508.

Smith, V. L. (2008). *Rationality in Economics: Constructivist and Ecological Forms*, Cambridge University Press.

Soltan, K. (2011). A Civic Science. *The Good Society*, **20**(1), 102–119.

Sproule-Jones, M., Allen, B., and Sabetti, F. (Eds.). (2008). *The Struggle to Constitute and Sustain Productive Orders*, Lanham, MD: Lexington Books.

Steinberg, R. (2003). Economic Theories of Nonprofit Organizations. In H. K. Anheier and A. Ben-Ner, eds., *The Study of Nonprofit Enterprise*, New York: Springer US, pp. 277–309.

Steinberg, R., and Gray, B. H. (1993). The Role of Nonprofit Enterprise. *Nonprofit and Voluntary Sector Quarterly*, **22**(4), 297–316.

Steinberg, R., and Powell, W. W. (Eds.). (2006). *The Nonprofit Sector: A Research Handbook*, 2nd edition, New Haven, CT: Yale University Press.

Stigler, G. J., and Becker, G. S. (1977). De Gustibus Non Est Disputandum. *American Economic Review* **67**(2), 76–90.

Storr V. (2008). North's Underdeveloped Ideological Entrepreneur, in E. Chamlee-Wright, ed., *Annual Proceedings of the Wealth and Well-Being of Nations*, Vol. 1, Beloit, WI: Beloit College Press, pp. 2008–2009.

Storr, V. H., Haeffele-Balch, S., and Grube, L. E. (2015). *Community Revival in the Wake of Disaster: Lessons in Local Entrepreneurship*, New York: Palgrave Macmillian.

Swedberg, R. (1990). *Economics and Sociology: Redefining Their Boundaries: Conversations with Economists and Sociologists*, Princeton University Press.

Thaler, R. H., and Sunstein, C. R. (2003). Libertarian Paternalism. *The American Economic Review*, **93**(2), 175–179.

Thaler, R. H., and Sunstein, C. R. (2008). *Nudge: Improving Decisions About Health, Wealth, and Happiness*, revised and expanded edition, New York: Penguin Books.

Thompson, C. (2013). *Smarter Than You Think: How Technology is Changing Our Minds for the Better*, New York: Penguin.

Todd, P. M., and Gigerenzer, G. (2003). Bounding Rationality to the World. *Journal of Economic Psychology*, **24**(2), 143–165.

Tomasi, J. (2012). *Free Market Fairness*. Princeton University Press.

Toonen, T. (2010). Resilience in Public Administration: The Work of Elinor and Vincent Ostrom from a Public Administration Perspective. *Public Administration Review*, **70**(2), 193–202.

Tully, J. (2013). Two Ways of Realizing Justice and Democracy: Linking Amartya Sen and Elinor Ostrom. *Critical Review of International Social and Political Philosophy*, **16**(2), 220–232.

Valentinov, V., and Iliopoulos, C. (2013). Economic Theories of Nonprofits and Agricultural Cooperatives Compared: New Perspectives for Nonprofit Scholars. *Nonprofit and Voluntary Sector Quarterly*, **42**(1), 109–126.

van de Haar, E. (2009). *Classical Liberalism and International Relations Theory: Hume, Smith, Mises, and Hayek*, New York: Springer.

van de Haar, E. (2015). *Degrees of Freedom: Liberal Political Philosophy and Ideology*, New York: Transaction Publishers.

Vanberg, V. J. (2002). *The Constitution of Markets: Essays in Political Economy*, London: Routledge.

Vanberg, V. J. (2005). Market and State: The Perspective of Constitutional Political Economy. *Journal of Institutional Economics*, **1**(01), 23–49.

Wagner, R. E. (1966). Pressure Groups and Political Entrepreneurs: A Review Article. *Papers on Non- Market Decision Making*, **1**(12), 161–170.

Wagner, R. E., (Ed.). (2016). *Politics as a Peculiar Business: Insights from a Theory of Entangled Political Economy*, Cheltenham, UK: Edward Elgar Publishing.

Walker, J. (2012, June 12). Elinor Ostrom, Scholar Who Argued for Decentralization, RIP. Hit & Run Blog at Reason.com, retrieved from http://reason.com/blog/2012/06/12/elinor-ostrom-scholar-who-ma

Walzer, M. (1983). *Spheres of Justice: A Defense of Pluralism and Equality*, New York: Basic Books.

Weisbrod, B. A. (1975). Toward a Theory of the Voluntary Nonprofit Sector in a Three-Sector Economy. In E. S. Phelps, ed., *Altruism, Morality, and Economic Theory*, New York: Russell Sage Foundation, pp. 171–196.

Weisbrod, B. A. (1977). *The Voluntary Nonprofit Sector*, Lexington, MA: D.C. Heath & Co.

Weisbrod, B. A. (1991). *The Nonprofit Economy*, Cambridge, MA.: Harvard University Press.

Young, D. R. (2000). Alternative Models of Government–Nonprofit Sector Relations: Theoretical and International Perspectives. *Nonprofit and Voluntary Sector Quarterly*, **29**(1), 149–172.

Young, D. R. (2013). *If Not for Profit, for What? A Behavioral Theory of the Nonprofit Sector Based on Entrepreneurship* (1983 print edition), Lanham, MD: Lexington Books.

Index